Smart Cities at Play

This book explores how smart cities enable new and playful ways for citizens to experience, inhabit, and socialise within urban environments.

It examines how the functionality of digital technologies within municipal settings can extend beyond environmental pragmatism and socio-economic concerns, to include playful approaches to urban spaces that co-constitute and reinvigorate the experience of place through location-based applications and games. Chapters highlight the varied ways the city, as both a conceptual and lived space, is changing because of this confluence of technologies. This book also considers the extent to which these transformations form an armature upon which more playful approaches to the urban domain are emerging, while exploring what effect these ludic formations might have on related understandings of sociability.

Smart Cities at Play: Technology and Emerging Forms of Playfulness will be a key resource for scholars and researchers of information technology, urban planning and design, games and interactive media, human-centred and user-centred design, human centred interaction, digital geography, and sociology. This book was originally published as a special issue of *Behaviour & Information Technology*.

Prof. Papangelis is Assistant Professor at the Rochester Institute of Technology, USA, specialising in interactive games and media. He directs the Niantic X RIT Geo Games and Media Lab, focusing on locative media, extended/hybrid reality, and the metaverse. He has published extensively in renowned journals and conference proceedings.

Dr. Saker is Senior Lecturer at City, University of London, UK. He is the co-author of *From Microverse to Metaverse* (2022), *Intergenerational Locative Play* (2021), and *Location-Based Social Media, Space, Time and Identity* (2017) and the co-editor of *The Changing Face of VR* (2022).

Dr. Jones is Assistant Professor in Digital Human Geographies in the Faculty of Human, Education and Social Sciences at the University of Luxembourg, Luxembourg.

Smart Cities at Play

Technology and Emerging Forms of Playfulness

Edited by
**Konstantinos Papangelis, Michael Saker and
Catherine Jones**

CRC Press
Taylor & Francis Group
Boca Raton London New York

CRC Press is an imprint of the
Taylor & Francis Group, an **informa** business
AN AUERBACH BOOK

First edition published 2024
by CRC Press
4 Park Square, Milton Park, Abingdon, Oxon, OX14 4RN

and by CRC Press
2385 NW Executive Center Drive, Suite 320, Boca Raton FL 33431

© 2024 Taylor & Francis

CRC Press is an imprint of Informa UK Limited

British Library Cataloguing-in-Publication Data
A catalogue record for this book is available from the British Library

ISBN: 978-1-032-60850-1 (hbk)
ISBN: 978-1-032-60855-6 (pbk)
ISBN: 978-1-003-46104-3 (ebk)

DOI: 10.1201/9781003461043

Typeset in Minion Pro
by codeMantra

Publisher's Note
The publisher accepts responsibility for any inconsistencies that may have arisen during the conversion of this book from journal articles to book chapters, namely the inclusion of journal terminology.

Disclaimer
Every effort has been made to contact copyright holders for their permission to reprint material in this book. The publishers would be grateful to hear from any copyright holder who is not here acknowledged and will undertake to rectify any errors or omissions in future editions of this book.

Contents

Citation Information

The chapters in this book were originally published in the journal *Behaviour & Information Technology*, volume 39, issue 6 (2020). When citing this material, please use the original page numbering for each article, as follows:

For any permission-related enquiries please visit:
http://www.tandfonline.com/page/help/permissions

Notes on Contributors

Andre G. Afonso, The Bartlett School of Architecture, University College London, UK.

Duha Alsmadi, Faculty of Information Technology, University of Petra, Amman, Jordan.

Paloma Cáceres, ETS Ingeniería Informática, Universidad Rey Juan Carlos, Madrid, Spain.

M. Cavada, Manchester School of Architecture, University of Manchester, UK.

José María Cavero, ETS Ingeniería Informática, Universidad Rey Juan Carlos, Madrid, Spain.

Carlos E. Cuesta, ETS Ingeniería Informática, Universidad Rey Juan Carlos, Madrid, Spain.

Ava Fatah gen Schieck, The Bartlett School of Architecture, University College London, UK.

Abdulrahman Habib, Toulouse Graduate School, University of North Texas, Denton, USA.

Kate Hennessy. School of Interactive Arts and Technology, Simon Fraser University, Surrey, Canada.

Catherine Jones, Faculty of Human, Education and Social Sciences, Luxembourg University, Luxembourg.

Sanna Lehtinen, School of Engineering, University of Helsinki, Finland.

Karyn Moffatt, School of Information Studies, McGill University, Montreal, Canada.

Carman Neustaedter, School of Interactive Arts and Technology, Simon Fraser University, Surrey, Canada.

Rui Pan, School of Interactive Arts and Technology, Simon Fraser University, Surrey, Canada.

Carolyn Pang, School of Information Studies, McGill University, Montreal, Canada; School of Interactive Arts and Technology, Simon Fraser University, Surrey, Canada.

Konstantinos Papangelis, Applied Critical Thinking, Rochester Institute of Technology, USA.

Victor R. Prybutok, Toulouse Graduate School, University of North Texas, Denton, USA.

C. D. F. Rogers, Department of Civil Engineering, School of Engineering, University of Birmingham, UK.

Michael Saker, School of Policy and Global Affairs, City, University of London, UK.

Almudena Sierra, ETS Ingeniería Informática, Universidad Rey Juan Carlos, Madrid, Spain.

Belén Vela, ETS Ingeniería Informática, Universidad Rey Juan Carlos, Madrid, Spain.

Vesa Vihanninjoki, School of Engineering, University of Helsinki, Finland.

Introduction to smart cities at play: technology and emerging forms of playfulness

Konstantinos Papangelis, Michael Saker and Catherine Jones

Smart cities are commonly described as 'places where information technology is combined with infrastructure, architecture, everyday objects, and even our bodies to address social, economic, and environmental problems' (Townsend 2013, 15). In recent years, this notion of smart cities has become the focus of a mounting body of scholarly work (see Campbell 2013; Deakin and Al Waer 2012; Goldsmith and Crawford 2014; Kitchin 2014; Obaidat and Nicopolitidis 2016; Picon 2015; Stimmel 2015). As a corollary to this research, an increasingly important facet of this development has been mobile media embedded with other technologies, such as the global positioning system (GPS). These technologies, and the data they gather, have provided the platform for new forms of urban analysis (Ratti et al. 2006; Shoval 2008), municipal planning (Becker et al. 2011; Steenbruggen, Tranos, and Nijkamp 2015), as well as the production of more efficient spaces. To this end, locative data has been recursively used to interpret levels of traffic, forecast the arrival of mass transit vehicles, and assist ridesharing services . In this vein, locative technologies can be employed to better understand human mobilities (Becker et al. 2013), monitor crowds during large gatherings (Blanke et al. 2014; Draghici, Agiali, and Chilipirea 2015; El Mallah et al. 2015, and theorise the physical behaviours of tourists (McKercher et al. 2012; Pettersson and Zillinger 2011; Shoval and Isaacson 2009). At the same time, the advancement of smartphones—equally embedded with all manner of technologies, including GPS—has led to an array of locative media, including hybrid reality games (HRG), as well as—more generally—the mainstreaming of locative features into the broader media landscape (Evans and Saker 2017).

Importantly, then, digital technologies, in a variety of forms, are part of our daily lives. Likewise, these technologies increasingly co-constitute our phenomenological experience of the urban environment. While this might be the case, '[in] the rush to create so-called 'smart cities' … much of the attention has been on how to technically create and implement suitable smart city technology' (Kitchin 2014:1). What is, therefore, missing from these discussions is a deeper engagement with the lived perspective (De Certeau 1984) of these supposedly 'smart spaces', experienced on 'the ground', and the extent to which this confluence of the physical and digital are currently configuring new forms of play that can be contextualised within the wide field of smart cities. Certainly, smart cities can produce different degrees of playfulness. HRGs like Pokémon Go, for instance, can allow users to explicitly interact with their environment in a playful manner, while impacting sociality, and altering how users feel about themselves and their environment (Evans and Saker 2019; Saker and Evans 2020). Equally, digital technologies have the power to configure emerging approaches to space and place that may not be as overtly ludic, but are playful nonetheless. Take the social value of lodging services, such as Airbnb, for example. These services challenge how short-term accommodation is understood; moving beyond the sterility of standard hotels and towards something that is markedly—on the surface at least—different.

Whether explicit or implicit, then, it is our contention that smart cities can produce a meaningful suite of both planned and unplanned forms of play and playfulness that are not immediately accounted for in the context of 'efficiency' or pragmatism, but are still important in the context of illuminating the contours of this field and the extent to which the phenomenology of the urban environment presents different revealings of place. To be clear, this importance extends beyond simply describing emerging instances of municipal play amidst the physical and the digital. Many observers have helpfully demonstrated that not everyone experiences related services in the same way. For example, Airbnb has come under various criticism, with hosts reportedly cancelling reservations because of the ethnicity of their occupants, or occupants being asked to leave without being given sufficient reason (Mosbergen 2019). Again, these stories are significant for researchers and practitioners alike. And it is only by addressing the lived experience of smart cities through these stories that we are able to reveal *the* manifold ways these spaces are—at times playfully—experienced, as well as the varied inconsistencies that often remain just beneath the surface when related discussions simply focus on technology and the physical infrastructure framing smart cities.

Our special issue, therefore, covers a broad range of topics and explores how experiences of the city might be changing as a result of new technological practices that are currently creating both explicit and implicit playful possibilities, as well as the various social ramifications of this. In the article titled 'Factors That Determine Residents' Acceptance of Smart City Technologies', the authors propose a Smart Cities Stakeholders Adoption Model (SSA) to determine the influence of seven factors—effort expectancy, self-efficacy, perceived privacy, perceived security, trust in technology, price value and trust in government—on behaviour intention, specifically the decision to adopt smart-city technologies. The results demonstrate that each of these factors significantly influences citizen intention to use smart-city services. The results also reveal perceived security and perceived privacy to be strong determinants of trust in technology, while price value is a determinant of trust in the government. In turn, both types of trust are shown to increase user intention to adopt and use smart-city services. These findings offer city officials an approach to gauging residential intention to use smart-city services, as well as identify those factors critical to developing a successful smart-city strategy. The SSA model, therefore, makes an important contribution to the literature on smart-city services in the context of patterns of adoption.

Moving forward, the authors of the article entitled, 'The Role of a Location-Based City Exploration Game in Digital Placemaking' explore how location-based games (LBGs), can support urban residents in community awareness, city exploration, and placemaking. To examine this topic, the authors investigate the various challenges urban residents face in finding information about their community, while implementing and evaluating an LBG called City Explorer that supports city exploration using gamification and the viewing and sharing of community information. The results of this exploration demonstrate that residents value fun, competition, and rewards afforded through locative play in public spaces, creating opportunities for placemaking through location services, alongside knowledge sharing. Players also appreciate additional knowledge about their transit commutes, including data about the

frequency and route of their transit rides. Collectively, such ridership data offers the potential for smart city initiatives and illustrates that careful design considerations are required to balance peoples' needs for play, personal data, privacy, and the acquisition of community information.

Building upon this theme through an innovative framework of urban philosophy and everyday aesthetics, the authors of the article entitled 'Seeing New in the Familiar: Intensifying Aesthetic Engagement with the City through New Location-Based Technologies' explore the impact of mobile application on experiences and appreciations of urban environments. Significantly, the authors highlight that new digital tools can increase the quality of fun when moving through familiar surroundings. To be clear, fun—understood here through the lens of the aesthetic—precedes the experience of playfulness; that is, it alters the existing affordances of the urban environment in a way that allows more complex aesthetic qualities to emerge.

In a similar vein, the authors of the paper entitled 'Play in the Smart City Context: Exploring Interactional, Bodily, Social and Spatial Aspects of Situated Interfaces' examine how the digital and the physical facets of urban media installations can produce enjoyable and socially thriving playscapes. Accordingly, two case studies of urban media installations featuring high levels of interactivity and playfulness are presented: the Appearing Rooms, a seasonal art installation in London, and the Mirror Pool, a permanent, large-scale urban installation in Bradford, UK. Each of these interfaces incorporates a design paradigm that differs from the other in terms of context, duration of implementation, and scale. Following a longitudinal approach based on non-participant observations and time-lapse photography, the authors analyse emergent interactions and focus in particular on playful encounters at different levels and scales: from the micro scale of the bodily engagement to the macro scale of the spatial and social configurations. Their case studies highlight that the urban spatial layout is a key element in defining the emerging interactions and encounters around the urban situated interfaces. The authors suggest, within the premise of the 'smart city', that digital technologies can have an active role, with a great potential to encourage playful experiences and shared encounters in urban spaces; yet the digital should be coupled with a careful consideration of the spatial, physical, material and bodily aspects of interactions, that are fundamental to our lived experience of the city.

In the context of accessibility, the article 'Smart Data at Play: Improving accessibility in the urban transport system' the authors describe findings from the

Access@City Research Project, which seeks to improve the accessibility in the public transport system by using available information (open data, semantic-aware knowledge) provided by transport organisations in combination with a hybrid reality crowdsourcing game (HRG) to enrich information regarding the accessibility of subway stations. Their results illustrate that in a relatively short time this combination can provide an accurate description of the accessibility of these stations. After reflecting on their experiments and experiences with the Access@City project the authors suggest that playful approaches, such as the ones employed in this article, have the potential to capture accessibility data that the city couldn't capture otherwise.

Finally, the last article of our special issue is entitled 'Serious Gaming as a Means of Facilitating Truly Smart Cities: A Narrative Review'. Here, the authors fittingly review the ways that gamification can be used to understand the effects of 'smart initiatives' on cities and their operation. The authors conclude that gaming has considerable potential to affect individual and societal practices by profoundly influencing the gamers themselves, while technology and the game design play a central role in how gamification is implemented and used. Further, based on their analysis of the surrounding literature, the authors propose that way-finding games, when designed with sustainability, resilience and liveability agendas in mind, can potentially lead to increased citizen participation. Consequently, this article will serve as a useful platform to survey potential avenues for future research in the field.

References

Becker, R. A., R. Caceres, K. Hanson, J. M. Loh, S. Urbanek, A. Varshavsky, and C. Volinsky. 2011. "A tale of one city: Using cellular network data for urban planning." *IEEE Pervasive Computing* 10 (4): 18–26.

Becker, Richard, Chris Volinsky, Ramón Cáceres, Karrie Hanson, Sibren Isaacman, Ji Meng Loh, Margaret Martonosi, James Rowland, Simon Urbanek, and Alexander Varshavsky. 2013. "Human mobility characterization from cellular network data." *Communications of the ACM* 56 (1): 74–82.

Blanke, U., G. Tröster, T. Franke, and P. Lukowicz. 2014. "Capturing crowd dynamics at large scale events using participatory gps-localization." In *Intelligent Sensors, Sensor Networks and Information Processing (ISSNIP), 2014 IEEE Ninth International Conference on*, 1–7. Singapore: IEEE.

Cambell, Tim. 2012. "Beyond Smart Cities: How Cities Network, Learn and Innovate." In *From intelligent to smart cities*, edited by M. Deakin and H. Al Waer. New York: Routledge.

Campbell, T. 2013. *Beyond smart cities: how cities network, learn and innovate*. New York: Routledge.

De Certeau, M. 1984. *The Practice of Everyday Life, trans. Steven Rendall*. Berkeley: University of California.

Draghici, A., T. Agiali, and C. Chilipirea. 2015. "Visualization system for human mobility analysis." In *2015 14th RoEduNet International Conference-Networking in Education and Research (RoEduNet NER)*, edited by - -, 152–157. IEEE.

El Mallah, J., F. Carrino, O. A. Khaled, and E. Mugellini. 2015. "Crowd Monitoring." In *International Conference on Distributed, Ambient, and Pervasive Interactions*, 496–505. Springer International Publishing.

Evans, L., and M. Saker. 2017. *Location-based social media: Space, time and identity*. London: Springer.

Evans, L., and M. Saker. 2019. "The playeur and Pokémon Go: Examining the effects of locative play on spatiality and sociability." *Mobile Media & Communication* 7 (2): 232–247.

Goldsmith, S., and S. Crawford. 2014. *The responsive city: Engaging communities through data-smart governance*. London: John Wiley & Sons.

Kitchin, R. 2014. "The real-time city? Big data and smart urbanism." *GeoJournal* 79 (1): 1–14.

McKercher, B., N. Shoval, E. Ng, and A. Birenboim. 2012. "First and repeat visitor behaviour: GPS tracking and GIS analysis in Hong Kong." *Tourism Geographies* 14 (1): 147–161.

Mosbergen, D. 2019. Airbnb Host Kicks Out Black Guests After Calling Them 'Monkeys'. *Huffpost*. https://www.huffingtonpost.co.uk/entry/airbnb-host-black-guests-monkeys-racist_n_5cf635e4e4b0e346ce845be3.

Obaidat, M. S., and P. Nicopolitidis. 2016. *Smart Cities and Homes: Key Enabling Technologies*. New York: Morgan Kaufmann.

Pettersson, R., and M. Zillinger. 2011. "Time and space in event behaviour: Tracking visitors by GPS." *Tourism Geographies* 13 (1): 1–20.

Picon, A. 2015. *Smart Cities: A Spatialised Intelligence-AD Primer*. New York: John Wiley & Sons.

Quercia, D., N. Lathia, F. Calabrese, G. Di Lorenzo, and J. Crowcroft. (2010, December. "Recommending social events from mobile phone location data." In *2010 IEEE International Conference on Data Mining*, 971–976. IEEE.

Ratti, C., D. Frenchman, R. M. Pulselli, and S. Williams. 2006. "Mobile landscapes: using location data from cell phones for urban analysis." *Environment and Planning B: Planning and Design* 33 (5): 727–748.

Saker, M., and L. Evans. 2020. "Personalising the Urban: A Critical Account of Locative Media and the Digital Inscription of Place." In *Mediated Identities in the Futures of Place: Emerging Practices and Spatial Cultures*, 39–55. Cham: Springer.

Shoval, N. 2008. "Tracking technologies and urban analysis." *Cities* 25 (1): 21–28.

Shoval, N., and M. Isaacson. 2009. *Tourist mobility and advanced tracking technologies*. New York: Routledge.

Steenbruggen, J., E. Tranos, and P. Nijkamp. 2015. "Data from mobile phone operators: A tool for smarter cities?" *Telecommunications Policy* 39 (3): 335–346.

Stimmel, C. L. 2015. *Building Smart Cities: Analytics, ICT, and Design Thinking*. New York: CRC Press.

Townsend, A. M. 2013. *Smart cities: Big data, civic hackers, and the quest for a new utopia*. London: WW Norton & Company.

Factors that determine residents' acceptance of smart city technologies

Abdulrahman Habib ⓘ, Duha Alsmadi and Victor R. Prybutok ⓘ

ABSTRACT

While some cities attempt to determine their residents' demand for smart-city technologies, others simply move forward with smart-related strategies and projects. This study is among the first to empirically determine which factors most affect residents' and public servants' intention to use smart-city services. A Smart Cities Stakeholders Adoption Model (SSA), based on Unified Theory of Acceptance and Use of Technology (UTAUT2), is developed and tested on a mid-size U.S. city as a case study. A questionnaire was administered in order to determine the influence of seven factors – effort expectancy, self-efficacy, perceived privacy, perceived security, trust in technology, price value and trust in government – on behaviour intention, specifically the decision to adopt smart-city technologies. Results show that each of these factors significantly influenced citizen intention to use smart-city services. They also reveal perceived security and perceived privacy to be strong determinants of trust in technology, and price value a determinant of trust in government. In turn, both types of trust are shown to increase user intention to both adopt and use smart-city services. These findings offer city officials an approach to gauging residential intention to use smart-city services, as well as identify those factors critical to developing a successful smart-city strategy.

1. Introduction

Big cities like New York, Chicago, and Barcelona have implemented many smart-city projects. They can be presented as role models for small and medium-sized cities similarly interested in improving the efficiency and quality of their services. For example, New York smart and equitable projects added high-speed internet infrastructure for low-income communities. They installed Link-NYC kiosks with charging stations and free public Wi-Fi. Similarly, Barcelona, Spain, was recognised for the city-wide fibre optic implementations, installed parking sensors that manage on-demand parking and availability. A network of sensors was installed for water sprinklers, temperature, sound levels, pollution, and foot traffic. At the same time, many are skeptical that increased use of technology will have a measurable impact on citizen engagement, especially since their disuse would be a waste of resources (Nam and Pardo 2011b; Thomas et al. 2016; Townsend 2013). There are then fiscal reasons for determining resident interest before any significant investment is made. Researchers such as Chatterjee, Kar, and Gupta (2018), Luarn and Lin (2005) and Venkatesh, James, and Xu (2012) have stressed the importance of identifying and understanding user acceptance behaviour towards Information and Communication Technology (ICT). Our study continues in this tradition, by posing a simple question: what factors most affect user adoption of smart-city technologies?

To answer this question, we have applied an extension of the Unified Theory of Acceptance and Use of Technology (UTAUT2) to the City of Denton as a case study. Denton is a mid-size U.S. city located in north-central Texas, on the northern edge of the Dallas-Fort Worth metropolitan area with a population of just over 131 thousand. The City of Denton has two universities, the University of North Texas and Texas Women University. Denton was the seventh fastest-growing city in the U.S. in 2011. The universities' rapid growth played a significant rule in the City's economy and culture. In the past, Denton has focused on sustainability and digital governance, with the goal of reaching 100% dependency on renewable energy by 2019. By 2017, it could claim that 78% of its energy came from clean wind sources. In terms of digital governance, it has received four national Digital City Survey awards in its size group: 3rd place in 2003, 1st place in 2004 and 2005, and 7th place in 2016.

The remaining sections of this paper are organised as follows: a literature review on the importance of smart cities and technology adoption; a development of the Smart-city Stakeholders Adoption (SSA) model; the development and administration of a complementary survey; and an analysis of our findings. It concludes with an overview of its contributions to the field, its implications and limitations, and opportunities for future research.

2. Literature review

The proposed SSA model used in this study is based primarily on research of the past 10 years in the areas of technology adoption in e-government and smart-city development as well as input garnered from early interviews with the city stakeholders.

2.1. Smart cities

Nam and Pardo (2011a) define smart-city as (a) the integration of infrastructures and technology-mediated services, (b) the use of social learning for strengthening human infrastructure, and (c) governance for institutional improvement and citizen engagement. Like any other city, smart cities have social, environmental and economic dimensions. The difference is that technology plays a much larger role. Smart cities are more than digital cities: Whereas over time electricity and broadband characterised the modern metropolis, ICT and the Internet of Things (IoT) now serves as its technical backbone (Mohanty, Choppali, and Kougianos 2016).

The word 'smart' has become the prefix du jour for phones, homes, buildings, traffic systems, and beyond. 'Smart' implies the ability to solve problems and adapt to change, which is in turn associated with 'user-friendly' as noted by Hollands (2008). Becoming a smart city means not only adding technology but combining it with social innovation. ICT act as an enabler to the city to help it become innovative, efficient, responsive, resilient and innovative (Cavada, Hunt, and Rogers 2014). The goal is to enhance services, solve urban migration challenges, increase urban capacity, manage resources more efficiently and, most importantly, improve its residents' quality of life.

2.2. Technology-related challenges

The relationship between technology and the smart-city is not always straightforward. A city with advanced ICT-like connectivity like fibre optics, 5G wireless network, connected IoT devices, or use Artificial Intelligence (AI) is not necessarily smart. As Townsend (2013) argues, when IBM and Cisco promote their technologies as the solution to all problems, they presume a wide range of technologies and industries are doing just that. It is true that ICT-based infrastructures provide

cities with an array of sensors, allowing them to respond to problems much faster than before. However, sensors alone cannot improve either quality of life or economic stagnation. This was the case with Rio de Janeiro, which some declared as a failure (Nam and Pardo 2011b; Thomas et al. 2016; Townsend 2013).

Since then, ICT companies have focused not only on sensory-based systems but on the value of those systems to the communities they serve, viewing them as a means to facilitate engagement with residents through cycles of sense, seize, align, and transform (Chong et al. 2018). The city senses the needs of its citizens as well as environmental changes and public safety concerns; seizes this input and turns it into information through the use of analytics and other data-science technologies; aligns the information with the city's goals, such as improving quality of life, increasing resident satisfaction or adapting to environmental change; and, finally, transforms the city itself (Chang, Wang, and Wills 2018).

2.3. Technology adoption model

Today, e-government services are considered a fundamental function of local and federal organisations, and have become an essential part of our social life. Smart cities then are expected to extend these services through increased integration with both resident and community (AlAwadhi and Scholl 2013; Hollands 2008). UTAUT, developed by Venkatesh et al. (2003), is a prominent theory that can be applied to e-government-services adoption, and has been extensively used to study information system acceptance and use (Dwivedi et al. 2017). It is composed of four critical determinants of adoption: Performance Expectancy (PE), Effort Expectancy (EE), Social Influence (SI), and Facilitating Conditions (FC). Later, Venkatesh introduced three additional determinants – Hedonic Motivation (HM), Price Value (PV), and Habit (HB) – to account for consumer behaviour. This new theory, UTAUT2, could now be used to assess an individual's intention to use a specific system and identify the key factors influencing its acceptance and adoption. UTAUT is built upon previous adoption models, characterised by a considerable level of validity and reliability, and describes up to 70% of the variance in behavioural intention to use technology (Alsmadi and Prybutok 2018; Venkatesh, James, and Xu 2012).

UTAUT2 is a plausible Theory for examining the acceptance of smart cities technology. First, UTAUT2 was built based on previous adoption models with an extensive body of research from psychology, sociology, and human behaviours (Carter 2008; Venkatesh et al. 2003). Second, it has been successfully used to study both e-government services adoption and information system acceptance (Dwivedi et al. 2017; Williams et al. 2011). Third, smart-city technologies are accepted as an extension to e-government services through increased integration with both residents and the community (Alawadhi and Morris 2008; Hollands 2008). Finally, UTAUT2 included some of the constructs identified in our interviews and allowed for the inclusion of additional constructs. For these reasons, UTAUT2 is well suited for identifying the factors that most affect adoption and intention to use of smart-city services, which in turn will assist city officials and vendors better plan for implementation and evaluation.

We also asked city officials, employees, and residents what other challenges might face the implementation and adoption of smart-city services (see Section 4.1). In addition to UTAUT2's seven determinant factors, and one represent behavioural intention to use smart-city technology, four additional areas of interest were identified: security, privacy, trust in technology and trust in government.

3. Theoretical framework

The proposed SSA model, as applied to the City of Denton, Texas, is composed of eight constructs; Self-Efficacy (SE), Effort Expectancy (EE), Perceived Privacy (PP), Perceived Security (PS), Trust in Technology (TT), Trust in Government (TG), Price Value (PV), and Behavioural Intention (BI). Three of these constructs – EE, PV and BI – are taken from UTAUT2. The remaining five constructs were developed through a careful review of city requirements, interviews with city officials and residents, and an analysis of similar applications (discussed in Section 4.3). A panel of eight information professionals evaluated the survey model, theoretical consideration, and the pilot survey was updated based on their feedback.

Figure 1 shows the relationships among these constructs. A structural equation model was constructed using SmartPLS 3 (partial least square, or PLS, software) to test a series of nine hypotheses, each of which is represented in the model as a straight line, all ultimately leading to the intended use of smart-city services (BI).

3.1. Self-efficacy

Human behaviour can be explained by its relationship with environment events, personal and cognitive factors, each of which operates as a determinant of the others (Bandura 1977; Yi and Hwang 2003). Among Bandura's contributions to social cognitive theory is his theory of self-efficacy, based on the assumption that 'psychological procedures, whatever their form, alter expectations of

personal efficacy' (p.79). In applying this concept to information technology, Venkatesh (2000) discovered a relationship between SE and the user's belief in their ability to perform a particular task, a finding corroborated by Yi and Hwang (2003) and Shiau and Chau (2016). SE has also been shown to be a significant determinant of user behaviour by Flavián and Guinalíu (2006) and Hsu and Chiu (2004) in the area of user adoption of online e-commerce; Hung, Chang, and Yu (2006) in the area of trust in technology with e-government tax filing and payment; and Luarn and Lin (2005) in the area of user adoption of mobile banking. We may then assume that, in terms of smart cities, their residents must believe themselves capable of using these new services even though, as Agha (2016) points out, they may be challenging for those of lower socio-economic status.

Ha1: SE is correlated with BI in the adoption of smart-city services.

3.2. Effort expectancy

Venkatesh et al. (2003) define effort expectancy as 'the degree of ease associated with the use of the system' (p.450). This construct is built upon the service user's perception of ease-of-use, which they found more salient in the early adoption stages (Venkatesh et al. 2003.) Similarly, Alawadhi and Morris (2008) found EE to be an essential factor in government adoption, since city officials often expressed concern that too much technology (e.g. mobile parking apps) might overwhelm some residents and prevent them from performing a previously simple task.

Ha2: EE is correlated with BI in the adoption of smart-city services.

3.3. Perceived privacy and perceived security

As cities become more technologically advanced, residents and policy makers may find their expectations of privacy and security sorely challenged (See Chen and Zhao 2012; Chourabi et al. 2011; Elmaghraby and Losavio 2014; Ozkan and Kanat 2011). Those in smart cities will face even greater challenges, as IoT sensors and analytics proliferate and users of their services prove increasingly risk-averse (Scuotto, Ferraris, and Bresciani 2016).

3.3.1. Perceived security

Perceived Security (PS) is the degree to which users believe that smart-city services are secure platforms for storing and sharing sensitive data. PS and the influence of privacy concerns on adoption behaviour have been investigated in the areas of cloud computing, e-

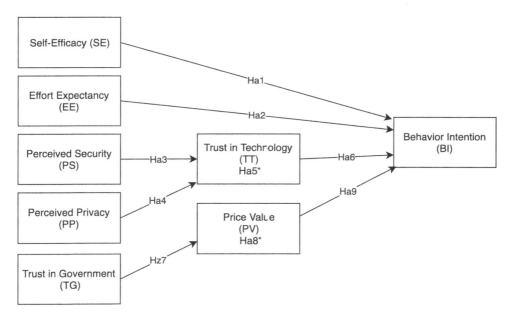

Figure 1. Smart-city stakeholders adoption model (SSA). *Ha5 and Ha8 represent mediation role of these construct in the subsequently introduced hypotheses.

Gov services and e-banking (see Arpaci, Kilicer, and Bardakci 2015; Pearson and Benameur 2010; Sarabdeen and Ishak 2015; Widjaja and Chen 2012). Smart-city service users have been found to value safety and security (Schumann and Stock 2014), quality of information and services quality (Chatterjee, Kar, and Gupta 2018), and increased government regulation (Edwards 2016; Van Zoonen et al. 2016). Couples with the recent ransomware attacks on Atlanta in 2018 and Baltimore in 2019 it is as yet unknown whether smart-city service users would tolerate some degree of security breach if the perceived benefits of using that service were sufficiently high.

Ha3: PS is correlated with TT in the adoption of smart-city services.

3.3.2. Perceived privacy

Arpaci, Kilicer, and Bardakci (2015) define perceived privacy as the degree to which users believe a given technology is sage and will protect their personal information. Privacy itself is considered a fundamental human right, by Pearson (2009) among others, a benchmark against which other violations can be measured. As a result, governments and businesses collecting their data – and potentially following their activities – may remind users of Big Brother (Manyika et al. 2011). In her study of technology acceptance in smart cities, Yeh (2017) found that citizens were willing to accept and use smart-city services so long as the services were innovative, their privacy assured, and the service themselves of high quality. This raises the question of whether smart-city service

users might accept a lower level of privacy if the benefits of using such services were sufficiently high.

Ha4: PP is correlated with TT in the adoption of smart-city services.

3.4. Trust in technology

Trust in technology measures how likely residents are to use smart-city technologies, and is in turn greatly dependent upon both PS and PP. According to Braun et al. (2018), any concerns regarding security and privacy must be addressed before infrastructure changes are initiated, if smart-city services are to be successfully adopted (Braun et al. 2018). However, any city seeking to add more technology to its operations is sure to sound like a nightmare to at least some of its residents. City officials too can have nightmares, given how easily 'outages could turn smart cities into zombies' (Townsend 2013) or cyber-attacks halt a city's entire information technology operation.

TT has also been shown to influence both consumer intention to buy as well as their purchasing behaviour (Flavián and Guinalíu 2006) and their intention to use e-government services (Ozkan and Kanat 2011). Our pilot test survey and interviews with city officials revealed similar results, with city officials, city employees, and residents expressing reservations in regard to how user data would be collected and used. At the same time, we found city officials were under the impression that only new generation and technology enthusiasts had any interest in smart cities, in keeping with Scuotto, Ferraris, and Bresciani (2016)'s discovery of a serious lack of technology knowledge among city planners and policymakers. These observations led us to examine the relationship between PS and PP, respectively, and BI, and the role of TT as a moderating effect.

> Ha5: TT moderates the relationship between PS and PP, respectively, on BI in the adoption of smart-city services.
>
> Ha6: TT is correlated with BI in the adoption of smart-city services.

3.5. Trust in government and price value

The investment in technologies such as IoT devices, especially when coupled with AI, allow governments to collect and analyse big data about its residents. Security and privacy matters aside, residents may also fear that the government's ability to track them will result in the rise of a surveillance state and supersede any commitment to public interest. For example: Could the government generate automated citations for incidents no one has witnessed? Or what if the vendors themselves proved unethical, using some or all of the data they collect for their own purposes? These challenges and more emphasise the important of resident trust in its government, despite how the two sides may differ in terms of their priorities. Similarly, as Hollands (2015) points out, cities must leverage their limited resources wisely, conscious that investing in smart-city technologies may hinder investment in other areas of operation. A better understanding of how residents perceive the price value of these technologies would enable city officials to better allocate scarce resources.

3.5.1. Trust in government

Almuraqab and Jasimuddin (2017) define trust in government as 'the public's assessment of government based on their perceptions of political authorities', agencies' and institutions' integrity and ability to provide services according to the expectations of citizens' (p.17). Similar to concerns over security and privacy, note Van Zoonen et al. (2016), that same public may be equally skeptical of an increased use of technology, questioning why and for what purpose their data are being gathered.

Along with TT, TG is a critical factor in a user's decision to access an e-government website or services. (See Almuraqab and Jasimuddin 2017; Roca, García, and Vega 2009; Shin 2010.) But while residents may be leery of IoT devices in government hands, the government itself more often appreciates the efficiencies IoT brings to service provision, such as improvements in public safety and emergency response. Its main concerns have to do with cost: those of adding these technologies and continuing to upgrade them over time can be prohibitive as well as of IT training and skills development (Chourabi et al. 2011).

3.5.2. Price value

Venkatesh, James, and Xu (2012) extended UTAUT to include price value, which they define as 'the consumers' cognitive trade-off between the perceived benefits of using a particular technology and the monetary cost of using it.' The resulting UTAUT2 has subsequently been applied in many technology acceptance studies.

Problems with PV arise when the benefits of a service do not match or exceed its financial costs, in which case users will neither adopt nor use it. In a smart-city context, where the residents as taxpayers are the funders, matters of cost (perceived or otherwise) residents' PV of smart-city services is clearly an essential factor in their adoption. The problem is putting a price tag on it. Several studies concluded that people who need to use a service tend to weigh the benefits against the costs. (See Hujran 2012; Susanto and Goodwin 2011; Sweeneya and Soutarb 2001). Almuraqab (2017) listed perceived cost as one of the factors affecting mobile or smart government adoption.

> Ha7: TG is correlated with PM in the adoption of smart-city services.
>
> Ha8: PV moderates the relationship between TG and BI in the adoption of smart-city services.
>
> Ha9: PV is correlated with BI in the adoption of smart-city services.

3.5.3. Behavioural intention

Behavioral intentions measure the strength of one's intention to do a specified behavior. For Venkatesh et al. (2003) it becomes the key predictor of technology use and has been widely applied in previous studies of individual acceptance. BI can determine the user's use of technology. For example, a resident who states that they will use a smart-city parking app when looking for parking spot is demonstrating intention to use that technology.

4. Methodology

4.1. Survey development

The process began with a series of semi-structured open ended interviews with city officials, employees, and residents to understand the underpinning challenges in smart-city and what factors affect their adoption to its services. Then a panel of eight information professionals (from the University of North Texas and the City of

Denton, plus several information system experts) evaluated the questionnaire and its theoretical underpinnings.

The city was interested in studying challenges residents might have concerning smart city initiatives if proposed. The researchers conducted interviews with city employees and residents to identify common themes to help develop the survey. The interviews reveal four dominant themes regarding the use of future city services. The first challenge is residents' confidence about their ability to use smart cities services or technologies. For example, using the mobile parking services if the city adopt a smart parking solution. The second theme is related to the resident's confidence in how much effort it will require them to be able to use smart city services. The third theme is an intertwining of how to trust technology with security and privacy concerns. The fourth theme is related to increasing technology expenditure, while many local government decisions are under scrutiny from residents. Some of these challenges were studied as part of the UTAUT2 model and the many extensions of that model into areas like e-government. The participating organisation was also concerned about survey fatigue and requested that the researchers focus primarily on the dominant themes. As a result of the need to address these themes and with consideration of the relevance of all the constructs within UTAUT2 it was deemed appropriate to eliminate factors that were less relevant to the context of the current study.

The resulting eight constructs of the SSA model were based on a combination of UTAUT2, an extensive literature search of cognate studies, and the aforementioned interviews. Each of these constructs was then broken down into three or four item statements, in order to determine the degree to which study participants agreed with them. In addition, two dichotomous (yes/no) questions of interest to city officials were appended, in order to determine resident familiarity with the concept of smart cities and awareness (or lack thereof) of smart-city services in Denton. Demographic information (age, gender, and education level) was also obtained.

4.2. Sampling and participants

The sample was selected from the resident population: 131, 097 according to the 2017 census. In keeping with the research design and available resources, snowball sampling was used to recruit participants. This method allowed us to draw a representative sample from among an interconnected group of people (Lin and Chen 2012). Of the 1787 responses received, 1444 were retained after removal of non-completed surveys.

4.3. Data collection

A pre-test was then performed by a group of 11 random UNT students, and IRB approval obtained. Next, two panels of four city officials each evaluated the item statements, followed by a pilot test randomly distributed to 55 residents of downtown Denton. Finally, limiting response options to three was a requirement of the participating organisation because they were concerned about survey fatigue among respondents. Therefore, the survey we changed from five-point Likert scale to three-point Likert like scale. This change help shorten the survey time by approximately 30%. Individual items were also added, deleted, or modified based on feedback regarding item clarity.

The questionnaire was distributed through five distinct channels: the City of Denton internal email system which targets City employees; the City's official website and social media pages; social media accounts belonging to one of our researchers; over Canvas, the University of North Texas' learning management system; and by placing the survey on iPads in public spaces around the city to facilitate an extra data collection point. To comply with city policy, the email to city employees was with no incentives. On the other hand, extra credit points were given to students participating via the fourth channel. Using iPads in public spaces helped recruit random residents who do not follow the city website or social media. Residents who completed the survey on the iPads received a free coffee coupon incentive for their participation in the study. Qualtrics survey software was used to collect user responses.

4.4. Analysis methods

A split sample technique was utilised to test and validate the SSA model. This involved randomly splitting the sample into two equal subsamples, where the Subsample1 (n1 = 722) was used to test the model and Subsample2 (n2 = 722) to test and validate the posited and developed model (Phillips, Peak, and Prybutok 2016).

A series of tests were performed to test for common method bias, non-response bias, validity and reliability. Results are analysed and discussed in Sections 5.2 and 5.3.

SMARTPLS 3 was used to test the distinctiveness of each construct (via Discriminate Validity Assessment and Convergent Validity Assessment), consistency in how each construct was measured (via Composite Reliability Assessment), and to verify the statistical significance of each of the hypothesised relationships shown in Figure 1 (via boot strap analysis). Results are analysed and discussed in Section 5.4.

Structural Equation Modelling was performed using SMARTPLS 3 to test the nine hypotheses illustrated in

Figure 1. Results are analysed and discussed in Section 5.5. Two questions were asked that were not part the SSA model. These are analysed and discussed in Section 6.2.

5. Data analysis

5.1. Demographics

Of the 1787 responses turned in to the research team 1444 were retained after removal of those surveys that were only partially completed. The sample was found to be representative of the composition of the residents. The 1444 usable surveys represent just over 1% of the 136,000 residents. Using the Qualtrics sample size calculator shows that sample size provides 99% confidence level with 5% margin of error for the purpose of estimating population characteristics. Among the responses, 50.2% were younger than 24, 32 were between 25 and 44, 15.8% were between 45 and 64, and 1.7 were older than 65 years. In addition, 41.2% were males, 55% were females, and 3.8% preferred not to answer. The educational levels varied among the respondents and 18.8% had a high school degree or less, 56.7% had an undergraduate degree, 20.1% had a graduate degree, and 4.4% had a professional certificate. Table 1 shows the demographic characteristics of the respondents.

5.2. Non-response bias

We employed the standard approach of comparing the early and late respondents, which treats late respondents as non-respondents reluctant to participate. If there is no significant difference between early and late respondents, we can then assume that non-respondents do not differ significantly from respondents (Peng et al. 2014).

In our study, the differences between early and late responders – specifically 90% of those who completed the survey the first week versus 10% of those who finished the last week – were examined and compared with an independent sample t-test (Armstrong and Overton

Table 1. Demographic characteristics.

Demographics	%
Gender	
Male	*41.2*
Female	*55.0*
Prefer not to answer	*3.8*
Age	
Younger than 24	*50.5*
25–44	*32.0*
45–64	*15.8*
Older than 65	*1.7*
Education	
High school & under	**18.8**
Undergrads	**56.7**
Graduate	**20.1**
Professional certificate	**4.4**

1977; Peng et al. 2014). A subsequent chi-square analysis revealed no significant difference between respondents on the basis of demographics (Hair et al. 2010).

5.3. Common method bias

Common response bias is deemed present when the first factor in an exploratory factor analysis accounts for most of the variance between all factors, or a single factor appears after factor analysis (Podsakoff et al. 2003). In order to determine whether common method bias exists, the eight constructs were entered into an exploratory factor analysis. The results were then assessed to determine if any one factor could account for the majority of the variance. Harman's (1976) single factor score showed that the first construct (self-efficacy) accounted for less than 50% of the variance, and that cumulatively the eight constructs explained less than 64%, both indications that such bias is unlikely to be present.

5.4. Reliability and validity measures

Validity and reliability of the eight SSA constructs and their respective item statements were assessed using SmartPLS 3. All constructs exceeded the minimum acceptable communality value of 0.5 (as determined by Child 2006), with the majority exceeding 0.70, evidence of a well-defined model. Results are given in Table 2. (See Fornell and Larcker 1981; Hair et al. 2014; Nunnally 1978; for further explanation).

5.4.1. Discriminate validity assessment

This test was performed to ensure that each construct has a stronger relationship with its associated item statements than it has with any other construct. It compares the Square Root of the Average Variance Extracted (AVE) value for each statement with the correlations between the constructs. The Fornell-Larcker criterion is satisfied in this data because the square root of the AVE is greater than any of the correlations.

Strong cross factor loading supports discriminant validity, with the AVE values of all constructs greater than 0.5 (or 50%) and, were also found consistent with the Fornell-Larker criterion.

5.4.2. Convergent validity assessment

This test was performed to ensure that each item statement presented to respondents is related to the construct it is meant to measure. Respondents were split randomly into two equal subsamples: Subsample1 (n1 = 722) was used to test the model, while Subsample2 (n2 = 722) was used for validation (Phillips, Peak, and Prybutok 2016). Factor loadings for each response were greater

Table 2. Reliability and validity measures.

Construct	Item	Reliability Measures		Validity Measures			R^2
		Composite Reliability	Item-total correlation	Factors loading	Commonality	Sq root of the AVE*	
SE		0.849				0.765*	
	SE1		0.457	0.662	.692		
	SE2		0.566	0.769	.728		
	SE3		0.609	0.815	.759		
	SE4		0.602	0.811	.736		
EE		0.915				0.853*	
	EE1		0.702	0.832	.692		
	EE2		0.731	0.853	.728		
	EE3		0.759	0.871	.759		
	EE4		0.737	0.858	.736		
PS		0.937				0.888*	
	PS1		0.785	0.880	.775		
	PS2		0.830	0.908	.825		
	PS3		0.805	0.894	.799		
	PS4		0.768	0.870	.757		
PP		0.778				0.744*	
	PP1		0.430	0.816	.666		
	PP2		0.304	0.672	.451		
	PP3		0.479	0.804	.647		
TT		0.951				0.911*	0.559
	TT1		0.837	0.910	.828		
	TT2		0.845	0.915	.837		
	TT3		0.820	0.899	.807		
	TT4		0.856	0.921	.849		
TG		0.894				0.824*	
	TG1		0.653	0.811	.658		
	TG2		0.717	0.853	.727		
	TG3		0.628	0.788	.621		
	TG4		0.704	0.842	.709		
BI						0.873*	0.407
	BI1	0.906	0.687	0.860	.740		
	BI2		0.698	0.866	.750		
	BI3		0.746	0.894	.799		

*Square root of the average variance extracted is less the construct correlations and shows the Fornell-Larker criterion test for discriminant validity is satisfied.

than the accepted threshold of 0.7 (or 70%), thus supporting convergent validity.

5.4.3. Composite reliability assessment
This test was performed to ensure, to the highest degree possible, that each item statement measures only the construct it was meant to measure. The squared correlation between a given item statements and the sum of the others produced values ranging from 0.778 to 0.951, demonstrating strong interrelatedness and supporting composite reliability.

5.5. Structural model and hypotheses testing

Using SMARTPLS 3, model path coefficients were examined, and a standard bootstrap error with the

Table 3. Hypotheses testing.

Hypothesis*	T-Statistics	2.5% CI	97.5% CI	P-Value	Supported?
Ha1: SE -> BI	5.802	0.147	0.296	0.000	Yes
Ha2: EE -> BI	6.056	0.159	0.314	0.000	Yes
Ha3: PS -> TT	10.761	0.329	0.477	0.000	Yes
Ha4: PP -> TT	11.450	0.347	0.490	0.000	Yes
Ha6: TT -> BI	5.580	0.132	0.274	0.000	Yes
Ha7: TG -> PM	13.23	0.382	0.514	0.000	Yes
Ha8: PV -> BI	5.83	0.151	0.3	0.000	Yes

*PLS table does not including hypothesis 5 and 8 related to mediation.

recommended 5000 bootstrap samples applied to generate the t-test values. All proposed hypotheses were tested and satisfied in both subsamples, with the results presented in Table 3.

Structural Equation Modelling (SEM) was then performed on SSA, as shown in Figure 2.

R^2 indicates the percentage of variance of the constructs TT, BI and PV. The beta coefficient (β), also known as the standardised regression coefficient, indicates each construct's strength of relationship. Of particular interest:

- SE ($\beta = 0.223$, $t = 5.802$) and EE ($\beta = 0.235$, $t = 6.056$) were each found to have a significant effect on BI;
- PP ($\beta = 0.405$, $t = 10.761$) and PS ($\beta = 0.416$, $t = 11.45$) were found to have a significant effect on Trust in Technology, where $R^2 = 55.9\%$; Trust in Technology ($\beta = 0.205$, $t = 5.580$);
- Trust in Government ($\beta = 0.446$, $t = 13.23$) was found to have a significant effect on Price Value, where $R^2 = 19.9\%$; Price Value ($\beta = 0.225$, $t = 5.830$).

These results show that the SSA model has statistical significance across all paths and explains over 40% of the variation in behavioural intention to use smart-city services.

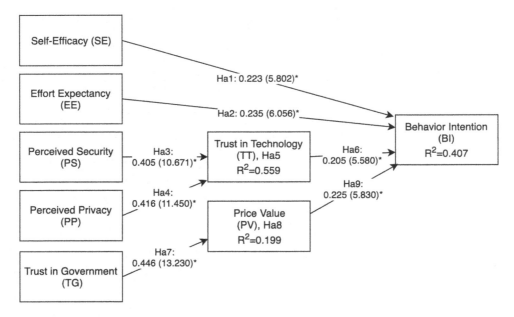

Figure 2. Results of the proposed research model.

6. Discussion & conclusion

This study explores factors affecting user adoption of smart-city services. While many cities have started or are looking to start a smart-city strategy or project, city officials want to be sure residents are willing to support such an effort, as well as that such an investment will improve their own position. The city we chose is an example of North American small-to-medium cities, with results drawn from a representative sample of residents and city employees.

6.1. SSA model

Relationships among the eight constructs were found to be significant, and support the value of the model in determining resident behavioural intention to use smart-city services.

One plausible explanation is that SSA accounted for many of the factors that would be important to a resident. These results suggest that at the very least, these factors should be considered when planning considered when planning smart-city services, including mobile, IoT, smart grid, smart lights, AI and other ICT technologies. The high statistical significance of all seven constructs leads us to confirm that they are strong predictors of the intention to use smart-city services. Results are given in Table 4.

6.1.1. Self-efficacy

A significant relationship between self-efficacy and behavioural intention supports Ha1. Respondents believe services such as sensor-based smart-traffic

systems and IoT devices that respond to traffic conditions are easy to use and would not vary greatly from what they are familiar with. Similar to other studies in e-government and internet cloud applications, residents show confidence in their ability to use smart cities services and technologies (Hsu and Chiu 2004; Hung,

Table 4. Results summary of factors affecting resident intention to use smart-city services.

#	Supported Hypothesis	Interpretation
1	Ha1: Self-Efficacy is correlated with Behavioural Intention in the adoption of smart-city services.	Residents are confident in their ability to use smart-city services.
2	Ha2: Effort Expectancy is correlated with Behavioural Intention in the adoption of smart-city services.	Residents believe smart-city services are similar to current commercial services they currently use today.
3	Ha6: Trust in Technology is correlated with Behavioural Intention in the adoption of smart-city services. Ha5: Trust in Technology moderates the relationship between Perceived Security and Perceived Privacy, respectively, on Behavioural Intention in the adoption of smart-city services. Ha3: Perceived Security is correlated with Trust in Technology. Ha4: Perceived Privacy is correlated with Trust in Technology.	Approximately 55% of trust in technology by residents is related to their perception of high degrees if security and privacy, which in turn influences their trust and adoption of smart-city services.
4	Ha7: Trust in government is correlated with Price Value of smart-city services. Ha8: Price Value is a moderating factor in the relationship between Trust in Government and Behavioural Intention. Ha9: Price Value is correlated with Behavioural Intention	Residents are influenced by the price value of smart-city services. More importantly, the price value of these services influences their trust in government.

Chang, and Yu 2006; Shiau and Chau 2016; Yi and Hwang 2003). The findings in these contexts suggest that residents believe themselves capable of using technology that is likely similar to smart city service adoption. Many already use similar technologies in their daily life, such as Google maps and Waze to monitor traffic congestion and avoid road closures in near-real time; and are accustomed to online or cloud-based security cameras for crime prevention and door locks that send notifications to their phones. They also believe smart-city services will help them achieve greater efficiency and contribute positively to their quality of life.

These results confirm that residents consider smart-city services similar to the commercial services they currently use, such as fitness wearables and tracking devices; and are consistent with research on mobile application adoption (Chang et al. 2016), the use of cloud and big data technology (Bhattacherjee and Park 2014; Verma, Bhattacharyya, and Kumar 2018) and e-government acceptance (Almalki, Duan, and Frommholz 2013; Hung, Chang, and Yu 2006).

6.1.2. Effort expectancy

A significant relationship between effort expectancy and behavioural intention supports Ha2. Ease of use was a significant factor in previous e-government studies (Alawadhi and Morris 2008; Hung, Chang, and Yu 2006). Similar studies referred to ease of use as convenience and it was the leading factor to adopt cloud technologies (Arpaci 2016; Gupta, Seetharaman, and Raj 2013). Respondents believe that smart-city services will be easy to understand and use. They are primarily interested in convenience, e.g. the convenience of finding a parking with the benefits of using 'push' notification such as ParkMobile services. However, they also recognise that these services offer savings in infrastructure cost as well as a potentially improved quality of life.

These results confirm that residents greatly value ease-of use, and are consistent with research on 311 non-emergency mobile reporting systems (Offenhuber 2015), as well as sensors for traffic monitoring, parking availability, flood level, and other areas (Chang, Wang, and Wills 2018). Moreover, the statistical significance of ease-of-use explains the importance of design the new services to be easy, intuitive, and provide convenience. At the same time, it shows how the ease of use can be a determinant factor to use and then later adopt a smart city service of not.

6.1.3. Privacy, security, and trust in technology

Smart-city service users have been found to value safety and security and support increased security government regulation (Edwards 2016; Schumann and Stock 2014;

Van Zoonen et al. 2016). Another study showed, residents' interest in using innovative and privacy assured smart cities services (Yeh 2017). The moderating effects of privacy and security concerns on the relationship between respondents' trust in smart-city technologies and their intention to use them supports Ha3, Ha4 and Ha5. A corresponding relationship between high levels of security and privacy and increased trust supports Ha6.

These results suggest that residents are willing to use smart-city technologies, provided they are assured their information is safe and their right to privacy guaranteed; and are consistent with research in e-government services and e-banking (Arpaci, Kilicer, and Bardakci 2015; Pearson and Benameur 2010; Sarabdeen and Ishak 2015; Widjaja and Chen 2012), mobile applications (Walravens 2015), and big data analytics (Krieg et al. 2018)

6.1.4. Price value and trust in government

The moderating effects of price value on respondents' trust in government and their intention to use smart-city services supports Ha7 and Ha8. A significant relationship between price value and behavioural intention supports Ha9.

These results suggest that residents expect the benefits of smart-city services to outweigh the cost, which in turn influences their trust in government. They are consistent with similar findings in the areas of SMS, internet and mobile usage (Venkatesh, James, and Xu 2012) and related to trust in government effects (Almuraqab and Jasimuddin 2017; Roca, García, and Vega 2009; Shin 2010). Residents wanted to make sure that smart cities investment should not hinder the investment in other operation areas (Hollands 2015). Trust in government found to be a critical factor in users decision to adoption to e-government (Almuraqab and Jasimuddin 2017; Roca, García, and Vega 2009; Shin 2010).

6.2. Additional questions

The two dichotomous questions the city was interested in revealed that the majority of residents might not be familiar with the term 'smart-city,' as only 34% of residents have heard of it. Similarly, only 24% of residents are aware of the city's current array of smart services.

In summary, results clearly show that four main factors affect residents' intention to use smart-city services: self-efficacy, effort expectancy, trust in technology (which is moderated with perceived security and perceived privacy) and price value (which is moderated by trust in government.) The additional qualitative questions reveal an overall lack of awareness that could and should be addressed in future.

7. Implications and limitations

7.1. Theoretical implications

The SSA model identifies those factors considered most likely to influence residents' adoption of smart-city services. While they all proved contributory to some degree, three were found to be exceptionally so: trust in technology (closely tied to their perceptions of privacy and security); trust in government; and price value.

7.2. Practical implications

SSA offers a modest contribution to academic research in model design. More importantly, it is an extension of UTAUT2 with the inclusion of trust (in technology and government, respectively) and expansion of perceived value to incorporate financial considerations.

For city officials, it verifies the strategic usefulness of SSA for planning and evaluation purposes. They can begin by choosing technologies in which residents exhibit a high degree of trust, and creating policies and investment opportunities that focus on the same.

7.3. Limitations

Our study explored an area – willingness to adopt smart-city services – that has yet to be clearly defined. Smart-city technologies and services remain esoteric terms for many residents and city officials. First forays are by definition brief excursions into new territory, and this one is no exception. By choosing to view overall adoption of technology within a single smart-city, we neither singled out individual services nor covered all aspects of what distinguishes smart cities from other urban environments. We also did not test other factors in UTAUT2 – hedonic values, performance expectancy, and facilitating conditions – or consider factors such as service quality, any of which could have influence the results as much or more.

7.4. Recommendations for future research

The SSA model can and should be used as a blueprint for the development of smart-city services; it might also be expanded to include more constructs from UTAUT2. If administered on a larger scale, the questionnaire could be re-designed to gauge resident demands for particular smart-city services. Finally, replication – both through case studies of specific cities and more generally across different types of urban environments – would lend credence to both SSA and its findings.

Disclosure statement

No potential conflict of interest was reported by the authors.

Funding

This research was supported by the City of Denton grant, to University of North Texas number GP40005.

ORCID

Abdulrahman Habib ⓘ http://orcid.org/0000-0001-5992-7490
Victor R. Prybutok ⓘ http://orcid.org/0000-0003-3810-9039

References

Agha, A. 2016. *A Stakeholder Based Assessment of Developing Country Challenges and Solutions in Smart Mobility within the Smart City Framework*. doi:10.13140/RG.2.1.3516.9689.

Alawadhi, S., and A. Morris. 2008. "The Use of the UTAUT Model in the Adoption of e-Government Services in Kuwait." Proceedings of the 41st Hawaii International Conference on system Sciences, 1–11. Waikoloa: IEEE. doi:10.1109/HICSS.2008.452.

AlAwadhi, S., and H. J. Scholl. 2013. "Aspirations and realizations: The Smart City of Seattle." *Proceedings of the Annual Hawaii International Conference on System Sciences*, 1695–1703. doi:10.1109/HICSS.2013.102.

Almalki, O., Y. Duan, and I. Frommholz. 2013. "Developing a Conceptual Framework to Evaluate e-Government Portals' Success." Proceedings of the 13th European Conference on e-Government, 19–26. Varese: University of Insubria

Almuraqab, N. A. S. 2017. "M-government Adoption Factors in the UAE: A Partial Least-squares Approach." *International Journal of Business and Information* 11 (4): 404–431. http://ijbi.org/ijbi/article/view/191.

Almuraqab, N. A. S., and S. M. Jasimuddin. 2017. "Factors that Influence End-Users' Adoption of Smart Government Services in the UAE: A Conceptual Framework." *The Electronic Journal Information Systems Evaluation* 20 (1): 11–23.

Alsmadi, D., and V. Prybutok. 2018. "Sharing and Storage Behavior via Cloud Computing: Security and Privacy in Research and Practice." *Computers in Human Behavior* 85: 218–226. doi:10.1016/j.chb.2018.04.003.

Armstrong, J. S., and T. S. Overton. 1977. "Estimating Nonresponse Bias in Mail Surveys." *Journal of Marketing Research* 14: 396–402.

Arpaci, I. 2016. "Understanding and Predicting Students' Intention to Use Mobile Cloud Storage Services." *Computers in Human Behavior* 58: 150–157.

Arpaci, I., K. Kilicer, and S. Bardakci. 2015. "Effects of Security and Privacy Concerns on Educational Use of Cloud Services." *Computers in Human Behavior* 45: 93–98. doi:10.1016/j.chb.2014.11.075.

Arpaci, I., Y. Yardimci Cetin, and O. Turetken. 2015. "Impact of Perceived Security on Organizational Adoption of Smartphones." *Cyberpsychology, Behavior, and Social Networking* 18 (10): 602–608.

Bandura, A. 1977. *Social Learning Theory*. Englewood Cliffs, NJ: Prentice-Hall.

Bhattacherjee, A., and S. C. Park. 2014. "Why End-users Move to the Cloud: A Migration-theoretic Analysis." *European Journal of Information Systems* 23 (3): 357–372. doi:10.1057/ejis.2013.1.

Braun, T., B. C. M. Fung, F. Iqbal, and B. Shah. 2018. "Security and Privacy Challenges in Smart Cities." *Sustainable Cities and Society* 39 (November 2017): 499–507. doi:10.1016/j.scs.2018.02.039.

Carlos Roca, J., J. José García, and J. José de la Vega. 2009. "The Importance of Perceived Trust, Security and Privacy in Online Trading Systems." *Information Management & Computer Security* 17 (2): 96–113. doi:10.1108/09685220910963983.

Carter, L. 2008. "E-government Diffusion: A Comparison of Adoption Constructs." In *Transforming Government: People, Process and Policy*, Vol. 2, pp. 147–161. doi:10.1108/17506160810902167.

Cavada, M., D. V. Hunt, and C. D. Rogers. 2014. "Smart Cities: Contradicting Definitions and Unclear Measures." In *World Sustainability Forum*, 1–12. MDPI AG.

Chang, I.-C., P.-C. Chou, R. K.-J. Yeh, and H.-T. Tseng. 2016. "Factors Influencing Chinese Tourists' Intentions to use the Taiwan Medical Travel App." *Telematics and Informatics* 33 (2): 401–409. doi:10.1016/j.tele.2015.09.007.

Chang, V., Y. Wang, and G. Wills. 2018. "Research Investigations on the Use or Non-use of Hearing Aids in the Smart Cities." *Technological Forecasting and Social Change* (November 2017), 0–1. doi:10.1016/j.techfore.2018.03.002.

Chatterjee, S., A. K. Kar, and M. P. Gupta. 2018. "Success of IoT in Smart Cities of India: An Empirical Analysis." *Government Information Quarterly* 35 (3): 349–361. doi:10.1016/j.giq.2018.05.002.

Chen, D., and H. Zhao. 2012. "Data Security and Privacy Protection Issues in Cloud Computing." *International Conference on Computer Science and Electronics Engineering* 1 (973): 647–651. doi:10.1109/ICCSEE.2012.193.

Child, D. 2006. *Essentials of Factor Analysis.* 3rd ed. New York, NY: Continuum International Publishing Group.

Chong, M., A. Habib, N. Evangelopoulos, and H. W. Park. 2018. "Dynamic Capabilities of a Smart City: An Innovative Approach to Discovering Urban Problems and Solutions." *Government Information Quarterly* (May): 1–11. doi:10.1016/j.giq.2018.07.005.

Chourabi, H., T. Nam, S. Walker, J. R. Gil-Garcia, S. Mellouli, K. Nahon, and H. J. Scholl. 2011. "Understanding Smart Cities: An Integrative Framework." *Proceedings of the Annual Hawaii International Conference on System Sciences*, 2289–2297. doi:10.1109/HICSS.2012.615.

Dwivedi, Y. K., N. P. Rana, A. Jeyaraj, M. Clement, and M. D. Williams. 2017. "Re-examining the Unified Theory of Acceptance and Use of Technology (UTAUT): Towards a Revised Theoretical Model." *Information Systems Frontiers*, 1–16. doi:10.1007/s10796-017-9774-y.

Edwards, L. 2016. *Privacy, Security and Data Protection in Smart Cities: A Critical EU Law Perspective.* https://heinonline.org/HOL/LandingPage?handle=hein.journals/edpl2&div=8&id=&page=.

Elmaghraby, A. S., and M. M. Losavio. 2014. "Cyber Security Challenges in Smart Cities: Safety, Security and Privacy." *Journal of Advanced Research* 5 (4): 491–497. doi:10.1016/j.jare.2014.02.006.

Flavián, C., and M. Guinalíu. 2006. "Consumer Trust, Perceived Security and Privacy Policy: Three Basic Elements of Loyalty to a web Site." *Industrial Management & Data Systems* 106 (5): 601–620. doi:10.1108/02635570610666403.

Fornell, C., and D. F. Larcker. 1981. *Structural Equation Models with Unobservable Variables and Measurement Error: Algebra and Statistics.*

Gupta, P., A. Seetharaman, and J. R. Raj. 2013. "The Usage and Adoption of Cloud Computing by Small and Medium Businesses." *International Journal of Information Management* 33 (5): 861–874.

Hair, J. F., W. C. Black, B. J. Babin, and R. E. Anderson. 2010. *Multivariate Data Analysis: A Global Perspective.* Upper Saddle River, NJ: Pearson.

Hair, J. F., G. T. M. Hult, C. Ringle, and M. Sarstedt. 2014. *A Primer on Partial Least Squares Structural Equation Modeling (PLS-SEM). Long Range Planning*, Vol. 46. Sage Publications, Inc. doi:10.1016/j.lrp.2013.01.002.

Harman, H. H. 1976. *Modern Factor Analysis.* Chicago: University of Chicago Press.

Hollands, R. G. 2008. "Will the Real Smart City Please Stand up? Intelligent, Progressive or Entrepreneurial?" *City* 12 (3): 303–320. doi:10.1080/13604810802479126.

Hollands, R. G. 2015. "Critical Interventions Into the Corporate Smart City." *Cambridge Journal of Regions, Economy and Society* 8 (1): 61–77. doi:10.1093/cjres/rsu011.

Hsu, M. H., and C. M. Chiu. 2004. "Internet Self-Efficacy and Electronic Service Acceptance." *Decision Support Systems* 38 (3): 369–381. doi:10.1016/j.dss.2003.08.001.

Hujran, O. Al. 2012. "An Assessment of Jordan's e-Government Maturity: A User-Centric Perceptive." *International Journal of Electronic Governance* 5 (2): 134–150. http://www.inderscience.com/info/inarticle.php?artid=49801.

Hung, S. Y., C. M. Chang, and T. J. Yu. 2006. "Determinants of User Acceptance of the e-Government Services: The Case of Online Tax Filing and Payment System." *Government Information Quarterly* 23 (1): 97–122. doi:10.1016/j.giq.2005.11.005.

Krieg, J. G., G. Jakllari, H. Toma, and A. L. Beylot. 2018. "Unlocking the Smartphone's Sensors for Smart City Parking." *Pervasive and Mobile Computing* 43: 78–95. doi:10.1016/j.pmcj.2017.12.002.

Lee, I., B. Choi, J. Kim, and S. J. Hong. 2007. "Culture-Technology Fit: Effects of Cultural Characteristics on the Post-Adoption Beliefs of Mobile Internet Users." *International Journal of Electronic Commerce* 11 (4): 11–51. doi:10.2753/ JEC1086-4415110401.

Lin, A., and N. Chen. 2012. "Cloud Computing as an Innovation: Perception, Attitude, and Adoption." *International Journal of Information Management* 32: 533–540. doi:10.1016/j.ijinfomgt.2012.04.001.

Luarn, P., and H. Lin. 2005. "Toward an Understanding of the Behavioral Intention to Use Mobile Banking." *Computers in Human Behavior* 21 (6): 873–891. doi:10.1016/j.chb.2004.03.003.

Manyika, J., M. Chui, B. Brown, J. Bughin, R. Dobbs, C. Roxburgh, and A. H. Byers. 2011. *Big Data: The Next Frontier for Innovation, Competition, and Productivity.*

Mohanty, S. P., U. Choppali, and E. Kougianos. 2016. "Everything you Wanted to Know About Smart Cities: The Internet of Things is the Backbone." *IEEE Consumer Electronics Magazine* 5 (3): 60–70. doi:10.1109/MCE.2016.2556879.

Nam, T., and T. Pardo. 2011a. "Smart City as Urban Innovation: Focusing on Management, Policy, and Context." *Proceedings of the 5th International Conference on Theory and Practice of Electronic Governance*, 185–194. doi:10.1145/2072069.2072100.

Nam, T., and T. A. Pardo. 2011b. "Conceptualizing Smart City with Dimensions of Technology, People, and Institutions." In *Proceedings of the 12th Annual International Digital Government Research Conference on Digital Government Innovation in Challenging Times - Dg.o '11, 282*. doi:10. 1145/2037556.2037602.

Nunnally, J. 1978. *Psychometric Methods*.

Offenhuber, D. 2015. "Infrastructure Legibility—a Comparative Analysis of open311-Based Citizen Feedback Systems." *Cambridge Journal of Regions, Economy and Society* 8 (1): 93–112. doi:10.1093/cjres/rsu001.

Okumus, B., and A. Bilgihan. 2014. "Proposing a Model to Test Smartphone Users' Intention to Use Smart Applications When Ordering Food in Restaurants." *Journal of Hospitality and Tourism Technology* 5 (1): 31–49.

Ozkan, S., and I. E. Kanat. 2011. "E-Government Adoption Model Based on Theory of Planned Behavior: Empirical Validation." *Government Information Quarterly* 28 (4): 503–513. doi:10.1016/j.giq.2010.10.007.

Pearson, S. 2009. "Taking Account of Privacy When Designing Cloud Computing Services." In *Proceedings of the 2009 ICSE Workshop on Software Engineering Challenges of Cloud Computing, Vancouver, Canada, May 23–23*, pp. 44–52. IEEE Computer Society. doi:10.1109/CLOUD.2009.5071532.

Pearson, S., and A. Benameur. 2010. "Privacy, Security and Trust Issues Arising from Cloud Computing." In *IEEE Second International Conference on Cloud Computing Technology and Science, Indianapolis, USA, Nov 30-Dec 3*, pp. 693–702. doi:10.1109/CloudCom.2010.66.

Peng, X., R. Scott, V. Prybutok, and A. Sidorova. 2014. "Product Quality vs Service Quality in the Mobile Industry: Is There a Dominant Driver of Customer Intention to Switch Providers?" *Operations Management Research* 7 (3–4): 63–76. doi:10.1007/s12063-014-0093-x.

Phillips, B., D. Peak, and V. Prybutok. 2016. *SNSQUAL: A Social Networking Site Quality Model*.

Podsakoff, P. M., S. B. MacKenzie, J.-Y. Lee, and N. P. Podsakoff. 2003. "Common Method Biases in Behavioral Research: A Critical Review of the Literature and Recommended Remedies." *Journal of Applied Psychology* 88 (5): 879–903. doi:10.1037/0021-9010.88.5.879.

Ratten, V. 2012. "Entrepreneurial and Ethical Adoption Behaviour of Cloud Computing." *The Journal of High Technology Management Research* 23 (2): 155–164.

Roca, J. C., J. J. García, and J. J. D. La Vega. 2009. "The Importance of Perceived Trust, Security and Privacy in Online Trading Systems." *Information Management & Computer Security* 17 (2): 96–113. doi:10.1108/ 09685220910963983.

Sarabdeen, J., and M. M. M. Ishak. 2015. "Impediment of Privacy in the Use of Clouds by Educational Institutions." *Journal of Advances in Information Technology* 6 (3): 167–172. doi:10.12720/jait.6.3.167-172.

Schumann, L., and W. G. Stock. 2014. "The Information Service Evaluation (ISE) Model." *Webology* 11 (1): 1–20.

Scuotto, V., A. Ferraris, and S. Bresciani. 2016. "Internet of Things: Applications and Challenges in Smart Cities: a Case Study of IBM Smart City Projects." *Business Process Management Journal* 22 (2): 357–367. doi:10.1108/BPMJ-05-2015-0074.

Shiau, W. L., and P. Y. K. Chau. 2016. "Understanding Behavioral Intention to Use a Cloud Computing Classroom: A Multiple Model Comparison Approach." *Information and Management* 53 (3): 355–365. doi:10.1016/j.im.2015.10.004.

Shin, D. H. 2010. "The Effects of Trust, Security and Privacy in Social Networking: A Security-Based Approach to Understand the Pattern of Adoption." *Interacting with Computers* 22 (5): 428–438. doi:10.1016/j.intcom.2010.05.001.

Susanto, T. D., and R. Goodwin. 2011. "User Acceptance of SMS-based eGovernment Services." *Lecture Notes in Computer Science (Including Subseries Lecture Notes in Artificial Intelligence and Lecture Notes in Bioinformatics)*, 6846 *LNCS*, 75–87. doi:10.1007/978-3-642-22878-0_7.

Sweeneya, J., and G. Soutarb. 2001. "Consumer Perceived Value: The Development of a Multiple Item Scale." *Journal of Retailing* 77 (2): 203–220. doi:10.1108/ 17506121211243086.

Thomas, V., D. Wang, L. Mullagh, and N. Dunn. 2016. "Where's Wally? In Search of Citizen Perspectives on the Smart City." *Sustainability (Switzerland)* 8 (3): 1–14. doi:10.3390/su8030207.

Townsend, A. 2013. *Smart Cities: Big Data, Civic Hackers, and the Quest for a new Utopia*. WW Norton & Company.

Van Zoonen, L., T. Braun, B. C. M. Fung, F. Iqbal, B. Shah, E. F. Z. Santana, and D. S. Milojicic. 2016. "Security and Privacy Challenges in Smart Cities." *Government Information Quarterly* 33 (3): 472–480. doi:10.1016/j.scs.2018.02.039.

Venkatesh, V. 2000. "Determinants of Perceived Ease of Use: Integrating Control, Intrinsic Motivation, and Emotion into the Technology Acceptance Model." *Information Systems Research* 11 (4): 342–365. doi:10.1287/isre.11.4.342.11872.

Venkatesh, V., T. Y. L. James, and X. Xu. 2012. "Consumer Acceptance and Use of Information Technology: Extending the Unified Theory of Acceptance and Use of Technology." *MIS Quarterly* 36 (1): 157–178. doi:10.1111/ j.1540-4560.1981.tb02627.x.

Venkatesh, V., G. M. Michael, G. B. Davis, and F. D. Davis. 2003. "User Acceptance of Information Technology: Toward a Unified View." *Mis Quarterly* 27 (3): 425–478.

Verma, S., S. S. Bhattacharyya, and S. Kumar. 2018. "An Extension of the Technology Acceptance Model in the big Data Analytics System Implementation Environment." *Information Processing and Management* 54 (5): 791–806. doi:10.1016/j.ipm.2018.01.004.

Walravens, N. 2015. "Mobile City Applications for Brussels Citizens: Smart City Trends, Challenges and a Reality Check." *Telematics and Informatics* 32 (2): 282–299. doi:10.1016/j.tele.2014.09.004.

Widjaja, A. E., and J. V. Chen. 2012. "Using Cloud Computing Service: A Perspective from Users' Information Security, Privacy Concern, and Trust." Proceedings, 43rd Decision Sciences Institute Annual Meeting (DSI), California, USA, Nov 17–20, 9221–9231. San Francisco, CA.

Williams, M. D., N. P. Rana, Y. K. Dwivedi, and B. Lal. 2011. "Is UTAUT Really Used or Just Cited for the Sake of it? A Systematic Review of Citations of UTAUT's Originating Article." In *ECIS*, 231–243. Helsinki: AIS.

Yeh, H. 2017. "The Effects of Successful ICT-Based Smart City Services: From Citizens' Perspectives." *Government*

Information Quarterly 34 (3): 556–565. doi:10.1016/j.giq. 2017.05.001.

Yenisey, M. M., A. A. Ozok, and G. Salvendy. 2005. "Perceived Security Determinants in E-Commerce Among Turkish University Students." *Behaviour & Information Technology* 24 (4): 259–274.

Yi, M. Y., and Y. Hwang. 2003. "Predicting the Use of Web-based Information Systems: Self-Efficacy, Enjoyment, Learning Goal Orientation, and the Technology Acceptance Model." *International Journal of Human Computer Studies* 59 (4): 431–449. doi:10.1016/S1071-5819(03)00114-9.

Appendix. Survey instrument

Construct	Item	Supporting Literature
Self-Efficacy (SE)	Have you heard of Smart Cities before? To what extent do you agree with the following: SE1. I can see myself using smart city services to seek city information if I have used similar services before SE2. I can see myself using smart city services to seek information if someone teaches me how to SE3. I can see myself using smart city services to seek information if I have time to try it out SE4. I can see myself using smart city services to seek information if I can afford it	Thomas et al. (2016) Okumus and Bilgihan (2014) Shiau and Chau (2016)
Effort Expectancy (EE)	To what extent do you agree with the following: EE1. Learning how to use smart city services is easy for me. EE2. It is easy for me to interact with smart city services, it is clear and understandable. EE3. It is easy for me to become skilful at using smart city services. EE4. I find smart city services easy to use. (Ex. Online utility metering portal, Mobile Parking System)	Venkatesh et al. (2003) Venkatesh, James, and Xu (2012)
Perceived Security (PS)	To what extent do you agree with the following: PS1. I would feel secure to send my sensitive information via smart city services. PS2. A smart city website is a safe place to transmit sensitive information. PS3. I would feel safe storing sensitive information and document about myself over smart city services. PS4. I believe that smart city services provide sufficient restrictions for unauthorised access.	Bhattacherjee and Park (2014) Arpaci, Yardimci Cetin, and Turetken (2015) Yenisey, Ozok, and Salvendy (2005)
Perceived Privacy (PP)	To what extent do you agree with the following: PP1. I believe that Smart city services have a strong policy to protect my sensitive information. PP2. I often look for and read privacy policies of smart city services PP3. I am careful not to give service providers more information online than I have to. PP4. Smart city providers only collect my personal information if necessary.	Arpaci, Yardimci Cetin, and Turetken (2015) Ratten (2012) Flavián and Guinalíu (2006)
Trust in Technology (TT)	To what extent do you agree with the following: TT1. I trust the security of the smart city services Legal/technical infrastructure of smart city services is sufficient in protecting my information TT2. I trust the devices that collect and process my data while I am using smart city services TT3. I can count on smart city services to protect my information	Almuraqab (2017) Shin (2010) Carlos Roca, José García, and José de la Vega (2009)
Price Value (PV)	To what extent do you agree with the following: PV1. A city can finance smart city services by Showing advertisements before using the service PV2. A city can finance smart city services by adding a small charge to your utility bill PV3. I am willing to share my information and usage data to cover the cost of smart city services PV4. I would be interested in vendors financing services instead of using bonds	Lee et al. (2007) Self-developed
Trust in Gov (TG)	To what extent do you agree with the following: TG1. I trust public departments and institutions TG. I trust city capabilities in providing safe, smart city services. TG3. I trust that citizens' interest is city's first priority. TG4. I trust City's procedures to protect my personal information	Almuraqab (2017) Self-developed
Behavioural intention (BI)	To what extent do you agree with the following: BI1. I intend to continue using smart city services in the future. BI2. I will always try to use smart city services in my daily life. BI3. I plan to continue to use smart city services frequently. Are you aware of any smart city services in Denton?	Venkatesh et al. (2003) Self-Developed
Demographics	Select your age Select your gender Select your highest or currently perusing education level	

The role of a location-based city exploration game in digital placemaking

Carolyn Pang, Carman Neustaedter, Karyn Moffatt, Kate Hennessy and Rui Pan

ABSTRACT

Many digital technologies, such as social media, community systems, and public displays, have been studied to explore how people engage with each other in their community. Yet little is known about how one form of technology, location-based games (LBGs), can support urban residents in community awareness, city exploration, and placemaking as they navigate spaces and places in their cities. To explore this topic, we investigated the challenges urban residents faced in finding information about their community along a transit network. We then designed, developed, and evaluated an LBG called City Explorer that supports city exploration using gamification and the viewing and sharing of community information. We found that residents valued the fun, competition, and rewards afforded through play in public spaces, creating opportunities for placemaking through location services and knowledge sharing. Players also wanted additional knowledge about their transit commutes, including data about the frequency and routines of their transit rides. Collectively, such ridership data offers potential for smart city initiatives and illustrates that careful design considerations are required to balance people's needs for play, personal data, privacy, and community information acquisition.

1. Introduction

Half of the world's population live in urban cities, a demographic reality that requires urban centres adopt an integrated view of public spaces, community services, and transportation to support engaged cities. Urban informatics explores the impacts of technology, systems and infrastructure on people in urban spaces (Williams, Robles, and Dourish 2009; Foth, Choi, and Satchell 2011). Research on urban informatics is far-reaching, with research spanning the study of social behaviours (communication studies, cultural studies, etc.), urban communities (urban planning, architecture, etc.), and computing (computer science, human–computer interaction, etc.) (Foth et al. 2011). Community participation has often been studied within the field of urban informatics where systems have been designed to encourage playful civic engagement and communication with government organisations (Schneekloth and Shibley 1995; Grasso et al. 2003; Schroeter and Foth 2009; Foth et al. 2011). Public transit within urban cities forms a network that connects suburbs within a metropolitan region and can move many people within confined spaces. Within this network and spaces exist opportunities for people to interact with each other, whether it is through densification near transit exchanges, or through more personal conversations with fellow riders.

For our area of focus, we see little work on how mobile technology supports community awareness by understanding the challenges people face in learning about their communities tied to public places along an urban transit network. Given this, we chose to design a transit-focused location-based game (LBG) as it offered opportunities to rethink ways in which people playfully engaged with others in their community. Location-based games (LBGs) are games played on mobile devices where content is tied to specific locations and accessed by players when they are there (Rashid et al. 2006; Williams, Robles, and Dourish 2009; Laureyssens et al. 2014). By connecting people with others in their community, LBGs could act as a catalyst for *placemaking*: broadly defined as the shaping of an environment to facilitate social interaction with the intention of creating public spaces that promote people's quality of life (Montola, Stenros, and Waern 2009; López and Butler 2013; Fredericks et al. 2015; Sun 2015; Foth 2017).

The aim of this article is to explore the role of a location-based city exploration game in digital placemaking to understand if and how LBGs may be able to increase awareness of community happenings, support real-time information sharing, and cultivate a sense of community participation. Digital placemaking augments physical places with location-specific services to create informal, playful, and meaningful opportunities for participation (Sun 2015; Foth 2017; Sun, McLachlan, and Naaman 2017; Peacock, Anderson, and Crivellaro 2018). While the concept of placemaking has a long history in urban studies and urban practice, several perspectives exist upon which placemaking in cities have been studied (Blokland 2017; Foth 2017). The combination of digital technology and urban places within the context of digital placemaking plays an important role in HCI research but has been underexplored to date (Willis et al. 2009; Sun and Naaman 2018; Carroll 2019; Freeman et al. 2019). As such, there is a need to better understand how playful technologies can affect how people perceive place and change their relationships with public spaces. This in turn offers opportunities for people to interact with the city, from learning about the history of places, to understanding how future developments could affect individual and collective human experiences. Both of these aspects are the focus of our research.

Our first research goal was to understand the community information needs of urban residents and to explore how best to present such information to them using a location-based system. While there are many possible types of technologies and designs that could facilitate the presentation of such information, we explore LBGs as one type of design genre, given a lack of research in this space. Our second research goal was to then investigate how and when urban residents would play an LBG and whether such a game would encourage community awareness, city exploration, and digital placemaking. To address these two goals, we conducted three stages of research: (1) an exploration of urban residents' needs for community information; (2) the design of a location-based game to support these needs; and, (3) an evaluation of the location-based game as it is experienced by residents in an urban city. Our exploratory study involved diaries and interviews with 18 participants living in the metropolitan area of Vancouver, British Columbia, Canada. We wanted to understand how, when and where residents found information about their local community, which tools they preferred to use to manage and share such information, and the challenges they faced in acquiring and sharing this information. The results revealed two main types of community information that people were interested in: *location-based information* – knowledge tied to specific places – and *time-based information* – knowledge of upcoming events and happenings. The former was used throughout daily life to understand one's community and how it was changing (where people often did not even realise they were interested in the information before they saw it). The latter was used to plan family activities within one's community, an aspect of digital placemaking that explores the social aspects of city life. Together, these results outline the challenges that future communication technologies should try to overcome along with lessons for how to begin to approach such design challenges. Detailed results of this study have been previously published (Pang et al. 2015); here, we summarise them in a reflective manner to demonstrate how it informed our design work.

Play systems have been previously designed for public spaces to support placemaking, such as 21 Balancoires and Ingress (Sun 2015). Building on our first study, we designed an LBG called City Explorer that provides people with a means to explore areas within their city and to share locally relevant information about one's community along an urban transit network. A challenge with placemaking includes the struggle to identify meaningful experienced geographies within cities in which people live (Freeman et al. 2019). The goal of our system was to increase community awareness through playful exploration of areas and the sharing of user-generated content related to players' transit trips. With City Explorer, people used their mobile phones to collect points as they rode public transit, where the overarching goal was to collect the most points and earn a spot on the leaderboard. Players created geo-tagged posts to describe and share community-related information. They also completed route-specific challenges and collaborated with other riders to multiply their points by riding the same route.

We deployed City Explorer with 12 participants over a 4-week period. Here, we explored when and how people would play a transit-based LBG and whether such a game would encourage community awareness, playful city exploration, and digital placemaking. Our results revealed that players valued learning about their personal transit routines and community information at the start and end of their routes based on its geographic importance to them (e.g. at home or work). We discuss these findings and reflect on both the successes and challenges they pose for future technology design and research that considers enabling residents to seamlessly integrate their daily lives with urban spaces through the use of personal devices and location-based services. This is especially critical in the context of smart cities and digital placemaking, where technologies make cities more manageable and more personal by deploying sensing capabilities and adopting data-driven approaches, yet face much criticism for privacy concerns (Roche and Rajabifard 2012; Barth and de Jong 2017; Zheng et al. 2018). Meaningful placemaking proposes community attachment as a strategy for building emotional connections to a place that affords satisfaction (Freeman et al.

2019). Detailed results of this study have also been previously published (Pang et al. 2019).

This article extends our prior work on community information needs and the presentation of such information through a location-based game (Pang et al. 2015; Pang et al. 2019). In those papers, we examined the types of community information and services urban residents wanted to know about and how this information should be presented to them. A recurring theme that emerged across that body of research was the role of digital placemaking. This extended article complements our body of knowledge on community information needs through a location-based game by examining both studies together and specifically reflecting on the work through a placemaking lens. It is through this larger lens that we can begin to understand and analyse community information needs and play, where technology can be used not just as a means to improve existing communications, but also as an unprecedented opportunity to improve the lives of urban residents through community engagement and attachment.

Next, we detail the related research around studies of public spaces, placemaking, and play, along with literature on community, information and communications technology (ICT) and engaging people within their communities. Following this, we describe each research stage: our requirements analysis study of community information needs, our design work of City Explorer, and then our field deployment. We conclude with a discussion of the implications from our research and the role of LBGs in city exploration and digital placemaking.

2. Related work

2.1. Public spaces, placemaking and play

In recent years, the Internet of Things has gained interest due to smaller sensor and device sizes and lower costs of chips and sensors (Reinfurt et al. 2016). As a result, there have been developments in concepts such as smart homes (Röcker et al. 2005), smart offices (Le Gal et al. 2001), and smart cities (Nam and Pardo 2011). More recently, the term *Internet of Places* was introduced as an extension of the Internet of Things. Where the Internet of Things makes the Internet accessible through physical objects, the Internet of Places aims to support awareness, engagement, and interaction related to human experiences in places (Carroll et al. 2017). Because mobile devices are constantly connected to the Internet, the boundaries between physical and digital spaces are often seamless, creating a hybrid urban space (De Souza e Silva 2006).

The distinction between *space* and *place* first emerged in the HCI field in 1996, when Harrison and Dourish

proposed a re-evaluation of spatial models to support computer-supported collaborative work (Harrison and Dourish 1996). The key principle, 'space is the opportunity; place is the understood reality', was introduced, along with their argument that properties of space were rooted in mutually-held cultural understandings about behaviour and action (Harrison and Dourish 1996). In our everyday experiences, we are physically located in *space*, but behave and act in *place*. Thus, people value spaces where the sense of place has a personal meaning or attachment. Cities have now become hybrid spaces with physical buildings, people, and social structures where location-based applications have become increasingly pervasive in our everyday lives. As such, opportunities exist for the exploration and sharing in the everyday activities that people encounter as they move around public spaces.

Placemaking is broadly defined as the shaping of an environment to facilitate social interaction with the intention of creating public spaces that promote people's quality of life (Montola, Stenros, and Waern 2009; López and Butler 2013; Fredericks et al. 2015; Sun 2015; Foth 2017). It describes the role that people play in turning public spaces into socially and culturally meaningful places (Foth 2017). Natural placemaking can emerge from the ways people occupy cities and leave their mark on the city, arising through grassroots initiatives, where communities come together with minimal involvement of city officials (Fredericks et al. 2015; Foth 2017). Here, urban residents can establish a shared vision and collectively implement and build the type of shared public space desired. This goes beyond the creation of permanent physical improvements to the embedding of community pride and promotion of environmental sustainability. For example, community gardens promote community building and offer a place for residents to develop friendships and build social capital (Wang et al. 2015). A more top-down approach occurs in accelerated placemaking, which occurs when city officials plan and build new urban developments and defined liveable communities (Foth 2017). Yet another form of placemaking may occur when arts and culture are used to shape the physical and social character of a place (creative placemaking) (Foth 2017). Digital placemaking explores the combination of location-based digital technologies in urban spaces to foster a connection to community and a sense of belonging, encouraging residents to value, cherish, and experience where they live (Foth 2017; Mushiba and Heissmeyer 2018; Carroll 2019; Freeman et al. 2019). Within the field of HCI, we have seen examples of digital placemaking where researchers have explored public displays (Grasso et al. 2003; Fortin, Neustaedter, and Hennessy 2014; Claes and Moere

2015), digital kiosks (López and Butler 2013; Fredericks et al. 2015), connected street furniture (Nam and Pardo 2011; Lea 2017; Howell, Niemeyer, and Ryokai 2019), and mobile and personal devices, including smartphones and personal wearables (De Souza e Silva 2006; Bilandzic, Foth, and De Luca 2008; Andone et al. 2017; Sun, McLachlan, and Naaman 2017). Yet, placemaking can be challenging in cities due to the struggle to identify the personal needs of those who live within, along with the complexities in balancing large-scale urban developments, sometimes at the expense of smaller, loosely connected neighbourhoods (Freeman et al. 2019).

Play in public spaces offers opportunities for placemaking in several ways. For example, urban art environments are often integrated within the landscape design, architecture, and planning of public spaces (Innocent 2016). Pervasive games extend the digital gaming experience into the real world and offer opportunities for community building based on principles of non-competitive game design such as collaboration over competition (Montola, Stenros, and Waern 2009; López and Butler 2013; Mushiba and Heissmeyer 2018). Such games have the potential to strengthen the link between cities and their residents through community participation, engagement and interaction with elements embedded in real spaces. Play in communities can be used as a formative element to bring people together through a productive element of culture and defining strategies for city exploration (De Koven 2013; Innocent 2016; Mushiba and Heissmeyer 2018). Gamification is defined as the use of game design elements in non-game contexts and often serve as good motivators when focused on pleasure, rewards, and time (Deterding et al. 2011; Zichermann and Cunningham 2011). Gamification is shown to motivate; this is important for the context of our research as we wanted to motivate people to share community information, explore areas along their commute, and engage with others and the information.

More recently, the ubiquity of mobile devices has enabled the emergence of location-based games (LBGs) that build on GPS maps and paints the city as a space in which to play, see, and explore. An example of a popular LBG is geocaching, created in 2000 and enjoyed by over 4 million players worldwide (Neustaedter and Judge 2012). Geocaching is a GPS-enabled treasure hunt that takes place in the real world (O'Hara 2008). In the game, players use the coordinates of a map on their mobile phones to find a physical, hidden container. Since then, many LBGs have been designed, including *Feeding Yoshi* (Bell et al. 2006), *Can You See Me Now?* (Benford et al. 2006), and *GEMS* (Procyk and Neustaedter 2014). In *Feeding Yoshi*, teams of players explore public and private Wi-Fi networks across urban environments with the goal of collecting points. Points can be earned by finding virtual on-screen Yoshis, sowing seeds, harvesting fruit, and feeding Yoshis (Bell et al. 2006). In *Can You See Me Now?*, online players are chased through a virtual city by 'runners' (street players equipped with GPS technology) (Benford et al. 2006). Online players can see the positions of other players and the runners and can also communicate via text messaging. *GEMS* was a location-based storytelling game where geotagged photos and videos can be shared with family and friends (Procyk and Neustaedter 2014). The game narrative encourages players to create geo-located digital memories that other players can then collect and view. Across all of these LBGs, location has been found to elicit a sense of discovery through exploration, sharing, and collaboration. We also see the idea of discovery emerge in commercial LBGs such as Foursquare. For example, users of Foursquare have been found to change their travel routes and mobility decisions in order to earn badges and other rewards such as 'mayorships' (Frith 2013). In sum, location-based games provide the opportunity to leverage location and gamification, offering a novel approach that could be used while travelling via public transit to encourage digital placemaking; we explore the extent to which this is possible and how transit riders use a LBG custom-designed for their travels.

2.2. Technologies for community information and engagement

Community is a broad term for a variety of social arrangements, including communities of practice, communities of interest, social communities (e.g. Facebook, Twitter, etc.), and neighbourhood communities (Ackerman et al. 2004; Cramer, Rost, and Holmquist 2011). Communities often overlap in large cities and are not necessarily bound by geographic locations or neighbourhoods; often, people subscribe to a number of communities, determined by occupation, hobbies, or religion, to name a few (Charles and Crow 2012; Blokland 2017). Community information spans a breadth of topics, including neighbourhood events, municipal activities, traffic, and leisure activities, where such information helps manage one's everyday activities (Unruh, Pettigrew, and Durrance 2002; Pang et al. 2015; Carroll et al. 2017). Community information is widely available through multiple traditional and digital channels, including local newspapers, social media, television, and radio news broadcasts.

Increasingly, ICT, such as social media, community systems, and public displays, have introduced ways for people to learn about community events. For example, social media tools have played a strong role in letting people share information within communities as well as foster social capital, defined as a set of properties of a social entity within communities that enables joint activities and cooperation for mutual benefit (Ackerman et al. 2004). Tools such as Facebook, Twitter, and Reddit offer ways to communicate and connect within groups, where social exchanges build social capital and establish credibility within the group (Alt et al. 2011; Budak, Agrawal, and Abbadi 2011; Jaeger, Bertot, and Shilton 2012; Zannettou et al. 2017).

Community systems and public displays have been studied as a means for playful civic engagement with local government (Benford et al. 2006; Satchell et al. 2008; Foth, Schroeter, and Anastasiu 2011) and content sharing in public spaces (Seeburger and Foth 2012; Reinfurt et al. 2016). Community systems can be loosely described as ICT that enables urban residents to interact with other residents, visitors, and local government. Earlier studies showed that such systems helped people maintain an awareness of activities occurring in the community. The *Fix-o-Gram* programme enabled residents to submit photos of issues to be fixed to the city (Foth, Schroeter, and Anastasiu 2011). *CityFlocks* offered residents the ability to stay informed and to learn about their city by accessing local residents' comments about different places within the city (Benford et al. 2006).

Public displays are large ambient information displays in public settings (Huang, Koster, and Borchers 2009). Public displays of information already play a prominent role in community life. Road signs, billboards, and bus timetables are prevalent throughout the city. Traditional (paper-based) community bulletin boards have been shown to support communities and culture (Cramer, Rost, and Holmquist 2011). Placing the displays in areas that already have a culture of participation and strong sense of local character helped to support and provide content of local relevance (Cramer, Rost, and Holmquist 2011). Placement in well-considered places would mean that people were more inclined to participate and interact. We also know that people value seeing user-generated content and being provided with controls to moderate content (Cramer, Rost, and Holmquist 2011; Seeburger and Foth 2012). People were valued as content producers, where they are empowered to contribute to their own community and can share their opinions with content owners with minimal limitations (López and Butler 2013; Cornet et al. 2017). People want to be active creators of information for others to see, comment on, and share. This is also evident with the current mass use of social media tools to post, comment, and share digital information with those in our social networks.

Common findings across these previous studies indicate that it can be difficult for residents to learn about their communities, further challenging their awareness of engagement opportunities. Moreover, as the number of information sources (and technology platforms) grow, so does the opportunity for misleading, false, or opinion-driven information (Zannettou et al. 2017). People are challenged with parsing and filtering the abundance of information publicly available, especially as many social media platforms have become tools for which users can initiate and propagate information (Alt et al. 2011; Budak, Agrawal, and Abbadi 2011; Zannettou et al. 2017). Amidst a perceived proliferation of online negativity, many users have decreased their consumption of news via social media, turning towards more credible journalistic organisations that have invested significant efforts to high-quality fact-checking of online content (Alt et al. 2011; Budak, Agrawal, and Abbadi 2011; Lampe et al. 2012; Zannettou et al. 2017). As such, the challenge becomes how to curate content, manage it, and add a degree of trust when sharing community information. Additionally, while studies have shown that social media usage can support opportunities for government-citizen interactions, many cities have limited their active participation with social media due to corporate policies, concerns about the privacy of citizen information and security of government information (Kavanaugh et al. 2011; Jaeger, Bertot, and Shilton 2012; Falco, Kleinhans, and Pereira 2018). As a result, people who are accustomed to timely and interactive dialogue afforded through social media tools are turning to other technologies to interact with others. At the same time, we acknowledge that information privacy concerns are an ongoing concern in the development of new ICTs.

Overall, our work extends the literature on public spaces, placemaking, and ICT for community engagement by weaving the hard, physical layers of the city with the softer layers of information flows, culture, play, and community.

3. Identifying community information needs

A goal of our research was to understand the types of community information and services urban residents wanted to know about and how this information should be presented to them. We were specifically interested in communities that residents defined within the cities in which one lives or visits as a part of everyday domestic life. By 'community information', we refer to information such as bylaws, community or municipal events, elections, traffic, construction, etc. While described here, we were largely interested in having participants define this type of information as part of our study. Specifically, we wanted to explore when, where, how, and why such information or services were sought out and what challenges people faced in acquiring and sharing this information. We wanted to use this information to understand if a mobile technology could better present relevant information to urban residents and evaluate its impacts, if any, on placemaking. The study was approved by our university research ethics board.

3.1. Participants

We recruited 18 people (10 female, 8 male) through snowball sampling, word-of-mouth, and by posting ads on an online classified advertisements forum, Craigslist. Participants ranged in age between 30–59 (median = 42) and resided in multiple suburbs within the Metro Vancouver area, located in British Columbia, Canada. Participants were all fluent in English and frequent users of technology, including desktop computers and mobile smartphones. We were specifically interested in exploring the coordination of family activities. As such, we included families where one or more adults had full-time jobs and who were primarily responsible for a household and coordinating their children's schedules with recreational activities (15 of 18 participants had children whose ages ranged from 8 months to 27 years old). Our participants had diverse full-time professions, including work as stay-at-home parents and employment in the public sector, technology and sales industries. Participants were each entered into a draw for one of four gift cards (valued at $50 each) as compensation for their participation in our study.

3.2. Methods

Participants first completed an online survey that gathered basic demographic information, such as age, gender, education, and profession. Survey questions also explored participants' current living situation (e.g. homeowner, home renter, shared accommodations, etc.) and how connected participants considered themselves to be with their community. We asked participants to briefly describe the types of community information they were most interested in and how they currently found such information.

Over a period of three weeks, participants kept an online diary to note any points of interest within their environment. This could be in the form of physical objects, places, billboards, public notices, or any socially related interests, such as instances of homelessness, vandalism, or crime. Participants were also able to record their thoughts as it related to any ideas or concerns surrounding their community, thoughts on becoming

involved and interacting with others, or searching for information online about their city. We chose this experience sampling method (Hormuth 1986; Consolvo and Walker 2003) in order to reduce the need for participants to recall their practices; instead, participants were able to capture their current activities, thoughts, and feelings in-the-moment with their mobile phone while they were amidst their normal daily activities.

We created private Twitter accounts that we asked participants to use as online diaries to record their thoughts using any form of post (text, links, photos, videos, or re-tweets). We expected that allowing multimedia formats within the diary method would enable us to understand both the actual point of interest and the surrounding environment. Twitter was chosen as our data collection tool as it offered privacy settings (where only the researchers could view their posts), location-tagging, photo, and video abilities. This gave participants a variety of capturing and recording options. Twitter was also available for multiple platforms (e.g. Android, iPhone, BlackBerry, Windows).

Following the diary period, we conducted semi-structured interviews (that lasted between 30 and 60 min with each participant) in-person or over Skype. Interview questions explored participants' daily routines and interactions with their local community. For example, questions included, 'Describe your commute to and from work'; 'Describe what types of community events you participate in, if any'; and 'Tell me about the last time you shared community information with someone'. Questions also sought to understand participants' community interests by reviewing their posts from their diary and asking them to further elaborate more about their thoughts at that time. This process helped us understand what it was they were specifically interested in and why they were interested in that particular aspect of their community. We also asked participants how they retrieved such information, and how they managed and shared such information with their social network.

3.3. Data collection and analysis

All interviews were audio-recorded and transcribed. We also kept typed notes for all interviews and downloaded all online entries from each participant's private study Twitter account. Using open, axial, and selective coding, we completed an analysis on the survey, diary, and interview data following grounded theory principles (Strauss and Corbin 1998). We also analysed a total of 293 textual posts and 67 photo posts captured during the diary stage (the range of posts was between 9 and 80; median number of posts was 32, and 5 for photo posts).

Our results first discuss the general themes we drew from our participants' online diaries, including what types of community information they were interested in and their sources of such information.

4. Results

An important aspect of digital placemaking considers the meaning of various public places to people and their lived experiences that shape their sense of belonging to the community. Overall, we uncovered that community attachment influenced people's sharing experiences and that people wanted to capture a personalised experience of space. Seven themes emerged that illustrated people's personal community information needs and routines for accessing such information: administrative, maintenance, recreational, legal, traffic, community, and environment. *Administrative* related to the more task-related act of paying bills, property taxes, or applying for licenses and permits. *Maintenance* surrounded information requiring services from local government, such as garbage collection, roads maintenance (e.g. construction, potholes), and parks maintenance (e.g. cleanliness). *Recreational* involved activities in parks, trails, or community centres. Information about noise bylaws and building permits were categorised as *legal*, while *traffic* was related to traffic conditions and regulations. *Community* surrounded events in the area or ways to become involved with others on a specific initiative. Finally, *environment* related to any developments within the community (including rezoning applications), and sustainability practices. At a surface level, the diary posts demonstrated thoughts about general community information during participants' daily activities. Beyond this basic pattern of information acquisition, a deeper analysis revealed interesting additional routines around how people gathered community information, when and why people thought about this information, and how such information was shared with family members or friends.

A common challenge with digital placemaking includes issues related to awareness, cohesion, and identity within communities. Location-sharing technologies have been pivotal in addressing this challenge, where mobile apps such as Foursquare and Facebook have facilitated community sharing of locations and places with others. Within the themes of community information desired by our participants, we found there was a large amount of *location-based information* that participants wanted to know about within their community and local surroundings, yet they often did not know about this until they saw something that piqued their interest. We refer to it as location-based information because it was tied to specific places in one's neighbourhood or city. A common type of location-based information that surfaced across many of our participants was thoughts surrounding *traffic* and road construction (*maintenance*) within their community. Participants expressed frustration with encountering road closures, construction zones, and traffic during their commute. Other types of location-based information included knowledge about services offered by local government, such as garbage collection (*administrative*), concerns with park services or facilities (*community, environment*), and items related to bylaws (*legal*).

We also found that participants were very interested in what we call *time-based information*. We define this as information that is needed 'before-the-moment' so one could plan activities based on it or around it. First, the most common type of time-based information related to *community* events and *recreational* activities for families. This information was needed to assist with household planning. Second, *traffic* information was also described by participants in a way that made it time-based and was desired 'before-the-moment'. Third, *administrative* tasks associated with one's community (e.g. property taxes, dog licensing) were also described as time-based activities. Many participants expressed frustration when caught in the middle of a construction zone or a traffic jam. In this case, people expected to become aware of this information before heading in that direction. Perhaps the most interesting aspect about time-based information (across all three of these information types) was an expectation by participants that this information would surface and present itself to them at the appropriate time and place. Thus, rather than feeling that they needed to go online and actively find the information themselves, in many ways, they expected this information to be 'delivered' or 'presented' to them by some source where someone else or another service would show them what was relevant to them given their location (e.g. where they lived) or their general interests.

Overall, these findings illustrate the need for systems to be designed to support information sharing amongst residents where information is surfaced both 'in-the-moment' and at later points in time at different places. A full description of our results is available in (Pang et al. 2015); here, we introduce the core findings that informed the design of our system, City Explorer. Next, we include a more detailed description of our design rationale, expanding our work in (Pang et al. 2019).

5. The design of City Explorer

The findings from our study showed two main types of community information that urban residents were interested in: *location-based information* (knowledge tied to specific places) and *time-based information* (knowledge of upcoming events and happenings). These types of information were used throughout daily family life to understand changes within one's community and to plan activities. Our goal was to explore the challenges residents faced in finding, retrieving, and sharing local community information and services with others in the community. Some of the challenges included the difficulty in finding information online where there often was an overwhelming amount of information to navigate. People also reported the routines of relying on traditional, paper-based media; however, they found it difficult to share or manage such artefacts over time.

Building on our first study, we designed a location-based game for urban residents that would focus on supporting community awareness and engagement in public spaces along a public transit network. We began our design process by reflecting on prior work around domestic routines, ICT for community awareness and engagement, and public spaces and placemaking. We were also inspired by popular games, such as Ticket to Ride and Pokémon Go, along with widely adopted mobile applications, Foursquare and Facebook. Based on this literature and existing technologies, three design requirements for the game emerged and formed the foundation upon which City Explorer was built.

The first design requirement was to incorporate location detection and the geotagging of community information. A criterion for digital placemaking involves the use of location-based services to enable place-based communication and flexibility to connect when and where needed. The second design requirement was to facilitate social collaboration, if desired. Here, we needed to balance the affordances of playing individually or collaboratively, where potential privacy concerns with location detection and/or sharing had to be considered, while preserving the ability to connect with those in close proximity. Lastly, our third design requirement was to borrow the mechanics from popular social media platforms to support community engagement. This included the ability to post geo-tagged information in multimedia formats (e.g. text, video, images) and to provide feedback to boost/promote posts. This is often a key aspect of digital placemaking.

In the remainder of this section, we first provide an overview of City Explorer, outline its key features, and then describe three scenarios to illustrate its use.

5.1. Features

City Explorer was built as a web application that users could access through their mobile phone browser. This allowed us to deploy the app to a variety of devices, which enabled us to include participants described in Section 6 who used a variety of O/S, including Apple and Android. The front-end of the game was developed using a combination of HTML5 and JavaScript. The back-end of the game was built with Spring MVC, AJAX, and Tomcat. It also integrated data from Translink's existing Open API (General Transit Feed Specification) to provide transit data, including bus stops, train stations, routes, and schedules. We designed our database using MongoDB to store the locations of the stops and added a geographic index for calculating the distance for challenges. The records of users were also stored in a remote MongoDB server. Finally, the geolocation detection of the user was implemented through the HTML5 API for accessing the current GPS data.

5.1.1. Location sharing

We incorporated location awareness to provide personalised, context-relevant information. Location-based systems have evolved to provide people with context-relevant information as well as to enable people to connect those in proximity. Doing so can support awareness at preferred times and within specific locations in people's local surroundings. For example, Google Maps detects one's location to provide navigational directions while Yelp uses one's location to offer information about businesses nearby. Many studies have identified the need to design for mobility as people move throughout their day (Paulos and Goodman 2004; Charles and Crow 2012). Users' searches on their mobile devices are highly influenced by geographic location, such as within the vicinity of their current location, while in transit, or about information related to their destination (Charles and Crow 2012). With people particularly interested in locally relevant news and events (Wouters et al. 2013; Claes and Moere 2015), it was important to incorporate location sharing and geotagging of community information. Incorporating location sharing offers a more tailored, personalised experience for the user by only presenting information that is relevant based on one's location.

City Explorer's map is the default screen for the game (Figure 1). Once signed in, a player's location and nearby transit stops are detected within a 100 m radius. Each transit stop offers potential points that can be earned by passing by the transit stop. Once the player passes the stop, the flag disappears, and the player earns the marked points. A player can only earn points for a stop every 30 min. This parameter was set to restrict players from earning duplicate points for the same stop while waiting for transit to arrive. We determined the expected maximum wait time for transit to be 30 min.

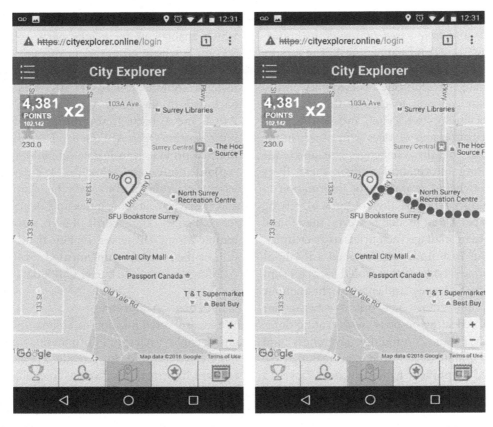

Figure 1. City Explorer's default home screen for the game includes a map and auto-detected geo-tagged location.

As the player moves, their route is tracked with a series of blue dots on the map.

As can be seen, City Explorer's core functionality is similar to existing applications such as Google Maps or transit-specific applications. That is, they all show a person's current location and the ability to search for and track transit routes. City Explorer differs in that it applies game mechanics to these core location features (e.g. points for travel). The intention was that by gaining points for travel, one may consider travelling more or finding different travel routes. Such travel may help aspects of digital placemaking where people may begin to see different types of location-specific services or events, or meet different people travelling along similar routes as oneself.

5.1.2. Local news and user-generated content

We provided local, curated news and user-generated content to offer a breadth of community information based on the seven themes from our initial study (Pang et al. 2015). We already know that traditional community noticeboards and local newspapers provide people with information and news that pertain to the local community (Alt et al. 2011; Fortin, Neustaedter, and Hennessy 2014). Yet, such traditional methods are slowly disappearing and much of the information and discussion related to one's neighbourhood is now available digitally, scattered across many websites and social media (Alt et al. 2011). Online news aggregators have become a popular source of news consumption, with search engines and aggregators (e.g. Google News, Yahoo!) being relied on to search for news (Alt et al. 2011). However, many of the news aggregators curate news at the level of a person's country or city, missing the mark on providing information related to one's direct neighbourhood or tied to one's regular routes throughout the day. Additionally, such information is often broadcast one-way; that is, the information is professionally authored and published from a news agency, and there are few opportunities to post user-generated content. User-generated content offers local knowledge based on experiences that is developed over time by people living in a given community (Cai and Tian 2016). Despite prior work revealing that people want to learn more about others who are in transit with them or who frequent the same areas (Camacho, Foth, and Rakotonirainy 2013a; Pang et al. 2015), we have yet to see a system that combines both local news from a news agency, with community information created by others nearby.

To support community awareness and discussions, we included a Posts feature in our game (Figure 2). Players can add content (text, links, photos, videos) to a location within a 150 m radius of their physical location.

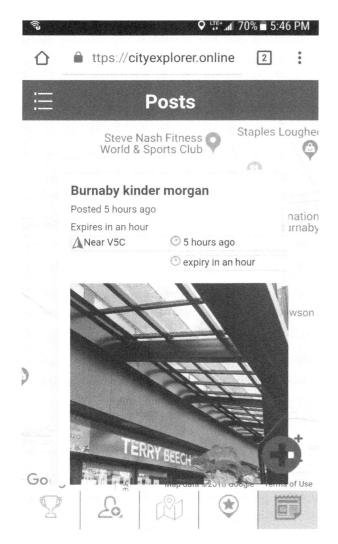

Figure 2. The Posts feature in City Explorer enables players to add geo-tagged content within 150 m of their location.

Information is surfaced to all players in the game when they are within 150 m from it and it is, hopefully, geographically relevant. We were interested in the types of information people chose to share with others during their transit commute. Because posts are geo-tagged and related to the players' locations (e.g. traffic condition, road detours, or construction, etc.), we set a default expiry period of one hour for all posts. Content was not moderated, though, players were able to 'boost' a post to keep it active for another hour. This allowed any players to determine the value of community information and whether it needed to remain available for others to view past the hour. For example, a traffic incident may only be needed for the hour whereas a petition for enhanced park security may need to remain active for several days. Boosting can only be done once every 12 h by a player for a specific post (this prevents players from continuously boosting the same post). Through these

posting features, we wanted to explore how City Explorer may help to create strong ties to place for players, thereby enhancing aspects of digital placemaking. Such features are not often available in transit applications (e.g. Vancouver's transit app only allows one to choose bus routes. There is no ability to share content related to routes). They are also not available in systems like Google Maps that users could use to select and track their transit route.

5.1.3. Community engagement and gamification

To support play, we provided challenging game elements linked to rewards. The play aspects of gaming support several intrinsic motivations. This includes pleasure that arises from a sense of accomplishment, excitement at the moment of discovery, and offers a way to connect and bond with people (Knaving and Björk 2013). Cities have public places where citizens can roam (Montola, Stenros, and Waern 2009). As such, gamification can enable people to see the city in a new way. Spatially expanded games leverage mobile technologies to trace player locations and movements or to create a virtual overlay on top of the real world (Montola, Stenros, and Waern 2009). For example, Ingress overlays its gameplay over the real world and incorporates elements of treasure hunts (Karpashevich et al. 2016). Pokémon GO also uses GPS to layer the players' real-world location with the virtual world (Paavilainen et al. 2017). Much of the work studying the use of gamification to foster public participation shows the use of reward-based gamification. Reward-based gamification involves the use of badges and points to show progress, as well as displays achievements against other users on leaderboards (Knaving and Björk 2013; Thiel 2016). These elements provide immediate feedback to the player and can often be shared on social media or be seen on the game leaderboard.

It was our aim to challenge players to explore nearby areas, atypical of their daily routine. As mentioned earlier, this could help to enhance aspects of digital placemaking for users. City Explorer offers destination challenges to players based on their geographic location (Figure 3). A destination challenge is a pre-determined route to a community centre, building or park that a player needs to take to score additional points. Details of all possible challenges for the player will display on this screen. Challenges included routes with multiple stops and were predetermined in the game's design by us where we created challenges around community centres, libraries, and public parks located in each of the suburbs within the city.

5.1.3.1. Difficulty. City Explorer automatically determines the difficulty of challenges based on a player's

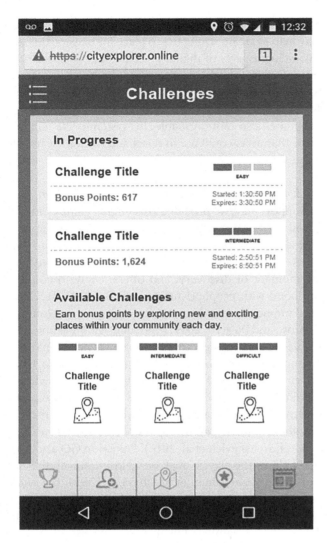

Figure 3. Challenges in City Explorer are based on players' geographic location and encouraged players to explore new destinations.

current location and a calculation of the number of vehicles (buses, trains) required for the player to arrive at the destination. An 'Easy' challenge requires a player to use one transit vehicle (e.g. one bus) within a single trip. An 'Intermediate' challenge requires more transit vehicles (e.g. one bus and one train) to complete the challenge. Finally, a 'Difficult' challenge contains more transfers and changes of vehicles (e.g. two buses and two trains). For example, a large park in the city's downtown core may be 'Easy' for a player currently located downtown as it is within 10 km away, but it may be 'Difficult' for a player located in a suburb 40 km away as the routes may involve the use of multiple vehicles.

5.1.3.2. Time limits. Many games employ a time limit to indicate how much time the player has to complete a level. We decided to set an expiry period based on the difficulty of the challenge: 2 h (Easy), 6 h (Intermediate), or 12 h (Difficult). As it is unlikely people will commute for more than 12 h to arrive at their destination, we set this as the time limit for the most difficult challenge. City Explorer's leaderboard allows players to see how they rank amongst other players in terms of game points. The leaderboard displays the *All Time Ranking* for the lifetime of the game for the top 10 players. It also shows *Today's Ranking* for the past 24 hours for the top 10 players. This offers players a sense of in-time competition to increase their engagement with the game.

5.1.4. Privacy control

Lastly, we offered privacy mechanisms to support partial and anonymous identities. Privacy plays a central role in our society, and an important aspect of managing one's privacy is the ability to control access to information about oneself (Velasco-Martin 2011). Anonymity and accountability on the Internet have been a widely debated controversy. Advocates for anonymous online identities argue the right to ensure privacy and free speech (Keesom 2004). Anonymity also lifts inhibitions, allowing groups of people who are stigmatised by society (e.g. victims of violence, survivors of child abuse, etc.) a safe zone to share information without fear of embarrassment or harm (Kang, Brown, and Kiesler 2013). There are several reasons why people prefer anonymity versus being identified. Anonymity absolves accountability, where people can act without consideration and misuse the Internet for misconduct (Farkas et al. 2002). Anonymity can also make it difficult for people to establish trust, maintain credibility, or hinder community building (Kraut, Resnick, and Kraut 2011). Given the degree of privacy enabled is often a personal choice, we wanted to design the game in such a way to support certain activities (such as location-sharing) so that people will choose the social benefits over the risk trade-offs.

The Friends feature was designed to support awareness of other players within a 150 m range (Figure 4). We wanted to explore whether such a feature would strengthen existing ties or create new relationships with other transit riders. Again, such aspects are tied to concepts of digital placemaking whereby players could develop enhanced feelings of connection to people within the places they frequent or travel through. If a player set their game visibility to 'ON', all players within a 150 m range were able to see them in the *All Players* list. To connect with them, one needs to click on the 'Add' player button. Thus, players can connect with other players who are strangers to them. If they wanted to connect with a player who was further away than 150 m, they were able to type in their email address and select 'Add Friend'.

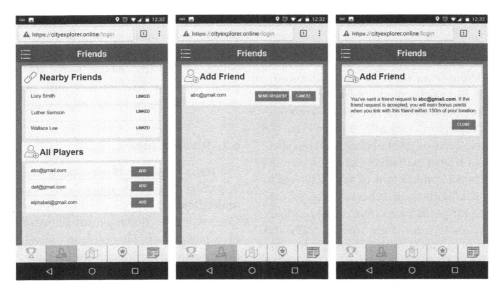

Figure 4. The Friends feature in City Explorer enabled players to play anonymously, connect with nearby players (left), add friends by email (centre), and receive confirmation of a sent friend request (right).

5.2. User scenarios

We now present several scenarios that were created based on the demographic data from participants in our initial study. These scenarios describe basic gameplay and individual stories behind how and why residents would play City Explorer.

5.2.1. Scenario 1

Sally was just dropped off at the bus exchange in the morning and stands in line at her usual bus stop. She notices a new billboard has been posted across the street by the empty lot, announcing a new development permit application had been filed at city hall. She pulls up City Explorer and switches to the news area to see if anyone has posted information about the new development. No one has posted anything yet, so Sally takes a photo of the billboard and adds a post with it, noting that the public hearing is scheduled for next month. As soon as the post is saved, she sees someone has already boosted it, adding another hour to the expiry time.

5.2.2. Scenario 2

Karen is on her way to work. She launches City Explorer which automatically geo-tags her current location as she walks to her usual bus stop. While waiting for the bus, she accepts the (easy) challenge for the day, which has her stopping at the new coffee shop that opened two blocks from her work. As she travels on the bus, she earns points for each bus stop passed. She checks the leaderboard to view her points balance, which has a running total of 760 points. She is currently in 17th place, with the 1st place player having accumulated 1,320 points. After picking up her morning coffee, she earns 570 bonus points for completing her challenge.

5.2.3. Scenario 3

Roger and Kyle are at the central transit exchange downtown, waiting for their train to head to school. They are acquaintances, having seen each other on their daily commute since the beginning of the semester. Roger asks Kyle if he may add him as a friend on City Explorer so that they can receive double the points for their ride to school. Kyle accepts his friend request. They board the train and begin collecting points as they pass each station. Instead of individually earning 380 points for their commute, they have now each earned 760 points. When they arrive at their destination, they are notified with a City Explorer post that a student bake sale is happening that afternoon. The post is set to expire in 35 min. Kyle boosts this post, keeping it active for 1 hr 35 min, hoping other students stay informed of the sale.

6. Field deployment

We investigated how urban residents living in the Vancouver regional area of British Columbia, Canada played City Explorer through a field deployment that took place in March and April 2018. Our goal was to understand when and how people would play a transit-based LBG, to gain insight into the types of community information desired, and, to evaluate whether such a game would encourage community awareness, city exploration, and digital placemaking. The study was approved by our university research ethics board.

6.1. Participants

We recruited 12 participants (7 female, 5 male) through snowball sampling and community forums. These participants were different from those in our earlier study. We created email and social media posts and shared them within our social networks via email lists at our university, Facebook, Instagram, LinkedIn, and Twitter. We also placed advertisements on public boards and bus shelters located at major transit exchanges calling for participants who took transit a minimum of four days/week. Table 1 describes details about each person who participated in the study. Our participants were urban residents between the ages of 23–35 years of age (median = 27), and lived within Metro Vancouver in BC, Canada. Five participants lived in the city for less than 4 years (five for 4–9 years, and two for 10+ years). Seven (of our twelve) participants had children as we wanted to explore if and how their transit routines affected family activities and compare these to the five participants who did not have children. All participants owned a mobile device with adequate data coverage to play, used GPS services, and had previously played LBGs (e.g. Pokémon GO, geocaching, etc.). These formed part of the recruitment criteria as we wanted participants who were familiar with their own mobile devices, including location sharing and LBGs in order to minimise any time required to learn how to use a different mobile device.

Participants selected were not meant to represent all residents within the city. Instead, our 12 participants were representative of residents' commuter times and distances. For example, we included participants who had short commute times with minimal exchanges between buses (e.g. 20 min.). We also included participants who had lengthy commute times that required exchanges between buses and/or trains (e.g. 45 min.).

6.2. 4-Week usage

We started the 4-week field deployment by conducting in-person interviews individually with participants to understand their prior gaming experiences. During this time, we also conducted an onboarding process with each participant. This included installing the game on their personal device, reviewing City Explorer features and game rules. Participants had staggered start dates based on availability for the in-person interviews, though everyone started playing City Explorer within a week's timeframe of each other. Although participants started at staggered times, this had little effect because content was seeded to give the experience of a much larger participant pool.

To provide a realistic environment of gameplay where our participants could not detect that they were the only ones playing the game, we needed a way of seeding content within the game that was systematic, automatic, and minimally interfered with the participants as they played. We chose to use Twitter (and its API) due to its capability of being integrated with current, concise, community-based content. We searched for Twitter accounts that mentioned our city, the city tourism group, or the city police Twitter handles. We found 31 accounts that contained factual and opinion-based content that prior work has shown people are interested in knowing about in their community, e.g. recreational information, traffic data, municipal government information, and selected these accounts for our study. Content was automatically pulled from these accounts once daily and added into City Explorer. Using Twitter accounts to seed content offers several advantages. First, content is current, sometimes even real-time, and offers players with information that is locally relevant. Second, Twitter is already a popular platform that people use to share thoughts and links to other items. Its format of a maximum 280-character limit mapped well to our post size in City Explorer. Lastly, Twitter allows us to easily bootstrap the system as it provides a source of content at a time when there are not sufficient users. This supports exploratory research at an early design stage.

While all participants had prior experiences playing LBGs, seven participants noted they did not play as frequently now as in the past, given their work and family schedules. During the interviews, we were interested in

Table 1. Summary of participants based on our demographic survey.

	Gender	Age	Household	Lived in city	Children	Uses GPS services
P1	M	26	Lives w/family/single	<1 year		At least 5 days per week
P2	M	23	Lives with housemates/single	<1 year		At least 5 days per week
P3	M	32	Lives w/spouse/married	10+ years		A few times a month
P4	F	32	Lives w/spouse/common-law	4–9 years		At least 5 days per week
P5	F	35	Lives w/partner/common-law	10+ years	6 yr old	1–3 days per week
P6	F	23	Lives with housemates/single	<1 year		At least 5 days per week
P7	M	33	Lives w/spouse	4–9 years	5 yr old	At least 5 days per week
P8	F	29	Lives w/spouse	1–3 years	2 yr old	1–3 days per week
P9	F	34	Lives w/spouse	4–9 years	3 yr old	1–3 days per week
P10	M	34	Lives w/spouse	4–9 years	5 yr old	At least 5 days per week
P11	F	33	Lives w/spouse/married	4–9 years	1 yr old	1–3 days per week
P12	F	35	Lives w/spouse	1–3 years	1 yr old	At least 5 days per week

how they defined 'community', what types of community information they currently sought, and what challenges they faced in acquiring this information. We wanted to understand if and how City Explorer might affect these practices. Questions also focused on exploring participants' weekly schedules and routines, understanding what their existing transit experience was like, including what types of activities they currently do on their commutes. For example, we asked, 'Tell me more about what your transit experience is like – do you take the same buses/routes'; 'What kinds of things do you like to do while on your transit commute?'; and, 'When do you use location-based services on your phone?'.

We asked our participants to play City Explorer on their own personal mobile devices to ensure they were comfortable and adjusted to using the device. During this time, participants would sign in to the game at the start of their commute and City Explorer would detect their location while they travelled on public transit within the city. Participants played for four weeks during which time we asked them to play during at least five of their transit trips. Following the first week, we encouraged participants to play as frequently as they desired, and this was monitored by us through system logs.

6.3. Weekly surveys

At the end of the first and second weeks of the study, we sent participants an email with a set of 10 questions to answer. Questions included understanding the features played in City Explorer during their transit rides, what they thought worked well (and did not work well) within the game, and how often they were able to play the game that week. For example, we asked why they added or linked with players that week (or why not); how frequently they read posts in the game; and to describe the types of city exploration challenges they attempted.

6.4. Semi-structured and contextual interviews

Following the third week of the study, we interviewed participants over the phone to ask more probing questions about their experiences playing City Explorer. Upon completion of the four-week gameplay period, we conducted one-on-one interviews with each participant. Qualitative interviews enabled us to ensure relevant data was captured and ideas were fully expressed. Half (six) of the interviews were conducted in person or via Skype and lasted approximately 60–90 min each. While completing these first six interviews, we noted participants had challenges re-creating their experiences. As such, we decided to conduct the remaining six as

contextual interviews on transit buses, while riding alongside the participants during one of their commutes.

Conducting contextual interviews yielded even richer data as we interviewed participants in-situ on their transit routes. The six contextual interviews were a blend of observation and dialogue, as we accompanied these participants on their commutes to and from work. These commutes ranged between 30–45 min each and offered rich observations of activities of interest, including insights into the routines leading up to their transit ride, and observations of events and encounters during their commutes. These contextual interviews enabled us to examine the physical environments and assess participants' usage of City Explorer as it related to location, environment, and surroundings. We gathered insights into people's experiences riding transit, including their walk to and from the bus stops and the environment and behaviours observed while on the buses. Though it was more time consuming than surveys, it allowed us to maximise description and discovery of participants' experiences, where we accessed their ideas, thoughts, and memories in the moment. This would not have been attainable if conducted solely via weekly surveys or semi-structured interviews over the phone.

The interview protocol included questions about people's game experiences, their views on content quality and ownership, their community information needs and search behaviours; their motivations for playing the game (aside from being in a study); feedback on the features of the game, including privacy and location-sharing; and, how they shared the information they found in City Explorer. For example, we asked, 'How did you use the friends feature, if at all?'; 'What prompted you to boost certain news posts?'; and, 'How did City Explorer affect your interactions with people you recognized on your commutes, if at all?'.

6.5 Data collection and analysis

Usage data, such as number and duration of game sessions, along with dates and times of gameplay, was collected through system logs, weekly surveys, and interviews. All interviews were audio recorded, transcribed, and analysed to obtain a detailed qualitative description of needs and behaviours surrounding community information preferences, as well as an in-depth understanding of participants' experiences playing the game. We performed open, axial, and selective coding on all interview data collected as part of our analysis following grounded theory principles (Strauss and Corbin 1998). Open codes described the specific benefits and challenges of City Explorer, along with the various activities being performed. For example, codes included 'track their commutes' and 'check their player ranking' as activities residents engaged in. Axial codes grouped open codes into categories, such as 'tools', 'information', 'reasons', etc. During our selective coding stage, we saw main themes emerge around technology use (providing contextual information of their commutes), personal community information needs, challenges with learning about community events, and concerns with acquiring and consuming quality information.

Our results first show that the gamification aspects were positive and contributed to digital placemaking and the exploration of new areas. We also reveal an unanticipated use of our game where people used City Explorer as a means of tracking their daily transit commutes and routine travel. Lastly, our study explores the desire for factual community information presented at the right time and place. A full description of our results is available in (Pang et al. 2019); here, we summarise the core findings to better situate our meta-analysis of our work described in our discussion.

7. Results

7.1. Play and city exploration

In general, we saw patterns of gameplay that fluctuated week by week. Only three participants showed a steady increase of points, suggesting they played City Explorer more over time as they became more comfortable with the game and began to incorporate it into their transit routines. Other players showed varied interest in the game over time with likely an initial period of novelty for players who had high point values in Week 1 and low point values following it (e.g. P6, P8–P12). Subsequent weeks with larger amounts of play were likely a result of us conducting phone calls and interviews with participants, which may have acted as a reminder to play (e.g. P8–P10). Our interviews revealed that participants valued seeing their points accumulate while playing City Explorer, as well as seeing how they ranked amongst other players. This included seeing points collected throughout the duration of the entire gameplay history and over the course of each day. Players earned points by passing bus stops and by completing challenges while playing the game.

We learned that while people were much less willing to deviate from their weekday routines to explore nearby areas for the sake of exploring, people did attempt challenges that encouraged the exploration of areas that were near to their end destinations. This was evident in when and how frequently challenges were attempted. City exploration (i.e. challenges) was either considered or attempted on the weekends, when participants were

walking or biking (and not while on transit to their destination) or when they had time to spare when waiting for their bus. Participants were more willing to start a challenge when they had time to pass and if it was a short distance from where they were (or needed to be). For example, a participant described having just missed his bus and then having to wait for the next one, during which time he took the opportunity to see what was nearby in City Explorer and which challenges were easily attainable within this time.

> Last Sunday, I missed my bus and saw I had 40 minutes until the next one. I checked City Explorer to see what was in the area and within walking range so I wouldn't miss the next bus. I kinda aimed for low hanging fruit … I wanted the bonus points. – P10, Male, 34 years

Four participants described having more awareness of community activities through the challenges feature of City Explorer. One participant described using the challenges with neighbourhood community centres as destinations to guide his regular evening run. As a result, he learned more about the nearby centres and various services offered.

> When I was on my evening runs, sometimes I'd take a break and would walk around to complete challenges, but not too much. During my commute, I didn't because I wanted to be somewhere on time. – P7, Male, 33 years

Such place discovery is often seen in digital placemaking and offers opportunities for community awareness wherein participants were encouraged to explore the city and contribute to the community through sharing locations.

7.2. Interest in residents' commuting patterns and routines

An important aspect of digital placemaking considers people's sense of place that supports personal meaning and attachment in spaces. We learned that people enjoyed the mapping feature of City Explorer, where one's location was detected, and their route was drawn in real-time on the map. While some participants had used existing transit applications or map apps (e.g. Google Maps) to plan their transit routes or understand when the next bus or train would arrive, most participants did not actually track their routes as they went using these applications. Moreover, participants appreciated the game mechanics of earning points with minimal interaction during their commute. Several participants described learning more about how frequently they travelled, as recorded by the running tally of points and the leaderboard. They valued seeing their routes on the map as a way to learn more about their personal commutes, rather than trying to gain more points than others. For this reason, the capturing of their personal commutes became meaningful for them and helped them become more aware of their transit habits, often described in a way that was similar to journaling. Eleven of our twelve participants noted that this allowed them to understand how frequently they travelled and where. Compared to other applications that show transit routes (e.g. Google Maps), City Explorer caused users to think about their routes given that there were points attached to them. One participant described playing the game in a way that was like personal goal trackers, such as a Fit-Bit, step and/or calorie counters. The idea of being able to track transit routines, keep records, and have a higher-level view on one's day-to-day was valued.

> City Explorer fell into a camp of practice that I do a lot of, actually … using tools to track data about the self, about your day. Versus a game experience. It fell into more of a journaling thing for me, so like, for example; when I take walks, I use a walk tracker that tracks where I go. That logs my steps. That does all that stuff. I use calorie counters. Right? So, I log if I eat half cup of rice and six carrot sticks. I enter all that information. And then usually, the end goal of a lot of quantified self-experiences are to go back over the data to review it. – P4, Female, 32 years

People appreciated learning more about their transit routines, including the routes, times, and frequency of their trips. Another participant suggested that gamification and journaling were both routine and habitual, and that through playing City Explorer, she could see a pattern of her commutes. This was desirable. Doing so created more awareness around patterns of travel in the city and also contributed to participants' sense of attachment in areas that they often visited. This is often the goal of digital placemaking, where technologies are used to bring people and places together. Such location awareness also permitted our participants to learn about happenings that either negatively or positively affected their routines. While participants were less interested in community information throughout their commute, they were interested in their personal tracking data for this time period. For example, they were interested in data from the moment they left their home until they arrived at work, including walking to a transit stop, travelling, and arriving at their final destination. Providing such data to residents offered opportunities for them to mentally link contextual details about their life, including knowledge of their frequency of travel, length of commutes, how much time they spend at home vs. away from it, and what activities they are able to do outside of work time.

While participants valued transit-specific apps that offered the real-time status of transit vehicles (such as Transit and Google Maps), they noted that such apps lacked context around any delays and did not provide alternate routes proposed based on personal travel routines. They also do not provide people with a broader understanding of the impact of commute time on their personal lives. As such, transit-specific apps were seen as a form of one-way communication and did not support digital placemaking as there was little motivation to strengthen the social, cultural, and environmental experiences of those living in and travelling through urban spaces. Such applications were focused on route knowledge, rather than community-based information and placemaking.

7.3. Presenting factual community information at the right time and place

Digital placemaking offers value in large-scale urban developments, including the planning, design, construction and use of urban spaces. Yet, for cities to be successful in soliciting feedback, engagement with residents becomes important. We found that the timing in which factual community information was presented was relevant in engaging with residents. People consumed community information in City Explorer when they were relatively stationary prior to or after commuting. Information tied to the start and end points of their commutes was valuable, especially as it related to real-time impacts on their imminent route. In City Explorer, people were often uninterested in content that appeared to be based on personal, opinion-based information. Instead, they valued succinct informative information that had clear factual data. Further analysis of the gameplay in City Explorer revealed trends around the types of community information people were interested in before, during, and after their commutes. Community information that was transient (made available during travel) through City Explorer was less relevant for people. People often settled into routine activities during their commutes and were rarely interested in any community information that surfaced as they traversed different areas/cities during their commutes. Their interest was fleeting and information in transient locations that they moved through on their commute was of little importance or impact to them.

> I know I see things when I'm on the bus or Skytrain but my thoughts are somewhat fleeting. I mean, I'll see an ad or something being built and I think to myself, that's interesting. But I don't really do more than that. – P9, Female, 34 years

People tended to rely on technologies that they used prior to the study because they were already familiar to them. For example, while walking to their first transit stop, 8 of our 12 participants used applications such as Transit and Google Maps to scan for any delays or accidents affecting their commute, allowing them to choose alternate routes if required. Upon arriving at their destinations, participants were interested in nearby services (such as convenience stores, grocery stores, and coffee shops), describing it as convenient to fit into their routines.

In contrast to the location-specific information that City Explorer was providing them, participants said they valued information from communities of people with shared interests, such as hobbies, work, or culture, where participants could gain support, resources, or feel a sense of belonging. For example, participants described feeling like they belonged to communities with those who shared interests, such as scuba diving or photography, or groups with whom they shared a similar cultural background (e.g. country of origin, language, religion). This becomes important in fostering a sense of community attachment with others who share similar social and cultural values. Participants also contrasted City Explorer's way of presenting location-based community information to the way that they normally obtained such information through other apps, which was often based on their personal interests. For example, news curators, such as Google News and Flipboard, were used to tailor current news for the person, displaying content that was deemed to be about relevant information. These were found to be more useful than City Explorer as the content (although general) was based on personal interests.

> I also use Google News to stay up-to-date on current events on my phone. You know what, the information I consume there is more things I read in passing. Like, things that I'll read but not retain. It's just casual browsing. It's different from the information from Flipboard. That information sticks. I think it's so focused on my personal interests that I read it more often. – P10, Male, 34 years

For most participants, there was a desire to subscribe, search, and filter content based on personal interests and of immediate impact on their transit experiences. City Explorer had no way for users to filter content, unlike other apps people already used as part of their routines, including news curators (Flipboard, Google News). Such features were especially useful for them as they had set their personal preferences on topics to filter for them.

8. Discussion

The goal of our research was to explore how urban residents would use location-based games (LBGs) and whether LBGs could support the exploration of public spaces and placemaking through an increased awareness of community information. We now complete our meta-analysis of our findings across our studies through a discussion of the implications of our work and opportunities for extensions of City Explorer moving forward.

8.1. The quantified self for smart citizens

Placemaking requires the collective actions of people living in urban communities to shape the spaces into meaningful places. We see the potential in leveraging urban residents' anonymized data as urban spaces become increasingly connected and networked. First, we found that people appreciated learning more about their transit routines, including the routes, times, and frequency of their trips. Tracking routine commutes was similar to the idea of the quantified self, where the use of technologies provides people with self-awareness and self-knowledge through the collection of personal data (Hilviu and Rapp 2015). Doing so created more awareness around patterns of travel and permitted our participants to learn about happenings that either negatively or positively affected their routines. However, a likely challenge is that of privacy, and the collection and usage of personal data by government and private organisations for reasons outside their knowledge and comfort. Some people, including those in our study, viewed sharing data with a particular group permissible if they believed that it would result in tangible benefits to themselves or their families (Zheng et al. 2018). Others had clear concerns about the disclosure of their personal data with any organisation, especially within the context of smart cities and government access and use of such data (Roche and Rajabifard 2012; Lea 2017). Yet, the concept of the privacy paradox considers the discrepancies between expressed privacy concerns and actual behaviours, where users claim to be concerned about their privacy but do very little to protect their personal data (Barth and de Jong 2017). Together, we see much to be explored to establish a balance between people's personal data collection, privacy concerns, tangible and social benefits, and empowering residents to easily safeguard their information.

As mobile phone technologies continue to advance, so too will its ability to harvest information about our whereabouts and activities. While we see the value at an individual level (the quantified self), this offers potential at even larger scales: our homes (smart homes) and public spaces (smart city). Previous work in the quantified self movement has suggested how multi-modal sensors and rich features of mobile devices can capture information about users' life experiences and enhance the process of memory' retrieval (Tjondronegoro and Chua 2012; Hilviu and Rapp 2015; Matassa and Rapp 2015). Although the activity of walking to a bus stop can be seen as a trivial aspect of one's life (Tjondronegoro and Chua 2012), our work shows that it would be valuable for people to collect information about their commute to support personal reflection.

Smart home technologies, one of the more developed aspects within the Internet of Things (IoT), has already introduced new ways of providing personalised information to its residents. Smart home ecosystems, such as Apple HomeKit and Google Home, combine a number of devices to streamline domestic life. For example, smart thermostats can be controlled remotely and auto-adjust based on one's proximity to the home. Smart security cameras offer cloud storage services where historic security footage can be accessed and shared. Smart appliances, like fridges, connect to the Internet and allow for the sharing of messages for family members and the remote viewing of fridge contents by way of a camera.

At an even larger scale, smart cities offer opportunities for the usage of vast amounts of individual data at a collective level. A smart city is a complex ecosystem made up of many aspects, including human aspects (social capital, lifestyle), institutional aspects (urban planning, governance, communities), and technology aspects (sensors, data analytics) (Roche and Rajabifard 2012; Lea 2017). Information-gathering devices deployed in public spaces, can gather, aggregate, and regulate information from many city services, including lighting, parking, traffic and waste management, citizen engagement, safety and security. The data generated from such devices around us is then analysed to draw actionable and meaningful insights for streamlining and making city operations better, in turn improving the quality of life for its smart citizens.

While we recognise the success of smart cities is contingent on institutional aspects and technology aspects, from an HCI perspective, the human aspects stand out as equally, if not more, critical for the transformation of cities. First, user-generated content empowers citizens as both producers and consumers of local information. Citizens then act, in a way, as sensors, where they provide their real-time information about their spatial experiences: recording and sharing personal memories, reporting on inefficiencies and problem areas within the city, or rating the services provided in different locations (Roche and Rajabifard 2012). Second, making citizens 'smart' requires teaching, encouraging, and changing the attitudes of residents (Lea 2017). This includes sharing the benefits of smart cities via public engagement discussions and campaigns. Yet, the more traditional ways of public town halls are less effective, as residents seek convenient, digital ways of providing their feedback. Lastly, in order for community engagement and attachment to occur (a key aspect of digital placemaking), mobility is essential. In urban cities where people are dependent on travelling large distances between work and home, commuter data and traffic combined with infrastructure have now become even more interdependent, needing to function and collaborate successfully together.

8.2. Inclusive communities through urban narratives and public spaces

Second, we found little interest by our participants to connect with fellow transit riders. While it may be that our sample size of 12 participants posed a challenge wherein it was unlikely that two participants would ever be sharing a route together, the preference to ride in isolation was common in our study. This presents a challenge for digital placemaking, which relies on the collective actions of people in shaping their communities. Many of our participants described seeing the same people on their regular commutes either while waiting at the same bus stop or while riding on the same train. This emerged as an interesting theme where co-located members of a geographic community were not necessarily interested in connecting with others while in transit. This suggests that while the game did not affect people's existing social practices of connecting with others (or a lack thereof), people described wanting to improve their sense of belonging within their own defined social communities based on where they live, and less in terms of their transit community. More specific to the context of public transit communities, research has suggested that social interaction between strangers offers a valuable opportunity for producing further engagement on transit journeys (Camacho, Foth, and Rakotonirainy 2013a, 2013b; Camacho et al. 2015; Andone et al. 2017). Our work found that people did not want to spend or invest the time in building this social connection. Thus, while there may be value in strengthening these connections, we found transit riders did not place much value on it. The focus then with digital placemaking initiatives may require a shift from communities based along one's transit and travel areas towards communities based around spaces aligned by common interest (e.g. geographic locations of personal meaning). People wanted to use their commute time to connect with family members and friends already in their social network and there was a desire to share community information, whether it was with a single person in their family or within their larger social network. As such, there exists opportunities to build on these existing social groups to bring people and places together.

From an HCI lens, digital placemaking offers many opportunities for civic engagement to improve and enrich communities. The emerging concept of the Internet of Places (IoP) places value in exploring collective experiences in urban spaces to tap into the meanings of local places to the people who inhabit them. While it may be the case that social interactions were not desirable during commutes, as we saw in our study, there is potential in leveraging the gamification aspects with physical public spaces rooted in the community. For example, physical interactions with tangible artefacts such as public displays or urban art installations can play an important role in helping residents gain a deeper understanding of information in the neighbouring area. These are meaningful places to residents if located near to their homes or workplaces. Tangible interactions also have great potential to providing a more engaging means of encouraging participatory activities such as the sharing of urban narratives.

Urban narratives support the sharing of digital stories, playfulness through gamification, and location-based scenarios, all of which require people to contribute through the use of their mobile devices. In addition to user-generated stories, innovations within smart cities, such as sensors in things (IoT) and places (IoP), have the potential of using data to detect environmental conditions. The intersection of these two streams provides a more complete urban narrative that is likely to provide richer, more human-centric and context-aware services.

Digital placemaking can transcend many dimensions in cities. While we have focused on public spaces and transit, digital placemaking can also be applied to housing, health, infrastructure, and environmental systems (Silberberg 2013; Fredericks et al. 2015; Foth 2017). As such, many stakeholders, including urban planners, city officials, developers, researchers and citizens, can contribute to the practice of improving communities. At its most basic, sharing community information, at the right time and place and with the relevant people, offers an important contribution to sparking public discourse, connecting neighbourhoods, and nurturing a sense of place. We also see opportunities for placemaking through active living. Healthy living initiatives that target chronic illnesses, mental health, obesity, and social isolation can support community health and safety. Sharing community information to create awareness around community health programs/groups, walkable routes, streets with bike lanes, and actively used public parks can encourage residents to choose active lifestyles and alternative, green ways of commuting. This in turn may encourage residents to leverage parks and recreation areas embedded within cities and facilitate a connected, active community.

9. Conclusion

This article presented the study of community information needs and the design and field deployment of a location-based game, City Explorer, in an urban city located in British Columbia, Canada. Our initial study showed that people wanted location-based and time-based information to support community awareness, engagement, and the planning of activities within their daily lives. These information needs informed the design of City Explorer, a location-based game designed specifically to support city exploration and the sharing of community information along the public transit network. Our design focused on digital placemaking: augmenting physical places with location-specific services to create informal, playful, and meaningful opportunities for participation (Sun 2015; Foth 2017; Sun, McLachlan, and Naaman 2017; Peacock, Anderson, and Crivellaro 2018). We did this in City Explorer by incorporating location awareness to offer personalised, context-relevant information; providing curated news and user-generated content; incorporating gamification to support play in public spaces and placemaking; and, ensuring privacy mechanisms supported partial and anonymous identities. These features all relate to aspects of digital placemaking where we designed City Explorer to try and enhance players' feelings of connection to information and other people around them, where both tied to locations and notions of place. Through our field study, we found that urban residents discovered an interest in learning and tracking their personal commuting patterns and routines, especially when done automatically with no interaction from their end.

Overall, we found that through playful design, LBGs can improve the experience for urban residents by tracking routine commutes via personal smartphones. Through this, it not only offers valuable data to help with personal data reflection but can also provide vast amounts of citizen data to offer a broader picture of the city, such as real-time information about traffic, congestion, and transit delays. Second, including the routines and patterns of movement of residents through the transit network can be helpful in designing smart city infrastructure developments, including 'smart networks' for ICT and 'smart mobility' for transportation and logistics. Third, LBGs support digital placemaking by allowing residents to interact with their physical surroundings and to identify places of interest as they traverse public spaces. This offers value in tapping into the meanings of local places to the people that inhabit them. Of course, LBGs are not the only technology that is able to support digital placemaking. Our work has provided new knowledge of how LBGs can do this, with the recognition that other technologies may be able to similarly support digital placemaking, perhaps in different and valuable ways.

Lastly, we reflect on how City Explorer would need to be expanded if it were to be used by people outside of the working demographic that we studied. Our demographic had a median age of 27, thus, those who are much younger or older than this median may offer additional perspectives as to what kinds of community information they would find valuable to support community awareness and placemaking. Our participants played one specific transit game, City Explorer, with a fixed set of game mechanics and structure. There is a chance that some of our results are tied in particular to the game and the way it was designed. For example, if different game mechanics were utilised, it could be the case that participants may have appreciated competing with other players for points more. Future work should consider such possibilities and explore different game mechanics. For example, given the benefit that participants found for using their transit data for personal reflection, one could consider game mechanics that reward users for such reflection (e.g. points for comparing transit usage over time, points for increasing transit usage compared to driving a car). One could also consider different incentives for gameplay where they move beyond leaderboards (like the one we provided) towards peer recognition for community engagement and improvement. Further studies are needed to evaluate these ideas with demographically diverse groups of participants over extended periods of time.

Given our studies represent a small sample conducted over a short period of time (two-four weeks in duration each), there are opportunities for future studies to be conducted involving a longer-term study over months or years where researchers can observe and interact with people in their real-life environment. Such studies would allow one to more deeply understand the nuances of urban residents' technology usage, and issues around adoption or adaptation of a technology. This should certainly be considered a caveat of the work and suggests further exploration of longer-term use to understand routines of persons in smaller rural communities, with mixed cultures, and diverse income levels.

Acknowledgements

We thank TransLink for their collaboration on this project. This research was funded by the Natural Sciences and Engineering Research Council (NSERC) of Canada.

Disclosure statement

No potential conflict of interest was reported by the authors.

Funding

This research was funded by the Natural Sciences and Engineering Research Council (NSERC) of Canada.

References

Ackerman, Mark, Marlene Huysman, John M. Carroll, Barry Wellman, Giorgio DeMichelis, and Volker Wulf. 2004. "Communities and Technologies: An Approach to Foster Social Capital?" In *Proceedings of the 2004 ACM Conference on Computer Supported Cooperative Work (CSCW '04)*, 406–408. New York, NY, USA: ACM.

Alt, Florian, Nemanja Memarovic, Ivan Elhart, Dominik Bial, Albrecht Schmidt, Marc Langheinrich, Gunnar Harboe, Elaine Huang, and Marcello P. Scipioni. 2011. "Designing Shared Public Display Networks: Implications From Today's Paper-Based Notice Areas." In *Proceedings of the 9th International Conference on Pervasive Computing (Pervasive'11)*, edited by Kent Lyons, Jeffrey Hightower, and Elaine M. Huang, 258–275. Heidelberg: Springer-Verlag, Berlin.

Andone, Ionut, Konrad Blaszkiewicz, Matthias Böhmer, and Alexander Markowetz. 2017. "Impact of Location-Based Games on Phone Usage and Movement: A Case Study on Pokémon GO." In *Proc. of the 19th International Conference on Human-Computer Interaction with Mobile Devices and Services (MobileHCI '17)*. New York, NY, USA: ACM. Article 102, 8 pages.

Barth, Susanne, and Menno D. T. de Jong. 2017. "The Privacy Paradox Investigating Discrepancies Between Expressed Privacy Concerns and Actual Online Behavior A Systematic Literature Review." *Telematics and Informatics* 34 (7): 1038–1058.

Bell, Marek, Matthew Chalmers, Louise Barkhuus, Malcolm Hall, Scott Sherwood, Paul Tennent, Barry Brown, et al. 2006. "Interweaving Mobile Games with Everyday Life." In *Proceedings of the SIGCHI Conference on Human Factors in Computing Systems (CHI '06)*, edited by Rebecca Grinter, Thomas Rodden, Paul Aoki, Ed Cutrell, Robin Jeffries, and Gary Olson, 417–426. New York, NY, USA: ACM.

Benford, Steve, Andy Crabtree, Martin Flintham, Adam Drozd, Rob Anastasi, Mark Paxton, Nick Tandavanitj, Matt Adams, and Ju Row-Farr. 2006. "Can You See Me Now?" *ACM Transactions on Computer-Human Interaction* 13 (1): 100–133.

Bilandzic, Mark, Marcus Foth, and Alexander De Luca. 2008. "CityFlocks: Designing Social Navigation for Urban Mobile Information Systems." In *Proceedings of the 7th ACM Conference on Designing Interactive Systems (DIS '08)*, 174–183. New York, NY, USA: ACM.

Blokland, Talja. 2017. *Community as Urban Practice*. Cambridge: Polity Press. ProQuest Ebook Central.

Budak, Ceren, Divyakant Agrawal, and Amr El Abbadi. 2011. "Limiting the Spread of Misinformation in Social Networks." In *Proceedings of the 20th International*

Conference on World Wide Web (WWW '11), 665–674. New York, NY, USA: ACM.

Cai, Guoray, and Ye Tian. 2016. "Towards geo-Referencing Infrastructure for Local News." In *Proceedings of the 10th Workshop on Geographic Information Retrieval (GIR '16)*. New York, NY, USA: ACM. Article 9, 10 pages.

Camacho, Tiago, Marcus Foth, and Andry Rakotonirainy. 2013a. "Pervasive Technology and Public Transport: Opportunities Beyond Telematics." *IEEE Pervasive Computing* 12 (1): 18–25.

Camacho, Tiago, Marcus Foth, and Andry Rakotonirainy. 2013b. "TrainRoulette." In *Proc. of the 2013 ACM Conference on Pervasive and Ubiquitous Computing (UbiComp '13 Adjunct)*, 1385–1388. New York, NY, USA: ACM.

Camacho, Tiago, Marcus Foth, Markus Rittenbruch, and Andry Rakotonirainy. 2015. "TrainYarn: Probing Perceptions of Social Space in Urban Commuter Trains." In *Proceedings of the Annual Meeting of the Australian Special Interest Group for Computer Human Interaction (OzCHI '15)*, edited by Bernd Ploderer, Marcus Carter, Martin Gibbs, Wally Smith, and Frank Vetere, 455–464. New York, NY, USA: ACM.

Carroll, John. 2019. "The Internet of Places." In *Social Internet of Things. Internet of Things (Technology, Communications and Computing)*, edited by A. Soro, M. Brereton, and P. Roe, 23–32. Cham: Springer.

Carroll, John M., Patrick C. Shih, Jess Kropczynski, J. Guoray Cai, Mary Beth Rosson, and Kyungsik Han. 2017. "The Internet of Places at Community-Scale: Design Scenarios for Hyperlocal Neighborhood." In *Enriching Urban Spaces with Ambient Computing, the Internet of Things, and Smart City Design*, edited by S. Konomi, and G. Roussos, 1–24. Hershey, PA: Engineering Science Reference.

Charles, Nickie, and Graham Crow. 2012. "Community Re-Studies and Social Change." *The Sociological Review* 60 (3): 399–404.

Claes, Sandy, and Andrew Vande Moere. 2015. "The Role of Tangible Interaction in Exploring Information on Public Visualization Displays." In *Proceedings of the 4th International Symposium on Pervasive Displays (PerDis '15)*, 201–207. New York, NY, USA: ACM.

Consolvo, Sunny, and Miriam Walker. 2003. "Using the Experience Sampling Method to Evaluate Ubicomp Applications." *IEEE Pervasive Computing* 2 (2): 24–31.

Cornet, Victor P., Natalie K. Hall, Francesco Cafaro, and Erin L. Brady. 2017. "How Image-Based Social Media Websites Support Social Movements." In *Proc. of the 2017 CHI Conference Extended Abstracts on Human Factors in Computing Systems (CHI EA '17)*, 2473–2479. New York, NY, USA: ACM.

Cramer, Henriette, Mattias Rost, and Lars Erik Holmquist. 2011. "Performing a Check-in: Emerging Practices, Norms and 'Conflicts' in Location-Sharing Using Foursquare." In *Proceedings of the 13th International Conference on Human Computer Interaction with Mobile Devices and Services (MobileHCI '11)*, 57–66. New York, NY, USA: ACM.

De Koven, Bernard. 2013. *The Well-Played Game: A Player's Philosophy*. Cambridge, MA: The MIT Press.

De Souza e Silva, Adriana. 2006. "From Cyber to Hybrid: Mobile Technologies as Interfaces of Hybrid Spaces." *Space and Culture* 9 (3): 261–278.

Deterding, Sebastian, Dan Dixon, Rilla Khaled, and Lennart Nacke. 2011. "From Game Design Elements to Gamefulness: Defining "Gamification"." In *Proceedings of the 15th International Academic MindTrek Conference: Envisioning Future Media Environments (MindTrek '11)*, 9–15. New York, NY, USA: ACM.

Falco, Enzo, Reinout Kleinhans, and Gabriela Viale Pereira. 2018. "Challenges to Government use of Social Media." In *Proceedings of the 19th Annual International Conference on Digital Government Research: Governance in the Data Age (dg.o '18)*, edited by Anneke Zuiderwijk, and Charles C. Hinnant. New York, NY, USA: ACM. Article 124, 4 pages.

Farkas, Csilla, Gábor Ziegler, Attila Meretei, and András Lörincz. 2002. "Anonymity and Accountability in Self-Organizing Electronic Communities." In *Proceedings of the 2002 ACM Workshop on Privacy in the Electronic Society (WPES '02)*, 81–90. New York, NY, USA: ACM.

Fortin, Claude, Carman Neustaedter, and Kate Hennessy. 2014. "Posting for Community and Culture: Considerations for the Design of Interactive Digital Bulletin Boards." In *Proceedings of the SIGCHI Conference on Human Factors in Computing Systems (CHI '14)*, 1425–1434. New York, NY: ACM.

Foth, Marcus. 2017. "Lessons From Urban Guerrilla Placemaking for Smart City Commons." In *Proceedings of the 8th International Conference on Communities and Technologies (C&T '17)*, 32–35. New York, NY, USA: ACM.

Foth, Marcus, Jaz Hee-jeong Choi, and Christine Satchell. 2011. "Urban Informatics." In *Proceedings of the ACM 2011 Conference on Computer Supported Cooperative Work (CSCW '11)*, 1–8. New York, NY, USA: ACM.

Foth, Marcus, Laura Forlano, Christine Satchell, and Martin Gibbs. 2011. *From Social Butterfly to Engaged Citizen: Urban Informatics, Social Media, Ubiquitous Computing, and Mobile Technology to Support Citizen Engagement*. Cambridge: The MIT Press.

Foth, Marcus, Ronald Schroeter, and I. Anastasiu. 2011. "Fixing the City one Photo at a Time: Mobile Logging of Maintenance Requests." In *Proceedings of the 23rd Australian Computer-Human Interaction Conference (OzCHI '11)*, 126–129. New York, NY: ACM.

Fredericks, Joel, Martin Tomitsch, Luke Hespanhol, and Ian McArthur. 2015. "Digital Pop-Up: Investigating Bespoke Community Engagement in Public Spaces." In *Proceedings of the Annual Meeting of the Australian Special Interest Group for Computer Human Interaction (OzCHI '15)*, edited by Bernd Ploderer, Marcus Carter, Martin Gibbs, Wally Smith, and Frank Vetere, 634–642. New York, NY, USA: ACM.

Freeman, Guo, Jeffrey Bardzell, Shaowen Bardzell, Szu-Yu (Cyn) Liu, Xi Lu, and Diandian Cao. 2019. "Smart and Fermented Cities: An Approach to Placemaking in Urban Informatics." In *Proceedings of the 2019 CHI Conference on Human Factors in Computing Systems (CHI '19)*. New York, NY, USA: ACM. Paper 44, 13 pages.

Frith, Jordan. 2013. "Turning Life Into a Game: Foursquare, Gamification, and Personal Mobility." *Mobile Media & Communication* 1 (2): 248–262. doi:10.1177/2050157912474811.

Grasso, Antonietta, Martin Muehlenbrock, Frederic Roulland, and Dave Snowdon. 2003. "Supporting Communities of Practice with Large Screen Displays." In *Public and*

Situated Displays. The Kluwer International Series on Computer Supported Cooperative Work. Vol. 2., edited by K. O'Hara, M. Perry, E. Churchill, and D. Russell, 261–282. Dordrecht: Springer.

Harrison, Steve, and Paul Dourish. 1996. "Re-place-ing Space: The Roles of Place and Space in Collaborative Systems." In *Proceedings of the 1996 ACM Conference on Computer Supported Cooperative Work (CSCW '96)*, edited by Mark S. Ackerman, 67–76. New York, NY, USA: ACM.

Hilviu, Dize, and Amon Rapp. 2015. "Narrating the Quantified Self." In *Adjunct Proceedings of the 2015 ACM International Joint Conference on Pervasive and Ubiquitous Computing and Proceedings of the 2015 ACM International Symposium on Wearable Computers (UbiComp/ISWC'15 Adjunct)*, 1051–1056. New York, NY, USA: ACM.

Hormuth, Stefan E. 1986. "The Sampling of Experiences in Situ." *Journal of Personality* 54 (1): 262–293.

Howell, Noura, Greg Niemeyer, and Kimiko Ryokai. 2019. "Life-Affirming Biosensing in Public: Sounding Heartbeats on a Red Bench." In *Proceedings of the 2019 CHI Conference on Human Factors in Computing Systems (CHI '19)*. New York, NY, USA: ACM. Paper 680, 16 pages.

Huang, Elaine M., Anna Koster, and Jan Borchers. 2009. "Overcoming Assumptions and Uncovering Practices: When Does the Public Really Look at Public Displays?" In *Proceedings of the 6th International Conference on Pervasive Computing (Pervasive '08)*, edited by Jadwiga Indulska, Donald J. Patterson, Tom Rodden, and Max Ott, 228–243. Heidelberg: Springer-Verlag, Berlin.

Innocent, Troy. 2016. "Play and Placemaking in Urban art Environments." In *Proceedings of the 3rd Conference on Media Architecture Biennale (MAB)*. New York, NY, USA: ACM. Article 2, 4 pages.

Jaeger, Paul T., John Carlo Bertot, and Katie Shilton. 2012. "Access Perspectives and Design Values in Government Social Media Usage." In *Proceedings of the 13th Annual International Conference on Digital Government Research (dg.o '12)*, 216–222. New York, NY, USA: ACM.

Kang, Ruogu, Stephanie Brown, and Sara Kiesler. 2013. "Why do People Seek Anonymity on the Internet?: Informing Policy and Design." In *Proceedings of the SIGCHI Conference on Human Factors in Computing Systems (CHI '13)*, 2657–2666. New York, NY, USA: ACM.

Karpashevich, Pavel, Eva Hornecker, Nana Kesewaa Dankwa, Mohamed Hanafy, and Julian Fietkau. 2016. "Blurring Boundaries Between Everyday Life and Pervasive Gaming: an Interview Study of Ingress." In *Proceedings of the 15th International Conference on Mobile and Ubiquitous Multimedia (MUM '16)*, 217–228. New York, NY, USA: ACM.

Kavanaugh, Andrea, Edward A. Fox, Steven Sheetz, Seungwon Yang, Lin Tzy Li, Travis Whalen, Donald Shoemaker, Paul Natsev, and Lexing Xie. 2011. "Social Media use by Government: From the Routine to the Critical." In *Proceedings of the 12th Annual International Digital Government Research Conference: Digital Government Innovation in Challenging Times (dg.o '11)*, 121–130. New York, NY, USA: ACM.

Keesom, Kristina A. 2004. "Anonymity, Accountability & John Doe." In *Proceedings of the 1st Annual Conference on Information Security Curriculum Development (InfoSecCD '04)*, 115–118. New York, NY, USA: ACM.

Knaving, Kristina, and Staffan Björk. 2013. "Designing for fun and Play: Exploring Possibilities in Design for Gamification." In *Proceedings of the First International Conference on Gameful Design, Research, and Applications (Gamification '13)*, 131–134. New York, NY, USA: ACM.

Kraut, Robert, Paul Resnick, and In Kraut. 2011. Encouraging Contributions to Online Communities.

Lampe, Cliff, Jessica Vitak, Rebecca Gray, and Nicole Ellison. 2012. "Perceptions of Facebook's Value as an Information Source." In *Proceedings of the SIGCHI Conference on Human Factors in Computing Systems (CHI '12)*, 3195–3204. New York, NY, USA: ACM.

Laureyssens, Thomas, Tanguy Coenen, Laurence Claeys, Peter Mechant, Johan Criel, and Andrew Vande Moere. 2014. "ZWERM: A Modular Component Network Approach for an Urban Participation Game." In *Proceedings of the SIGCHI Conference on Human Factors in Computing Systems (CHI '14)*, 3259–3268. New York, NY, USA: ACM.

Lea, Rodger. 2017. Smart Cities: An Overview of the Technology Trends Driving Smart Cities. doi:10.13140/RG.2.2.15303.39840.

Le Gal, Christophe, J. Martin, Augustin Lux, and James Crowley. 2001. "SmartOffice: Design of an Intelligent Environment. Intelligent Systems." *IEEE* 16: 60–66.

López, Claudia A., and Brian S. Butler. 2013. "Consequences of Content Diversity for Online Public Spaces for Local Communities." In *Proceedings of the 2013 Conference on Computer Supported Cooperative Work (CSCW '13)*, 673–682. New York, NY, USA: ACM.

Matassa, Assunta, and Amon Rapp. 2015. "Map-making: Designing a Mobile Application for Enhancing Memories' Retrieval." In *Proc. of the 17th International Conference on Human-Computer Interaction with Mobile Devices and Services (MobileHCI '15)*, 994–1001. New York, NY, USA: ACM.

Montola, Markus, Jaakko Stenros, and Annika Waern. 2009. *Pervasive Games: Theory and Design.* San Francisco, CA, USA: Morgan Kaufmann Publishers Inc.

Mushiba, Mark, and Holger Heissmeyer. 2018. "Dérive: An Exploration of Critical Play for Urban Place-Making." In *Proceedings of the Second African Conference for Human Computer Interaction: Thriving Communities (AfriCHI '18)*, edited by Heike Winschiers-Theophilus, Izak van Zyl, Naska Goagoses, Dharm Singh Jat, Elefelious G. Belay, Rita Orji, and Anicia Peters. New York, NY, USA: ACM. Article 65, 3 pages.

Nam, Taewoo, and Theresa A. Pardo. 2011. "Conceptualizing Smart City with Dimensions of Technology, People, and Institutions." In *Proceedings of the 12th Annual International Digital Government Research Conference: Digital Government Innovation in Challenging Times (dg.o '11)*, 282–291. New York, NY, USA: ACM.

Neustaedter, Carman, and Tejinder K. Judge. 2012. "See-It: A Scalable Location-Based Game for Promoting Physical Activity." In *Proceedings of the ACM 2012 Conference on Computer Supported Cooperative Work Companion (CSCW '12)*, 235–238. New York, NY, USA: ACM.

O'Hara, Kenton. 2008. "Understanding Geocaching Practices and Motivations." In *Proceedings of the SIGCHI Conference on Human Factors in Computing Systems (CHI '08)*, 1177–1186. New York, NY, USA: ACM.

Paavilainen, Janne, Hannu Korhonen, Kati Alha, Jaakko Stenros, Elina Koskinen, and Frans Mayra. 2017. "The Pokémon GO Experience: A Location-Based Augmented Reality Mobile Game Goes Mainstream." In *Proceedings of the 2017 CHI Conference on Human Factors in Computing Systems (CHI '17)*, 2493–2498. New York, NY, USA: ACM.

Pang, Carolyn, Carman Neustaedter, Jason Procyk, Daniel Hawkins, and Kate Hennessy. 2015. "Moving Towards User-Centered Government: Community Information Needs and Practices of Families." In *Proceedings of the 41st Graphics Interface Conference (GI '15)*, 155–162. Toronto, Ont., Canada: Canadian Information Processing Society.

Pang, Carolyn, Rui Pan, Carman Neustaedter, and Kate Hennessy. 2019. "City Explorer: The Design and Evaluation of a Location-Based Community Information System." In *Proceedings of the SIGCHI Conference on Human Factors in Computing Systems (CHI '19)*. New York, NY, USA: ACM. 15 pages.

Paulos, Eric, and Elizabeth Goodman. 2004. "The Familiar Stranger: Anxiety, Comfort, and Play in Public Places." In *Proceedings of the SIGCHI Conference on Human Factors in Computing Systems (CHI '04)*, 223–230. New York, NY, USA: ACM.

Peacock, Sean, Robert Anderson, and Clara Crivellaro. 2018. "Streets for People: Engaging Children in Placemaking Through a Socio-Technical Process." In *Proceedings of the 2018 CHI Conference on Human Factors in Computing Systems (CHI '18)*. New York, NY, USA: ACM. Paper 327, 14 pages.

Procyk, Jason, and Carman Neustaedter. 2014. "GEMS: The Design and Evaluation of a Location-Based Storytelling Game." In *Proceedings of the 17th ACM Conference on Computer Supported Cooperative Work & Social Computing (CSCW '14)*, 1156–1166. New York, NY, USA: ACM.

Rashid, Omer, Ian Mullins, Paul Coulton, and Reuben Edwards. 2006. "Extending Cyberspace: Location-Based Games Using Cellular Phones." *Computers in Entertainment* 4 (1): 1–18. Article 4.

Reinfurt, Lukas, Uwe Breitenbücher, Michael Falkenthal, Frank Leymann, and Andreas Riegg. 2016. "Internet of Things Patterns." In *Proceedings of the 21st European Conference on Pattern Languages of Programs (EuroPlop '16)*. New York, NY, USA: ACM. Article 5, 21 pages.

Roche, Stéphane, and Abbas Rajabifard. 2012. "Sensing Places' Life to Make City Smarter." In *Proceedings of the ACM SIGKDD International Workshop on Urban Computing (UrbComp '12)*, 41–46. New York, NY, USA: ACM.

Röcker, Carsten, Maddy D. Janse, Nathalie Portolan, and Norbert Streitz. 2005. "User Requirements for Intelligent Home Environments: a Scenario-Driven Approach and Empirical Cross-Cultural Study." In *Proceedings of the 2005 Joint Conference on Smart Objects and Ambient Intelligence: Innovative Context-Aware Services: Usages and Technologies (sOc-EUSAI '05)*, 111–116. New York, NY, USA: ACM.

Satchell, Christine, Marcus Foth, Greg Hearn, and Ronald Schroeter. 2008. "Suburban Nostalgia: The Community Building Potential of Urban Screens." In *Proceedings of the 20th Australasian Conference on Computer-Human Interaction: Designing for Habitus and Habitat (OZCHI '08)*, 243–246. New York, NY: ACM.

Schneekloth, Lynda H., and Robert G. Shibley. 1995. *Placemaking: The art and Practice of Building Communities.* New York: John Wiley & Sons.

Schroeter, Ronald, and Marcus Foth. 2009. "Discussions in Space." In *Proceedings of the 21st Annual Conference of the Australian Computer-Human Interaction Special Interest Group: Design: Open 24/7 (OZCHI '09)*, 381–384. New York, NY, USA: ACM.

Seeburger, Jan, and Marcus Foth. 2012. "Content Sharing on Public Screens: Experiences Through Iterating Social and Spatial Contexts." In *Proceedings of the 24th Australian Computer-Human Interaction Conference (OzCHI '12)*, edited by Vivienne Farrell, Graham Farrell, Caslon Chua, Weidong Huang, Raj Vasa, and Clinton Woodward, 530–539. New York, NY: ACM.

Silberberg, Susan. 2013. *Places in the Making, how Placemaking Builds Places and Communities.* Boston: MIT Department of Urban Studies and Planning, Massachusetts Institute of Technology.

Strauss, Anselm L., and Juliet M. Corbin. 1998. *Basics of Qualitative Research: Techniques and Procedures for Developing Grounded Theory.* Thousand Oaks: Sage Publications.

Sun, Emily. 2015. The Importance of Play in Digital Placemaking. International AAAI Conference on Web and Social Media, North America.

Sun, Emily, Ross McLachlan, and Mor Naaman. 2017. "MoveMeant: Anonymously Building Community Through Shared Location Histories." In *Proceedings of the 2017 CHI Conference on Human Factors in Computing Systems (CHI '17)*, 4284–4289. New York, NY, USA: ACM.

Sun, Emily, and Mor Naaman. 2018. "A Multi-Site Investigation of Community Awareness Through Passive Location Sharing." In *Proceedings of the 2018 CHI Conference on Human Factors in Computing Systems (CHI '18)*. New York, NY, USA: ACM. Paper 581, 13 pages.

Thiel, Sarah-Kristin. 2016. "Reward-based vs. Social Gamification: Exploring Effectiveness of Gamefulness in Public Participation." In *Proceedings of the 9th Nordic Conference on Human-Computer Interaction (NordiCHI '16)*. New York, NY, USA: ACM. Article 104, 6 pages.

Tjondronegoro, Dian, and Tat-Seng Chua. 2012. "Transforming Mobile Personal Life log Into Autobiographical Multimedia EChronicles." In *Proceedings of the 10th International Conference on Advances in Mobile Computing & Multimedia (MoMM '12)*, edited by Ismail Khalil, 57–63. New York, NY, USA: ACM.

Unruh, K. T., K. E. Pettigrew, and J. C. Durrance. 2002. "Evaluation of Digital Community Information Systems." In *Proceedings of the 2nd ACM/IEEE-CS Joint Conference on Digital Libraries (JCDL '02)*, 240–241. New York, NY, USA: ACM.

Velasco-Martin, Javier. 2011. "Self-disclosure in Social Media." In *CHI '11 Extended Abstracts on Human Factors in Computing Systems (CHI EA '11)*, 1057–1060. New York, NY, USA: ACM.

Wang, Xiaolan, Ron Wakkary, Carman Neustaedter, and Audrey Desjardins. 2015. "Information Sharing, Scheduling, and Awareness in Community Gardening Collaboration." In *Proceedings of the 7th International Conference on Communities and Technologies (C&T '15)*, 79–88. New York, NY, USA: ACM.

Williams, Amanda, Erica Robles, and Paul Dourish. 2009. "Urbane-ing the City: Examining and Refining the Assumptions Behind Urban Informatics." In *Handbook of Research on Urban Informatics: The Practice and Promise of the Real-Time City*, edited by M. Foth, 1–20. Hershey, PA: IGI Global. doi:10.4018/978-1-60566-152-0.ch001.

Willis, Katharine S., Kenton O'Hara, Thierry Giles, and Mike Marianek. 2009. "Sharing Knowledge About Places as Community Building." In *Shared Encounters*. 1st ed., edited by Katharine S. Willis, George Roussos, Konstantinos Chorianopoulos, and Mirjam Struppek, 291–308. London: Springer Publishing Company, Incorporated.

Wouters, Pieter, Christof van Nimwegen, Herre van Oostendorp, and Erik D. van der Spek. 2013. "A Meta-Analysis of the Cognitive and Motivational Effects of Serious Games." *Journal of Educational Psychology* 105 (2): 249–265.

Zannettou, Savvas, Tristan Caulfield, Emiliano De Cristofaro, Nicolas Kourtelris, Ilias Leontiadis, Michael Sirivianos, Gianluca Stringhini, and Jeremy Blackburn. 2017. "The Web Centipede." In *Proc. of the 2017 Internet Measurement Conference (IMC '17)*, 405–417. New York, NY, USA: ACM.

Zheng, Serena, Noah Apthorpe, Marshini Chetty, and Nick Feamster. 2018. "User Perceptions of Smart Home IoT Privacy." *Proceedings of the ACM on Human-Computer Interaction* 2, CSCW, Article 200 (November 2018), 20 pages.

Zichermann, Gabe, and Christopher Cunningham. 2011. *Gamification by Design: Implementing Game Mechanics in web and Mobile Apps*. Sebastopol, CA: O'Reilly.

Seeing new in the familiar: intensifying aesthetic engagement with the city through new location-based technologies

Sanna Lehtinen ⓘ and Vesa Vihanninjoki ⓘ

ABSTRACT

Understanding better the effects of the use of mobile apps to the use and appreciation of urban environments has been gaining more prominence as a research topic recently due to the increasing everyday use of these apps. Whether this type of digital mediation changes the lived experience is of interest in this article. The intention is to show that besides changing the prevailing practices and behaviour, new technologies also enhance and add positive value to the everyday urban experience. This positive experiential value is approached with the framework consisting of recent advances in philosophical urban and everyday aesthetics, which put emphasis on both *familiarity* and *fun* as important qualities that describe the everyday experience in urban environments. We claim that new digital tools increase the quality of fun when moving in familiar surroundings. Fun, understood through the lens of the aesthetic, precedes the experienced quality of playfulness. It alters the existing affordances of the urban environment in a way that make more complex aesthetic qualities emerge. The case examples are GPS-based wayfinding applications such as route planners and navigation tools for pedestrian use and related AR applications such as the popular game app Pokémon GO.

1. Introduction

The neologism 'technoference' has been used recently to describe, for example, the decreased quality of interhuman relations due to the increased use and reliance on mobile devices (McDaniel 2015). How this type of reliance is affecting the use and perception of urban space has still been less studied. However, it is clear that this type of absent-mindedness caused predominantly by increased technological mediation has become already an urban trope causing amusement and irritation in equal amounts. Seeing a place through one's screen is lamented to diminish the quality of the lived experience of that particular place. People walking on city streets while staring at their mobile devices has given rise to the derogatory term 'smartphone zombie' or 'smombie' in the contemporary urban culture (Chatfield 2016). Even though the users of mobile devices are physically present in the place, they seem to be less present and alert mentally in the situation, as the mobile device is indisputably at the focus of attention.

Acknowledging the potentially dangerous consequences of this new type of urban behaviour, it is of interest to understand in a more comprehensive way what exactly happens to the subjectively experienced engagement with urban places when they are increasingly perceived through their on-screen representations yet, at the same time, being physically present in them. This has become an especially important topic with the rapid increase in ubiquitous reliance on contemporary mobile route planning and wayfinding applications, which are designed to guide their users as smoothly and efficiently as possible from point A to point B.

The aim in this article is to show how philosophical urban everyday aesthetics could be used as a theoretical framework to study how the consequences of adding this layer of 'screen value' to experiential value of a place could be evaluated. Our hypothesis is that the change in behaviour does not need to be understood necessarily only as a threat to the more traditional understanding of the lived experience. The currently used new mobile technologies do not intrinsically alienate or detach the users from their most immediate physical surroundings. While this hypothesis is also backed up by research in mobile interface studies (De Souza E Silva and Frith 2012), the prejudices towards some recent advances in mobile interfaces defend the need to re-examine the topic also with new perspectives. With this hypothesis as the starting point, GPS-based technologies and the wider effects of their use might be studied in a more comprehensive way, taking cue also from the recent advances in humanistic and philosophical studies of the urban environment. We argue, for example, that based on recent research done in the context of everyday aesthetic values, the use of mobile location-based technologies can also *enhance* and add *positive value* to the experiential qualities of the urban environment. In order to study this further, we bring together how the notion of 'fun' has been treated as an aesthetic quality of everyday life (mainly by Thomas Leddy) and, on the other hand, how this definition of fun as an indispensable everyday aesthetic quality can help to assess some of the new, more complex forms of playfulness that stem from the technology-mediated engagement with the otherwise familiar urban environment.

As the theoretical framework coming mainly from the sphere of philosophical urban and everyday aesthetics does not discuss technology to any significant degree, the post-phenomenological approach to philosophy of technology as well as some recent strands in affordance theory have been indispensable for building the main arguments of this article. This article seeks to complement the recent studies in psychology (Dalton, Hölscher, and Montello 2019), social studies (Leorke 2019) and visual culture (Dibazar and Naeff 2019) which have shed light on how contemporary mobile technologies are changing how the city is perceived, experienced and further imagined and interpreted. A selection of recent GPS-based wayfinding applications such as route and journey planners and location-based AR games such as Pokémon GO have been used as references informing the current state of these widely-used technologies. The article aims at conceptualising how they enrich the urban experience with previously inhibited but now newly available opportunities for a wider variety of different types of aesthetic experiences, leading ultimately to an increase also in the creative use of urban space. Understood in this way, the use of mobile apps may enhance the aesthetically perceived value of the place even in the most familiar everyday environments.

2. New wayfinding practices in the urban environment

New wayfinding tools and the practices related to their use contribute in various ways to increasing the general accessibility of urban environments: previously unnoticed places become known and more alluring through their on-screen representations, route planners offer route options that we would not have otherwise considered and so on.[1] Navigation apps relying on Global Positioning System (GPS) consist of a wide range of route planners and wayfinding apps, but also increasingly of mobile augmented reality (AR) games which

integrate features from virtual and physical environments. These tools and games are gaining importance through mediating experience and engagement with the physical surroundings especially in the context of the everyday. For the purpose of this article, we have chosen to focus on the community-based route planner app Waze, walking directions in Google Maps, and on the Helsinki metropolitan area Journey Planner, which provides the official app by the Helsinki Region Transport Authority. We have been studying and using these apps within familiar urban environments and rely also on various empirical studies made with their users (Hunter, Anderson, and Belza 2016; Ishikawa 2016). The use and features of the chosen apps has been compared with the currently popular mobile game Pokémon GO, which employs the same location-based technology for gaming purposes.

Prevalent forms of human mobility within the urban context are understood to be changing due to the rise of new technologies, but without unanimity about the exact amount and desirability of this change. Spatial thinking as such is feared to be at risk due to the over-reliance on navigation apps (Grabar 2014). The transformative effect of new wayfinding tools is feared to take even evolutionary dimensions, starting to erode the human capacity to think and, as a consequence, to act spatially in a conscious and efficient way. It has been also widely suspected that the ubiquitous and skilful use of digital tools has far-reaching consequences for the relation with the physical environment: 'The habits, hubris and quirky predilections that once manipulated my movements are being replaced by the judgments of artificial intelligence' (Grabar 2014). As a result, the notoriously erratic human behaviour might become more rationalised or, in any case, more directed by extrinsic factors based on algorithms opaque to the end users of the apps.

Formally, the visual guidance provided by the currently used mobile app interfaces does not differ radically from that of portable paper maps. However, one clear difference from the user's perspective is acquiring the possibility of locating oneself reliably on the map at any given moment in time. With paper maps, locating oneself is one of the most difficult tasks and also the crucial moment when the physical surroundings and its two-dimensional representation in the map format are most clearly put into interaction through interpretative activity. Thus, contrary to the most negatively inclining scenarios, it could be argued based on implementation of previous navigation tools such as paper maps, that a gradual shift is a more likely alternative to disruptive change in this case. However, these various scenarios also in themselves attest that new mobile technologies seem to unleash previously unrealised possibilities in experiencing environments. This could refer to freedom of attention as much as to freedom of movement.

The consequences of new wayfinding practices, especially those relying on smart location-based technologies, may encourage creativity and playfulness in the use of city space through experiences definable as 'fun'. It is important to note, that in its current modes, wayfinding is also a social practice to a considerable extent, the psychology and behaviour behind which has been also recently studied (Dalton, Hölscher, and Montello 2019). There are two interesting lines of progression taking place currently in the individual, aesthetic experience of the urban environment, in both of them technology acts as an overall *agent of change* (Lehtinen and Vihanninjoki Forthcoming). First, something that can be described as the *aesthetic approach* to the environment is currently more possible and even likely to take place than previously, since the GPS technologies make us less reliant on the conventional locational markers and features of the environment. On the other hand, GPS-based wayfinding-related apps such as Pokémon GO make us see completely new place-based affordances in the environment, giving potentially rise to entirely *new forms of sense of place* (Lehtinen and Vihanninjoki Forthcoming).

Smartphone-based wayfinding practices might thus seem to support the specific type of attention that has in traditional aesthetic theories been described as *aesthetic attitude* towards one's surroundings: more intent and free forms of observation and experience are possible, as one can safely let go of the constantly present task of locating oneself geographically. In this paper, we have set out to speculate in which ways the place value and the lived experience develop when smartphones are used in urban wayfinding, particularly when one moves on foot in an urban environment. Experience of the city is understood here as a socio-culturally built set of conditions but also as an embodied, sensorially based and situated condition which is thus part of the intrinsically subjective realm. Embodiment in itself is always already a spatial practice (Farman 2012). In general, besides increased focus on the *details*, it can be argued that also the city as a large-scale *system* is gaining a new form of aesthetic appreciation, where functional and overflowing features all contribute to the diversity of the city and to the experience of it.

Pokémon GO as an AR game integrates virtual and physical environments. It is played with the mobile phone, most often in similar urban settings where wayfinding applications are used. The purpose for playing a game instead of finding a route from point A to point B is based on different intentions. Pokémon GO engages its player into a scavenger hunt in the urban space. Playing it is very much focused on areas which are already used to a great extent. More quiet areas of the city might not be that good for playing the game, but even in the most popular areas, game directs the attention of its players to previously unnoticed features of the environment. An architectural ornament, a memorial plate, a statuette or any visibly notable feature might gain new importance through the 'lens' of the game. In order to play the game, one is not required to know the place where one is playing it: Pokémon GO might be played at one's everyday environment as well as in places which one is only visiting. For the purposes of this article, we focus on those occasions, when the game is played in the familiar everyday environments.

Since its release in July 2016, Pokémon GO[2] has gained both positive and negative attention. Playing the game has been the main cause of some accidents, which has lead experts to exhibit worry over how the AR qualities of the game 'present genuine dangers especially to the more vulnerable, often easily distracted pediatric population' even though admitting at the same time that 'Pokémon GO can be a fun and entertaining game that encourages smartphone users of all ages to be active outside their homes, often outdoors, in order to explore and play' (Raj, Karlin, and Backstrom 2016). There are already numerous psychological studies on the behaviour or even the personality features of Pokémon GO players (Khalis and Mikami 2018; Tabacchi et al. 2017). However, more diverse analyses of the relation to the environment within which the play takes place seem to be missing in research literature.

The seamless continuity of the virtual and the physical environment is the goal in these types of mobile AR games. The hypothesis is that the relatively new location-based apps enable a new type of aesthetic interest towards the existing but unacknowledged qualities and features of the physical surroundings. This change in interest follows from how attention gets directed in more free and creative ways while engaged with the familiar environment in new, exciting and fun ways. As the intricacies of the interface qualities of these new modes of play are studied more closely in the field of human–computer interaction (HCI), it is still less clear in which ways the interaction with the new urban location-based technologies alters the relation with other components in the environment. Collateral consequences of using a particular technology are difficult to trace and this is why we are resorting to tools from a more speculative tradition of thinking in the form of philosophical aesthetics.

3. Technologically mediated urban experience understood through aesthetic engagement

In various disciplines, and even further in inter- and multidisciplinary constellations, there has been increasingly emphasis on making sense of the technology-induced changes in the urban experience. How the urban experience is mediated by technologies could be in many ways, but the most obvious dimension is often easiest to neglect. How many new urban technologies affect end up affecting the individual urban user is through the effect they have on the sensory and perceptual realm of the experience. Several new mobile technologies that have been adopted into the everyday use, for example, require intricate visual or visuo-spatial interpretation skills. This emphasis on perceptual capacities links these new technologies into the realm of *the aesthetic* in urban experience, aesthetics understood here as the study of subjective and sensori-emotional values. The aesthetic referring to the perceptual layer of the human existence has also uncontested but easily neglected epistemological value. Or, simply put: on an individual level, we get information about our surroundings through our senses in a complex process where it already gets mixed up with our previous knowledge and experiences, beliefs, expectations, cognitive biases, memories, emotions and imagination. The aesthetic is not used here in an evaluative sense (as a synonym for the beautiful for example) but as a grounding mode of the human experience.

Philosophical urban aesthetics focuses on studying to what extent and in which ways urban environments are experienced aesthetically and how these experiences could help in developing methods for qualitative assessment of urban environments (Lehtinen 2015; Vihanninjoki 2019). *Aesthetic engagement* has been established into the terminology or environmental aesthetics following from John Dewey's pragmatist philosophy. (Blanc 2013) Engagement explains in this context, not only how one interacts with the environment but also including in this more strongly the embodied, multimodal and experientially evolving, mode of being present in connection with the surroundings (Berleant 2007; Berleant and Carlson 2007). The urban environment is particularly interesting with aesthetic engagement in mind, since current global-scale megalopolises, for example, are dense with sensory stimuli and different types of perceptually cued affordances. This abundance of possibilities for experiential richness is also something, which might prove to be problematic: for example, if the excess of too many perceptually ambiguous high-level stimuli becomes unbearable. Advertisements, street signs, excessive traffic, other people and the overall look (e.g. chaotic, unorganised) or architectural elements (too diverse) of a part of a city have all been considered to contribute to this type of undesirable aesthetic overabundance and negatively experienced incoherence (Kolhonen 2005; von Bonsdorff 2008).

There has been substantial emphasis in the literature on aesthetics of the urban environment on the importance of *familiarity* for the aesthetic engagement with a place (Haapala 2005; Saito 2017). Arto Haapala's view, for example, puts 'forward an existential account of the phenomenon of the everyday and its aesthetic character' (Haapala 2005, 39). This focus on the existential importance of the everyday emphasises its familiar, experiential qualities. Aesthetics in this account refers to the human modes of acquiring and processing information about the world through the physical features of the particular environment in question. Since Haapala is focused on the everyday, the environment in question is that in which the everyday life takes place. For most people living currently and in the foreseen future on the planet Earth, the everyday life is equal to *urban life*. This urban way of living in turn, despite the obvious differences in cities, shares many elements and is thus comparable to a reasonable extent. These globally shared urban elements include phenomena such as the denseness of the built environment, proximity of other people and, increasingly, habituated use of refined and shared technologies.

Whereas Haapala focuses on studying the familiar spatial sphere of the everyday through the notion on *place*, the focus here is on what repercussions this type of thinking has for our understanding of *the city* at large. The city as the main 'arena' for the everyday encompasses both more and less familiar areas as well as places that we know well only through the news, stories and other people but rarely visit ourselves. The city also provides us with the unique yet quintessentially urban places that serve as starting points for our individual excursions into the city. Place is one useful concept in understanding this, since it is part of the common parlance, easy to grasp even though difficult to fully define. As Haapala points out, expressions such as 'sense of place' refer strongly to the 'senser': there is always someone to sense, perceive and interpret the place in question (Haapala 2005). This link to the experiential quality of urban space through the notion of the sense of place is central to our understanding of how new mobile apps are changing the underlying assumptions of how the physical qualities of the environment become or could and should become experienced.

In a passage on the sense of place, Haapala refers to Christian Norberg-Schulz' well-known formulation of *genius loci*, according to which environmental character as the essence of place comprises 'concrete things having material substance' (Norberg-Schulz 1980). It seems now inevitable to add that contemporary technologies are adding another layer to these physical features of the environment. How this process takes place and how these new elements become experienced needs further study. It seems clear that on the level of subjective experiences, the effects of technology-induced change in experiencing urban environments can also be dealt with through speculative practices such as different forms of play. The urban everyday is not only the realm of logical and rational efficiency but also open to the human qualities such as emotions, imagination and different types of unanticipated quirks. When it comes to these examples of 'the human factor', wayfinding technologies might induce more experiential variety in the already familiar urban environments since the need for rational attention for finding one's way is already less acutely present.

It seems obvious why location-based apps are needed in unfamiliar and new places and they have proven indispensable to those, who are visiting urban places. However, people use navigation apps in familiar environments for a much wider variety of reasons: navigation is needed in order to optimise and compare the already established routes, new route required by everyday activities starts from familiar settings, and apps are used also to increase the understanding of the spatial layout of their neighbourhoods. Cartographic literacy is on the rise due to the extensive use of contemporary navigation aids (Grabar 2014). Especially in the new global metropolises, it might be difficult to find new locations even in already familiar environments due to the density of these environments and the rapid pace of development which has not lead to increased *legibility* or *continuity* that usually enhance wayfinding (King and de Jong 2016). Location-based apps are also used increasingly for purposes of play and entertainment. The gamification trend within the familiar urban environment relies of fast-developing AR technologies and the new application possibilities are fascinatingly altering the way the most mundane elements of the familiar surroundings are seen. Games such as Pokémon GO encourage to spend time outdoors near home, and already this increased time in itself can prove to bring new facets out of the familiar places. The activity of mobile gaming provides an acceptable reason to stay and linger – hang out – in places that one has previously only passed by.

Besides these new indirect ways in which the new technologies affect the relationship with the familiar environment – closer study of existing routes, lingering in new places, increasing cartographic literacy – technological mediation[3] also seems to add something on a more fundamental and perceptual level to the elements of the everyday environment. Whether it is through a new way of representing a familiar place through computer-generated images (as in route planners) or pointing attention to previously unnoticed elements of the environment, this effect seems to be more fundamental in affecting the urban everyday experience and goes at least partially beyond how these technologies are planned in the first place. In this way, navigation technologies that are applied and used in the contemporary everyday act also as catalysts producing heightened attention regarding the aesthetically manifested values in the environment. Technological mediation in the form of these navigation tools make us look at the environment in a different way, not only when using the tools but also when strolling the familiar city streets without them. What is ultimately missing from these technologies, is, however, the multimodality of the experience. Their use is based on the multisensory qualities of the 'original' physical environment in which they are used: the smells and both haptic[4] and auditory qualities mostly come only from the actual physical surroundings in which these apps are used. Their use thus always necessarily merges with the elements of the concrete environment. The possibilities of this type of augmented engagement make these technologies all the more interesting from the perspective of urban aesthetics.

4. Elements of fun in the technologically mediated familiar environment

When it comes to the everyday life, joyful instances have not been traditionally at the forefront of research interest. The notion of the everyday itself seems to direct thoughts towards the functionally important, mundane tasks and chores or the habitually executed routines that belong to the inescapable realm of the everyday (Naukkarinen 2013). This kind of emphasis on the 'serious' and pragmatic features of the everyday has been predominant also in the study of the urban everyday. Whether leisure time and activities described with notions such as fun have been dealt as secondary due to the internal rational logic of more developed human societies, or, because fun and play as such are still often considered to be the domain of children – although interesting topics as such – are not in the scope of our inquiry here. However, it is worth to notice that how the city has been conceptualised for planning purposes has also focused on optimising the use and predictability of the functional elements of the city. *Efficiency* is a well-recognised value for example in transportation planning, but there has been surprisingly little interest in studying the ensuing experienced quality of this efficiently used quotidian time (Mladenović et al. 2019).

The negligence of perceiving 'fun' as an aesthetic category of interest in explaining human behaviour or values is to a certain extent due to it being interpreted as a predominantly hedonistic mode of experience. However, this lack has been alleviated by some recent advances in aesthetic theory, which (besides the sphere of art or entertainment) place fun into the core of those basal level aesthetic categories that characterise the everyday experience. The recent emphasis on aesthetics of the everyday has changed this and has brought to the discussion some concepts which have been previously considered too frivolous or otherwise of minor importance. In his account of aesthetics of everyday life, Thomas Leddy goes through the terminology relating to aesthetic experiences within the sphere of the everyday.

> Fun things might best be seen as a subset of things that are liked or pleasant. The word 'fun' is strongly associated with jokes and jocularity, but you can have fun without laughter. [...] The concept is also of great importance in the aesthetic lives of children and teens, and continues as a somewhat less important aspect of adult aesthetic experience. (Leddy 2012, 152)

'The term "fun" is applied mainly to activities, for example play, amusement and entertainment, although it may also be applied to things, for example jokes' (Leddy 2012, 153). Fun as a concept implying on activities in the urban environment seems thus to imply unconventional use of the city space. This activity in itself might be extraordinary (such as in the case of a parade) or it might be unconventional within a particular set of everyday habits. 'Fun' has not been considered traditionally a very valuable term for describing the human experience in other than the spheres or environments dedicated to play or entertainment specifically. The best-known examples come from commercialised entertainment environments such as amusement or activity parks. Everyday environments, on the opposite hand, are characterised through concepts such as practicality, functionality and efficiency. Familiar, everyday environments might not indeed be the obvious places for intriguing a sense of curiousness or adventure. However, the new layers of experiential affordances opened by location-based technologies might be changing this significantly. There are studies on how such practices as parkour or 'hanging out' contribute to the aesthetics and creative use of urban space (Tani 2014; Ameel and Tani 2012), but the increase in the use of GPS-based mobile applications would need to be further studied from the perspective of re-evaluation of the experiential horizon of previously familiar urban places.

'Fun' is 'a quality of an activity that involves pleasure'. It also 'fits the broadest definition of the aesthetic, the one that defines beauty as pleasure gained in the mere apprehension of something' (Leddy 2012, 153–154). Emphasis on the *aesthetic* experience means also emphasising the *immediacy* of experiences. Technological mediation makes the notion of immediacy more somewhat more complex, but nonetheless the experiential process develops in a similar way. Defined in this way, fun implies a range of creative flexibility in immediate experiences. In the case of urban aesthetic experience, this could refer to how the traditional qualities of urban environment are perceived and experienced in a new light or the experience of fun might stem from some entirely new form or quality present in the familiar context. The range of 'fun' yields also from the mildly amusing to that which is on the verge of full-blown absurdity.

According to Leddy, 'to say that something or some experience is fun can mean that it has a heightened significance, that it is more alive, that it seems to emanate meaning, and so forth' (Leddy 2012, 154). This type of definition would seem to support the idea that the experiences in the urban space that one would describe as fun are also symptomatic of a heightened attention towards the features of the surroundings. Leddy does not distinguish between the sources of these kinds of experiences in the everyday and neither is technology mentioned explicitly. In this sense, we are left to wonder, how technological mediation affects everyday experiences. All in all, technology is surprisingly little discussed in the main discussions on everyday aesthetics. This avoidance might be due to lack of knowledge about technology or because it is still seen as a hindrance and a form of alienation from the more authentic experiences that would take place without the use of technologies. This, however, is proving to be an increasingly problematic idea and in order to gain deep understanding of the aesthetics of the everyday, the theme of technology has to be introduced into the field of everyday aesthetics.

More flexible ways of using urban space have undeniably emerged during the last decades in the context of developed cities globally. This is also the result of changing social norms such as the development towards increase in gender equality. Especially interesting from the perspective of aesthetics is, how the new forms of urban technologies can lead to increased possibilities of *self-actualisation* in the urban environment. Self-actualisation is here understood widely as the realisation or fulfilment of one's creative or otherwise internally motivated talents and potentialities. This is considered to be a drive or need common and shared to a certain degree by all individual human beings. Games have traditionally provided medium and new opportunities for experimentation by providing a 'magic circle' in which new roles, rules and opportunities for actions have been possible

(Nguyen 2017). AR games are also forerunners in the use of new technologies and it is likely that many of the features that will define future urban wayfinding tools have first been experimented in the form of AR and advanced geospatial games.

The confluence of these particular technologies and the physical urban environments where they become used can from the vantage point of aesthetic analysis be seen as a moment for re-evaluation of the engagement with these environments. Whether new technologies enhance and reinforce the already existing forms of engagement, or whether they open up new possibilities is of interest also because these effects might have serious consequences not only for the use but also for the planning of urban environments.

It is possible to argue that urban dwellers especially in the affluent societies of the Global North have become able and more prone to appreciate urban environments through their distinctive *aesthetic qualities* that are not directly related to finding one's way in the city. This brings certain other types of unobtrusive or 'tacit' aesthetic qualities of the environment into focus also in the relation one has with various *urban places* – that is, compared to the locational qualities related to mere *place identification*. The argument is based on the fact that one does not depend anymore solely on the information provided by, e.g. roads and buildings to tell us where we are in a city: urban landscape or topography can cease to function principally as the guiding features in an environment. Instead, they are seen full of new possibilities, opportunities fuelled by their aesthetic potentiality or the inner logic of the game.

5. Conclusion

The aim of this conceptually focused article has been to describe how the increased use of mobile apps for navigation purposes is adding elements of fun and playfulness to the engagement with the familiar urban everyday environments. This has been done by using definitions for the aesthetic aspects of the categories of 'fun' and 'familiarity' that have been developed within the overlapping fields of philosophical urban and everyday aesthetics. The opportunities for fun and playfulness that new technologies insert into the urban everyday life have traditionally been considered difficult to assess, but we are hoping to contribute to an increase in the interdisciplinary study of the effects of the everyday use of these technologies.

Fun and playfulness as experienced qualities are in one form or another present in the everyday use of urban space. However, in discussions about developing cities they often remain on an implicit level due to overemphasised focus on measurable qualities such as efficiency. Such is the case with understanding end developing human mobility in cities, for example. Human mobility should not be understood merely through the notion of transportation which relies on quantifiable determinants such as efficiency and cost–benefit analysis. Regardless of these traditional tendencies in urban planning, fun and playfulness are intrinsically important for attaining a more comprehensive understanding of the human experience.

As digital mobile technologies are an increasingly important part of the everyday life globally, understanding what type of experiences they enhance or suppress is of crucial importance. The theory of technological mediation and philosophical urban aesthetics have been used here to explicate the primordially fun-based nature of the playful interactions that new tools bring forth. This leads to different new hypotheses, for example it could be stated based on this that efficiency alone is not a sufficient parameter to guide the design of the smart city solutions which are aimed at the everyday use of individuals. Focus on their creative usage through the notions of fun and playfulness would significantly increase the success of implementing new solutions into the everyday. Philosophical and applied approaches to everyday urban experience provide one way of conceptualising these inherently human qualities, which describe part of the immediate engagement with the urban environment.

Notes

1. It is important to take into consideration that there are also crucial limitations to the use of mobile apps, for example in militarized or politically controversial areas. Some large-scale extreme examples include Palestine, Gaza and North Korea.
2. *Harry Potter: Wizards Unite*, a game which was launched on 21 June 2019 is clearly aimed at a wide audience similarly to Pokémon GO, Niantic's previous success game.
3. The theory of technological mediation that we rely on in this context comes from post-phenomenological approach to philosophy of technology (Verbeek 2005).
4. Some apps use also haptic cues such as vibration to alert the users of certain features of the app.

Disclosure statement

No potential conflict of interest was reported by the authors.

ORCID

Sanna Lehtinen ⓘ http://orcid.org/0000-0003-1901-3584
Vesa Vihanninjoki ⓘ http://orcid.org/0000-0003-0815-5130

References

Ameel, Lieven, and Sirpa Tani. 2012. "Everyday Aesthetics in Action: Parkour Eyes and the Beauty of Concrete Walls." *Emotion, Space and Society August 2012* 5 (3): 164–173.

Berleant, Arnold. 2007. "Cultivating an Urban Aesthetic." In *The Aesthetics of Human Environments*, edited by Arnold Berleant and Allen Carlson, 79–91. Toronto: Broadview.

Berleant, Arnold, and Allen Carlson, eds. 2007. *The Aesthetics of Human Environments*. Toronto: Broadview.

Blanc, Nathalie. 2013. "Aesthetic Engagement in the City", Contemporary Aesthetics.

Bonsdorff, Pauline von. 2008. "Urban Richness and the Art of Building." In *The Aesthetics of Human Environments*, edited by A. Berleant, and A. Carlson, 66–78. Peterborough: Broadview Press.

Chatfield, Tom. 2016. "The new words that expose our smartphone obsessions." Accessed June 13 2019. http://www.bbc.com/future/story/20161129-the-new-words-that-reveal-how-tech-has-changed-us.

Dalton, Ruth Conroy, Christoph Hölscher, and Daniel R. Montello. 2019. "Wayfinding as a Social Activity." *Frontiers in Psychology* 10: 142.

De Souza E Silva, Adriana, and Jordan Frith. 2012. *Mobile Interfaces in Public Spaces*. London: Routledge.

Dibazar, Pedram, and Judith Naeff, eds. 2019. *Visualizing the Street: New Practices of Documenting, Navigating and Imagining the City*. Amsterdam: Amsterdam University Press.

Farman, Jason. 2012. *Mobile Interface Theory: Embodied Space and Locative Media*. London & New York: Routledge.

Grabar, Henry. 2014. "Smartphones and the Uncertain Future of 'Spatial Thinking'." Accessed February 15 2019. https://www.citylab.com/life/2014/09/smartphones-and-the-uncertain-future-of-spatial-thinking/379796/.

Haapala, Arto. 2005. "On the Aesthetics of the Everyday: Familiarity, Strangeness, and the Meaning of Place." In *The Aesthetics of Everyday Life*, edited by Andrew Light, and Jonathan M Smith, 39–55. New York: Columbia University Press.

Hunter, Rebecca H., Lynda A. Anderson, and Basia L. Belza, eds. 2016. *Community Wayfinding. Pathways to Understanding*. Switzerland: Springer.

Ishikawa, Toru. 2016. "Maps in the Head and Tools in the Hand: Wayfinding and Navigation in a Spatially Enabled Society." In *Community Wayfinding. Pathways to Understanding*, edited by Rebecca H. Hunter, Lynda A. Anderson, and Basia L. Belza, 115–136. Switzerland: Springer.

Khalis, Adri, and Amori Yee Mikami. 2018. "Who's Gotta Catch 'Em All?: Individual Differences in Pokèmon Go Gameplay Behaviors." *Personality and Individual Differences 1 April 2018* 124: 35–38.

King, Michael R., and Elise de Jong. 2016. "Legibility and Continuity in the Built Environment." In *Community Wayfinding. Pathways to Understanding*, edited by Rebecca H. Hunter, Lynda A. Anderson, and Basia L. Belza. Switzerland: Springer.

Kolhonen, Pasi. 2005. "Moving Pictures – Advertising, Traffic and Cityscape," in Contemporary Aesthetics, Special vol. 1.

Leddy, Thomas. 2012. *The Extraordinary in the Ordinary: The Aesthetics of Everyday Life*. Peterborough, ON: Broadview Press.

Lehtinen, Sanna. 2015. *Excursions Into Everyday Spaces: Mapping Aesthetic Potentiality of Urban Environments Through Preaesthetic Sensitivities*. Helsinki: University of Helsinki.

Lehtinen, Sanna, and Vesa Vihanninjoki. Forthcoming. "Aesthetic Perspectives on Urban Technologies: Conceptualizing and Evaluating the Technology-Driven Changes in the Urban Everyday Experience." In *Technology and the City: Towards a Philosophy of Urban Technologies*, edited by M. Nagenborg, M. González Woge, T. Stone, and P. Vermaas. Dordrecht: Springer (Philosophy of Engineering and Technology Series).

Leorke, Dale. 2019. "Wayfinding and Codemaking in the City of Melbourne." In *Location-Based Gaming*, 195–240. Singapore: Palgrave Macmillan.

McDaniel, Brandon T. 2015. ""Technoference": Everyday Intrusions and Interruptions of Technology in Couple and Family Relationships." In *Family Communication in the age of Digital and Social Media*, edited by C. J. Bruess, 227–243. New York: Peter Lang Publishing.

Mladenović, Miloš, Sanna Lehtinen, Emily Soh, and Karel Martens. 2019. "Emerging Urban Mobility Technologies Through the Lens of Everyday Urban Aesthetics: Case of Self-Driving Vehicle." *Essays in Philosophy* 20 (2), Article 3. doi:10.7710/1526-0569.1633.

Naukkarinen, Ossi. 2013. "What Is 'Everyday' in Everyday Aesthetics?" *Contemporary Aesthetics* 11.

Nguyen, C. Thi. 2017. "Philosophy of Games." *Philosophy Compass* 12 (8). doi:10.1111/phc3.12426.

Norberg-Schulz, Christian. 1980. *Genius Loci. Towards a Phenomenology of Architecture*. New York: Rizzoli.

Raj, Marc Alexander, Aaron Karlin, and Zachary K. Backstrom. 2016. "Pokémon GO: Imaginary Creatures, Tangible Risks." *Clinical Pediatrics* 55 (13): 1195–1196.

Saito, Yuriko. 2017. *Aesthetics of the Familiar: Everyday Life and World-Making*. Oxford: Oxford University Press.

Tabacchi, Marco Elio, Barbara Caci, Maurizio Cardaci, and Valerio Perticone. 2017. "Early Usage of Pokémon GO and its Personality Correlates." *Computers in Human Behavior July 2017* 72: 163–169.

Tani, Sirpa. 2014. "Loosening/Tightening Spaces in the Geographies of Hanging out." *Social & Cultural Geography* 03 September 2014: 1–21.

Verbeek, Peter-Paul. 2005. *What Things Do. Philosophical Reflections on Technology, Agency, and Design*. University Park, PA: Pennsylvania State University Press.

Vihanninjoki, Vesa. 2019. "Urban Places as Aesthetic Phenomena: Framework for a Place-Based Ontology of Urban Lifeworld," Topoi.

Play in the smart city context: exploring interactional, bodily, social and spatial aspects of situated media interfaces

Andre G. Afonso and Ava Fatah gen Schieck

ABSTRACT

Urban media interfaces can assume many forms, offering rich possibilities for interactions and social encounters. We focus on a particular type of urban interfaces, namely *urban media installations*, which are situated, fixed (i.e. non-mobile) and outdoor interactive interfaces enhanced by digital technologies. Drawing on research on play in the context of the smart city, we aim to clarify how the digital and the physical worlds of urban media installations can coalesce into enjoyable and socially thriving playscapes. Two case studies of urban media installations are presented: the *Appearing Rooms*, a seasonal art installation in London, and the *Mirror Pool*, a permanent, large-scale urban installation in Bradford, UK. Each of these interfaces incorporates a design paradigm that differs from the other in terms of context, duration of implementation, and scale. Following a longitudinal approach based on non-participant observations and time-lapse photography, we analyse emergent interactions and focus in particular on playful encounters at different levels and scales: from the micro scale of the bodily engagement to the macro scale of the spatial and social configurations. Our case studies highlight that the urban spatial layout is a key element in defining the emerging interactions and encounters around the urban situated interfaces.

1. Introduction

One important function of public space is providing citizens with a setting where they can encounter each other, interact with the environment and engage in playful activities. Yet, play as a mode for creative experimentation, can help us make meaning and understand how we can impact the world around us and affect change (Kress and Cowan 2017). As such the concept of 'urban play' emphasises a unique character of the urban experience: it is related to the ways people sense urban settings, move through them and act within them. Urban play embraces a wide variety of activities, which are spontaneous, irrational or risky, and often unanticipated by designers, managers and other users (Stevens 2007).

The growing use and implementation of digital technologies are redefining how people engage in urban spaces, with the environment itself and with other people (Fatah gen Schieck 2008; de Waal 2014; de Lange and de Waal 2019). The rise of urban media interfaces seems to stimulate a spatial shift: by coupling the digital with the physical, urban media can enable spaces for playful and social interactions that are more flexible and less dependent on the rigid structures of the built environment (Pop et al. 2016). At the same time, playful experiences

become available to a new public: children are no longer the sole players, as new agents and communities arise from playscapes enhanced by emergent technologies. Within this trend, and since technologies make it possible in some situations to re-configure new conditions for playful activities that can potentially transform the experience of any urban environment, conventional facilities such as dedicated playgrounds cease to be the only site for play.

New types of playful interfaces, whether mobile or fixed, have emerged over the years. In the context of mobile interfaces, Luke (2005) talks about the role of mobile phones in having a playful orientation to city spaces, while Saker and Evans (2016) point to the concept of the 'playeur' as an individual who reads city spaces as a site of play and who makes connections within the city contingent on mood or orientation. From a design standpoint, Verhoeff argues that media architecture technologies are inherently mobile and temporal, which makes the very process of designing them a performative process: the design does not merely precede the interface, but is rather *performed* in it; there is no rigorous distinction between 'process' and 'product' (Verhoeff 2015). However, playful interactions can also rely on other types of interfaces, such as the ones that remain fixed in their settings either temporarily or permanently. These fixed, and situated interfaces may carry a great potential to encourage not only playful behaviours, but also social encounters, bodily interactions and social learning and even act as platforms of socio-political critique. An interesting example of the latter case is the series of seesaws designed by Ronald Rael and Virginia San Fratello, which were installed at the steel border fence that separates the United States from Mexico. Once installed, the pink seesaws were promptly appropriated by children and adults located at either side of the border. Their playful interactions, locally and bodily performed, rapidly assumed a global meaning through the intangible interfaces of social media and communication networks. Among other aspects, this initiative is noteworthy because it responds to a serious political, social and spatial crisis in a playful, evocative and light-hearted fashion. According to Rael, besides bringing a sense of togetherness at the border fence, the project is about recognising that the actions that take place on one side have a direct consequence on the other side (The Guardian 2019).

One prominent example of interactive interface is the urban media installation: a fixed interface that creates an interaction space on a public open area, allowing several people to physically explore and share the interface at once. Urban media installations may be employed on a temporary or permanent basis. Those installed on a permanent basis tend to become embedded elements in the urban settings, just like a piece of architecture or landscaping feature. A central feature of urban media installations (and what distinguishes them from mere sculptures or conventional art installations) is the use of digital technologies – encapsulated in the term *media*, which ultimately mediate how people experience and share the interface and its surrounding space (Pop et al. 2016).

The types of urban media that are installed on a permanent, long-term or seasonal basis are becoming more common in recent years, due to recent technological innovations, coupled with a heightened awareness of the social, spatial and economic benefits brought about by these installations. From a socio-spatial perspective, these situated and fixed interfaces have given rise to new forms of bodily and playful interactions that, unlike those mediated through mobile media, present a highly situated character insofar as they are fixed interfaces, embedded in their places of interaction (Afonso, Ergin, and Fatah gen. Schieck 2019). Being fixed and embedded interfaces mean that players are often encouraged to interact with urban media installations not through a portable personal screen – as typified by mobile interfaces – but rather by using their whole bodies and

sensory apparatuses to explore the space, the materiality and the three-dimensionality of the installation. While engaging with urban media installations, people become aware not only of their own interactions, but also of other people's actions and behaviours; eventually, the entire socio-spatial environment becomes part of the playscape, with players' bodily positions and movements constantly negotiated, both in relation to other players, and in relation to the spatial arrangement of the installation, which defines different interaction spaces (Fischer and Hornecker 2012).

Urban media installations, as embodied and, to some extent, tangible structures situated in public settings, affect not only the behaviour of individual passers-by but also change the spatial and social dynamics around them (Behrens, Fatah gen. Schieck, and Brumby 2015; Fatah gen. Schieck, Briones, and Mottram 2008). At the same time, the existing physical space is not a passive 'platform' for the installation (Behrens et al. 2013): the spatial layout plays a vital role in defining how the interface will be approached, used and shared. Media architecture and urban digital interaction scholars have discussed the social and spatial aspects of introducing media installations in outdoor public settings, and key concepts have been proposed, such as 'Urban HCI' and 'social affordances' (Afonso, Ergin, and Fatah gen. Schieck 2019). On the one hand, most of these concepts emerge from studies of media interfaces that were only temporarily implemented, hence with little consideration of two fundamental aspects concerning urban spaces and the city context. Firstly, studies addressing temporary interfaces typically lack a more profound discussion regarding the wider urban context, with its various nuances, levels and scales of analysis. In terms of scale, for example, interactions with urban media range from the micro scale of the bodily engagement to the macro scale of the spatial and social configurations around the installation. Secondly, little attention is paid to the role of the physical space as enabler and generator of individual and shared encounters, in particular those that take place around urban interfaces installed on a permanent or long-term basis. On the other hand, research on interaction with permanent digital interfaces as part of architectural space (mostly in the form of vertical surfaces), addresses a situation that requires people to use another tangible device – a 'mediator' (Behrens et al. 2013) – to interact with the interface, which remains detached from a direct bodily connection and sensation.

We address the gaps in literature outlined above by exploring in depth two urban media installations in which water is an important feature, and whose permanent (or semi-permanent) character makes them embedded elements within their urban surroundings.

In this case, a range of factors concerning, for example, spatial layout, locational attributes, urban structure and pedestrian flows inform the design of the installations, which should fit the socio-spatial environment in which they are situated. Taking inspiration from the phenomenological assumption that our experiences in the world are inherently rooted in our perceiving, sensing and acting bodies, coupled with ideas from architectural research that draws on space (in terms of spatial configurations) as an enabler for shared encounters (in terms of spatial configurations),[1] we focus the discussion on urban interfaces supported by digital technologies and designed to encourage playful experiences and shared encounters through whole-body interactions.

Two case studies of existing urban media installations are presented: the *Appearing Rooms*, a seasonal interactive art installation in London, and the *Mirror Pool*, a permanent installation of a massive fountain which is the centrepiece of a project of urban regeneration in Bradford, UK. Each system incorporates a design paradigm which is markedly different from the other, both in terms of context (one as a self-contained artwork, the other embedded in a project of urban design), time (one as a seasonal installation, the other as a permanent addition to the city), and scale (one measuring approx. 50 square metre, the other approx. 3600 square metre). As situated and fixed media, the case studies also differ in the way they employ digital technologies: in the Appearing Rooms, players engage with the water, not with the computing device that controls the water behaviour (back-end model of interaction[2]), whereas in the Mirror Pool players can have a more direct experience of the digital technologies that mediate their interactions (back-end and front-end models[3]), particularly when the motion sensor-controlled laser lights of the installation are activated every night. We analyse how these playful interfaces help shape lived experiences at different levels and scales: from the micro scale of the bodily engagement to the macro scale of the spatial and social configurations unfolding on each urban context.

These case studies allow for a rich and nuanced discussion on playful interactions in urban spaces, particularly in the context of smart cities. We interpret 'smart' spaces as those enabling meaningful urban experiences, considered both from the perspective of the body (i.e. the physical, material, sensory qualities that render a space enticing for the lived body) and also from a socio-spatial perspective (the diverse community of players and other people who share and give life to these spaces, either temporarily – the case of *Appearing Rooms* – or through long-term relationships – the *Mirror Pool*).

Addressing the lived, bodily and playful experience of the city calls for an approach that foregrounds the material, tangible qualities of human interactions with situated technologies. In this regard, the two interfaces discussed in this paper share a significant feature: they exploit water as the basic material for interaction, following a long tradition in urban design (which has valued the water for its ecological, economic, topological and scenic qualities), yet reinterpreting the bodily experience of water in light of emergent digital interactive technologies. By analysing and comparing the bodily, social and spatial aspects that shape how people experience these two urban interfaces, we aim to clarify how the digital and the physical worlds can coalesce into enjoyable and socially thriving playscapes.

2. Background

We begin this section addressing urban design and providing a brief historical account of how the fields of architecture and urban design have discussed the concept of *play*, considered as the 'non-functional uses of public spaces'. This is followed by an outline of the effect of new technologies – specifically digital technologies – on urban design and their wide, potentially disruptive implications on all levels for the future of cities (Kitchin 2014; 2015). We sketch out the main trends in the literature of the so-called 'smart cities' initiatives; however, instead of focusing on data and information-heavy urban environments, we will re-think 'smart cities' as playable cities (Ackermann, Rauscher, and Stein 2016; Sicart 2016). This approach will be illustrated with examples of projects exploring playful interactions mediated by digital technologies that extend the conventional notion of 'play' into new dimensions, in which the sensory-kinaesthetic experience of the player assumes a central role. The section ends with a transition towards the use of water in urban design and how it supports playful forms of encounters and its manifestation through new digital forms, the typology of interface that will be later the focus of our discussions through our case studies.

2.1. Play and urban design

Dutch cultural historian Johan Huizinga, who coined the concept of *Homo Ludens*, stated that play is older than culture (1955). Yet, as far as urban design history is concerned, proper spaces for play were rare in the West, with the exception of classical Greek and Roman arenas. Until the late nineteenth century, play unfolded mostly in shared grounds, thus leaving no significant traces. Le Corbusier's 1933 *Radiant City* marked the turning point where play, and especially sport, became a core concern for urban design (Pérez de Arce 2018).

Among the core characteristics of play, scholars have identified its non-functional and non-utilitarian character. Stevens (2007), for example, links play to non-instrumental behaviour; for van Vleet and Feeney (2015), play involves a focus on the process of the activity and implicit learning, rather than end-goals, whereas for Kwastek (2013, 72), the common feature to all forms of play is the 'foundation of an experience on an activity that is not primarily purposeful'. However, in the context of urban settings, Stevens (2007) argues that, until not long ago, few relevant empirical studies had addressed the non-functional uses of public spaces – despite the importance of this subject to better understanding and developing the very concept of play.

An early study that acknowledged playful behaviour as a key element to create lively places is Suzanne and Henry Lennard's book *Public life in urban places*, in which the authors observe that 'providing an opportunity to relate in a playful and joyous mode is a contribution made by good public spaces towards the well being of their users' (Lennard and Lennard 1984, 9). Sicart, on the other hand, calls for scholars as well as designers to think about playful interactions as a valuable interface and design practice, and reminds us in his article *Play and the City* (2016), that playful engagement with urban environments has offered a mode of resistance and appropriation of cities for their citizens.

More recently, architectural research has paid more attention to the various forms of play in urban spaces, with important contributions arising from different perspectives, such as Iain Borden's work on skateboarding.[4] Although Borden's main interest does not lie in play itself, the notion of play is often revealed as the author discusses the history and practice of skateboarding, an activity that entails a playful approach to the city. Borden's research is particularly relevant to our discussion because the practice of skateboarding, as explored by the author, generates a domain of outdoor interactions that is deeply rooted in the idea of *bodily engagement*, which Borden uses to underpin a 'performative critique' of architectural and urban design: 'above all, it is in the continual performance of skateboarding – which, rather than reading or writing the city, *speaks* the city through utterance as bodily engagement – that its meaning and actions are manifested' (Borden 2001, 195, emphasis on original).

2.2. Play in the context of the smart city

As far as debates on digital cities are concerned, the turn of the millennium marked a shift in focus from 'cyber space' to 'ubiquitous computing'. Urban spaces have acquired a digital layer, which involves the design of organisations, services and communications. Digital technology is built into our environments and embedded in our devices, pervading our everyday lives. Increasingly, these technologies are networked and potentially disruptive, as exemplified by the notion of *smart city*, a highly debated model of urban development led by industrial and governmental initiatives.

Overall, literature on 'smart cities' seems to follow one of two trends: the first tends to promote a positive and rather simplistic view of smart urbanism with the focus on management and organisations; whereas the second trend represents a more critical view, focusing mainly on 'place' as location for political and socio-economic agency. Within the second trend, some authors have characterised the smart city model as a high-profile financial and political drive to smarten the built environment following a logic of technocracy (Carvalho 2015) and appraisals for progress (Catapult Future Cities 2017). A community-oriented alternative to such corporation-oriented notion of 'smart city' has informed the *Playable City* initiative. Spanning various cities across five continents, the Playable City aims to generate a worldview of 'smarter city' development by fostering creative technology-driven projects, which are sensitive to site-specific issues and opportunities (Playable City 2019). Such a site-specific, place-based approach to the concept of 'smart city' allows each community to tackle its own urban problems creatively.

Urban initiatives like the Playable City draw our attention to the importance of interactivity beyond the scale of the object and the task at hand. Key to this development is the notion of *space*, which calls for a coupling of urban design and interaction design. Such coupling may pave the way for novel approaches concerning how our cities are shaped, and how to deal with a variety of urban problems in light of emerging interactive technologies. From that viewpoint, it is important to explore other approaches to the implementation of digital technologies, and their impact on the practice of urban design.

Troy Innocent (2016, 2019), for instance, reframes the relationship of citizens to the city as 'players' and introduces three concepts that connect play and placemaking in cities: the 'urban art environment', a constructed playground in urban space; 'mixed realities and urban art', or the framing of the city as a playground; and the 'playful citizen', which reframes the relationship of the player to the city. Sicart (2016) reminds us that data created by smart cities can provide access to information-heavy urban environments on the level of human-scaled experiences, not necessarily presented as a service for citizens but rather as a support for play. According to him, data-rich cities can become playable cities, and, as such, more human and more inclusive spaces. Nijholt (2017, 2019) outlines the need to address other aspects of smart cities that relate to our daily life activities, activities that are undertaken without having any type of efficiency in mind and interactions in which we want to engage just for social, entertainment, and fun reasons, where residents have the possibility to hack the city and use the smart city's data and digital technology for their own purposes and applications. According to him, the infrastructure of a smart city can be adapted to playful applications that residents have in mind, or smart city residents can hack the environment and embed their own technology in an existing global network.

With regard to the practice of urban design, as projects increasingly embrace the idea of playfulness mediated through digital technologies, it becomes clear that playful spaces and interfaces do offer a great potential for creating activating urban spaces. However, as far as play is concerned, some recent projects have shown that the mere intention or indeed the presence of a playful infrastructure is far from assuring playful behaviours, let alone empirically observed benefits in terms of social encounters or urban livelihood. A good example of this is the Granary Square fountains,[5] part of an ongoing major project of urban redevelopment in central London (Argent St. George 2001; Zielinska-Dabkowska 2019). The Granary Square fountains incorporate a cutting-edge technology that enables members of the public to control the behaviour of their 1,080 water jets through a dedicated mobile app. (Figure 1).

Since this ingenious and playful feature was launched, a few years ago, we have been systematically visiting the site and, surprisingly, virtually no player was found engaging with the game. In the summer, plenty of social encounters and playful behaviours do take place within and around the fountains of Granary Square; yet none of these social activities were sparked by the site-specific game, no matter the season or weather conditions.

This gap between a designed experience (the urban game itself) and the ways people actually experience their everyday urban settings illustrates a relatively common situation in the fields of architectural and urban design. As philosopher Lefebvre (1991) explains through his concepts of 'conceived space' and 'lived space', when urban strategies, designs and mechanisms (the conceived space) do not meet basic requirements for the (playful) experience of local conditions (the lived space), the ideas or plans at stake – no matter how innovative they are – remain detached from the reality of embodied, situated urban experiences.

2.3. Spatial and social approaches to interactions with situated urban media

Within the context of smart cities, as we witness a new wave of implementations of situated urban media that run on a permanent or long-term basis, it seems necessary to engage in a much deeper and broader debate of the spatial and social implications of the urban media than those found in literature to date. In particular, it is fundamental to address the mechanisms whereby situated installations mediate an entire domain of urban experiences, with due attention to the role of the physical space as enabler and generator of individual and shared experiences and encounters. Previous research on urban media installations has already developed interaction frameworks that help to shed light on various aspects regarding the use and sharing of playful outdoor installations activated by digital technologies, and how this affects the surrounding physical space (Afonso, Ergin, and Fatah gen. Schieck 2019). A similar spatial concern informed the development of the 'media architectural interface' framework (Behrens, Fatah gen. Schieck, and

Figure 1. Views of the Granary Square fountains during the day (left) and at night, with the illuminated jets (right). After downloading the mobile app *Granary Squirt*, and accessing the local Wi-Fi network, people can use their mobile phones to play an urban-scale, water-based version of the game *Snake* – in which players control, in real time, a line of jets – or a 'water snake' – as it makes its way across the four fountain bays shown above.[8]

Brumby 2015), which provides a synthesis of situated and shared interfaces.

Research has also looked into interactions mediated through tangible interfaces (Müller et al. 2010), exploring the connections between various situated digital surfaces installed vertically and horizontally. They found that changing the properties of one component directly affects the other elements. These elements, in turn, set the level of participation (Fritsch and Brynskov 2011; Caldwell and Foth 2014) and, in some urban situations, may amplify participants' interactions, depending on the properties of the interface and its socio-spatial setting (for example, a busy high street or a transport hub). Other authors have focused on the social aspects of interactions with urban media interfaces, and how these interfaces support shared encounters in public spaces by bringing people together and by creating a setting for unplanned situations, conversations and site-specific experiences (Fatah gen. Schieck, Briones, and Mottram 2008).

Altogether, the body of research outlined above reinforces our argument that situated urban media installations represent a multi-layered phenomenon and, as such, have the capacity to mediate new experiences and stimulate new forms of engagements, both individually and collectively. At the individual level, urban installations lend themselves to numerous forms of bodily engagement: they encourage people to move, to feel and to *interact* – with the interface itself, with the spatial setting and with other people – as they wish, often triggering playful behaviours (Fatah gen. Schieck, Briones, and Mottram 2008; Urbanowicz and Lucyna 2012). At the collective level, urban installations are public and situated structures and, as such, they often function as a playful arena, able to spark many types of social encounters; these may take place via 'triangulation' (prompting strangers to talk to each other), or via 'shared encounters' (in which a sense of performative co-

presence is experienced) (Reeves 2011; Benford and Giannachi 2011).

2.4. Water in urban design: from contemplation to play

Urban design has a very long tradition in exploiting water features for manifold reasons. The very history of civilizations and urban societies is closely tied to the element of water; suffice it to say that the first known human settlements were established and developed alongside water streams: 'all civilization originally was a river civilization' (Niederland 1989, 43). Since those early settlements, water has been harnessed in cities for an ever-increasing variety of uses that exploit, for example, its utilitarian, economic, ecological, symbolic and scenic qualities. Especially relevant to this research, though, are the interactional and playful characteristics of water in public outdoor spaces, and how this notion has developed over time in light of new technologies.

A pedestrian crossing the lower level of the Trafalgar Square, in Central London, may feel enticed to approach one of the monumental fountains and, possibly, also spare some time lingering and resting on the fountain's borders, as shown in Figure 2. Trafalgar Square's aquatic facilities illustrate one of the most ubiquitous design typologies of fountains, which are essentially conceived as urban amenities that encourage passive, contemplative behaviours, and, to different degrees, also informal social encounters.

In the last decades, the emerging use of situated technologies has helped to bring whole new modes of social interaction and bodily engagement to urban spaces. And, in some cases, water has played a central role in encouraging these new social, spatial and experiential dynamics. One of these examples is the installation by Carlo Ratti Associati, built at the entrance of the 2008 Expo in Zaragoza, the Digital Water pavilion, an interactive structure

Figure 2. Trafalgar Square fountain, London: the non-playful design of a traditional water feature.

of digitally controlled water curtains. Supported by digital technologies, these interactive interfaces are operating a significant change in the place and role of water fountains – from monuments to look at structures to play with.

However, with the rapidly growing field of media and interactive art and its implementation within the urban context, many aspects relating to people's engagement with these new types of installations are not well understood. Using our case studies of the Appearing Rooms and the Mirror Pool as examples, we propose to build on this body of work and explore in depth an approach to mediated urban environments that focuses on spatial layout and whole-body interactions, allowing us to unpack significant socio-spatial implications of whole-body interactions in specific urban settings featuring urban media installations. Specifically, we discuss how designers and artists are deploying digital technologies to reinterpret the typology of urban fountains and, in so doing, they turn traditional contemplative fountains into playful and multi-layered platforms for bodily interactions and social encounters. We draw particular attention to the material and experiential qualities of water-based interactions – which are, in our view, two intertwined factors that help explain the long-standing popularity of urban water fountains.

Building on Lefebvre's concepts of 'lived space' and 'conceived space' outlined previously, the discussion of the Appearing Rooms and the Mirror Pool will also serve to illustrate how emerging digital technologies may be effectively used to foster active play in favour of liveable places – thus reconciling the conceived with the lived spaces, an outcome not easily attained by initiatives in this field.

3. Methodology

In this section we describe the initial exploratory studies that underpinned the selection of the two projects – the Appearing Rooms and the Mirror Pool – before proceeding with a description of the data collection process for each of the two projects.

3.1. Exploratory studies

The initial stage of our research consisted of a series of exploratory and observational studies of contemporary urban splash facilities, most of which located in London. Our primary interest at this stage was in surveying the overall environment and developing our first impressions on how the use of water features supported by digital technologies could bring about a variety of playful behaviours as well as shared experiences to specific urban settings. We were especially drawn to splash facilities featuring creative, interactive and fully accessible water features that encouraged a close bodily contact with the water. Over the course of one month, one of the researchers visited, observed and made a preliminary selection of the most relevant urban splash facilities, according to the research criteria outlined above. Altogether, nine splash facilities – spanning a wide range of sizes and technological sophistication – were selected, eight of which in London and one located in Bradford, England. These splash facilities are classified in Table 1 according to their main spatial and playful characteristics.

Following this preliminary selection, one of the researchers undertook systematic fieldwork in each splash facility. The principal methods of data collection at this stage are qualitative, non-participant observations, field notes, photographs and particularly the recourse to time-lapse photography. For this initial approach, the researcher applied the same protocol in all splash facilities: to avoid interfering with the spontaneous behaviours around the water features, the researcher stood in a secluded, inconspicuous position at all times, and used a small action camera, which was set to take photographs of the interactions at regular intervals of 30 seconds. These series of time-lapse photographs were then assembled into videos for further analyses.

This observational approach required a detached posture not to disturb people's natural behaviours and hence maximise the ecological validity of the study. Nonetheless, another crucial part of the research motivation was in understanding *what it is like* and *how it feels* to play with the water features; this involves an 'experiential bodily knowing' – a *knowing how* whose meaning is produced in and through movement (Larssen, Robertson, and Edwards 2007; Levisohn and Schiphorst 2011), and therefore can only be achieved through the first-hand experience of the water features and the urban setting immediately around them. In practical terms, this meant leaving the secluded position after the data collection was completed – leaving the role of detached observer – and taking part in the interactions on the splash facilities.

The first-hand experience of all splash facilities surveyed in this exploratory fieldwork, coupled with the analysis of the material collected at their locations (as indicated in Table 1), informed a reflection upon their significance and potential for further exploration, in light of our research questions and motivations. At the end of this stage, we selected two water features – the *Appearing Rooms*, in London, and the *Mirror Pool*, in

Table 1. Spatial and playful properties of the splash facilities surveyed in the initial stages of the research. By 'interface' (sixth column) we mean the design features that drive the interactions. The text in bold indicates the two case studies of this paper (the Appearing Rooms and the Mirror Pool) as well as the Granary Square fountains, another pivotal project for our discussion.

Splash facility	Location	Area (approx.)	Shape of the water feature	Spatial setting	Interface behaviour	Key playful elements
				Spatial properties	Playful properties	
Appearing Rooms	**Southbank Centre**	**50 m²**	**Square**	**Calm, empty open space used as a crossing site amid cultural/ leisure buildings; low pedestri-an traffic**	**Watery walls come up and down defining "rooms"**	**Enter and leave the inner spaces of the fountain without getting wet**
Edmond J. Safra Fountain	Westminster (Somerset House)	750 m²	Rectangular grid	Monumental courtyard of a major cultural venue; segregated from streets; low traffic of crossing visitors/ workers	Jets randomly appear and disappear at varying heights	Wander over the fountain while trying to predict what will happen next
Granary Square	**Kings Cross**	**400 m²**	**Four rectangular grids**	**Broad, scenic canalside plaza; crossing area amid mixed neighbourhood; steady flow of diverse communities**	**Animated jets, fog, app-based game; 1,080 LED-lit jets**	**Move around and follow the animated jets; use the mobile app to control the direction of the jets (at scheduled times only)**
Merchant Square Water Maze	Paddington	130 m²	Circular	Tranquil canalside thoroughfare in mostly residential area; low traffic of pedestrians	Groups of jets come up and down in a maze formation	Move across the water maze; traverse the fountain without getting wet
Mirror Pool	**City Park (Bradford, UK)**	**3400 m²**	**Oval**	**Massive scenic plaza in town centre; mixed-use neighbour-hood; transitional, integrated character (crossing/staying)**	**Reflection pool, fog, animated jets, geysers, 30m high water cannon; LED-lit jets**	**Walk around the various jets; get close and feel the fog and geyser effects; move across the pool or its causeways**
More London Riverside Fountains	Southwark (City Hall)	300 m²	Four linear banks	Partly segregated riverside area affording broad views; offices and shops nearby; high levels of pedestrian flows	Groups of 200+ jets appear and disappear	Move across the fountain while trying to predict which jets will appear and disappear
Peninsula Square Fountains	Greenwich (O2 Arena)	240 m²	Three circular pools	Vast open space by the entrance to a major music venue; occasional static activities and irregular pedestrian flows	Fog, geysers, lit jets	Get close and feel the jets, fog and geyser effects
Princess Diana Memorial Fountain	Knightsbridge (Hyde Park)	700 m²	Oval	Calm, picturesque area segre-gated in a vast central park; no crossing traffic; fenced site devoid of urban facilities	Cascading, bubbling stream runs through a stone ring	Walk along the watery pathway or sit on its borders to feel the stream
The Water Labyrinth	Stratford (Olympic Park)	350 m²	Winding ribbon	Large plaza next to a scenic walkway amid sports & leisure facilities; mid-to-low pedestrian flows; segregated from streets	195 LED-lit jets spring in varying sequences and heights	Race through the line of jets (following them to get wet or avoiding them to stay dry)

Bradford – for a more comprehensive study. The selection of these water features was based on three main reasons:

(1) Both are *fixed interfaces*, embedded in their urban surroundings – the Appearing Rooms is semi-permanent (activated every year during the summer), and the Mirror Pool is a permanent urban facility.

(2) *The broader 'social appeal' of playfulness* – the water features we observed in both the Appearing Rooms and in the Mirror Pool were actively *played with* by a varied population of different age groups, and not only by children, as observed in the other splash facilities surveyed. These broader levels of explicit social participation through play allow us to look deeper into the relationships between playfulness, bodily interactions and social encounters mediated by digital technologies.

(3) *The urban setting of the projects* – the spatial surroundings of the Appearing Rooms and the Mirror

Pool are characterised by a rich and diverse flow of people and social encounters. From an urban point of view, both projects occupy a privileged position, being set in highly accessible and visible areas of their cities; in Space Syntax terms, their locations are highly integrated into the spatial network of their urban fabric (Hillier and Hanson 1984). Other splash facilities that were surveyed, albeit featuring very creative designs and playful water choreographies, suffer from spatial segregation, that is, they are more or less detached from the core spaces of social activity in their urban neighbourhoods, the spaces which most people use on an everyday basis. The Princess Diana Memorial Fountain, for example, occupies a large, scenic yet secluded area in Hyde Park, hundreds of metres away from the main pedestrian routes of Central London. A similar situation is observed in the Somerset House fountain, set at the centre of a monumental courtyard, enveloped by the grand architecture of the cultural venue and detached from the bustling main streets further away. In contrast, the highly integrated urban locations of the Appearing Rooms and the Mirror Pool better respond to our objectives of finding out the social and spatial implications of smart playful technologies in the lived experience of contemporary cities.

4. Case studies – data collection

The case studies of the Appearing Rooms and the Mirror Pool were conducted following a longitudinal approach, which involved visiting and collecting data at the study sites over an extended period of time. The fieldworks were concentrated in the summers of 2015 and 2016 (Appearing Rooms), and from 2016 to 2017 (Mirror Pool). In both cases, one of the researchers collected data at different times of the day, on different days of the week, and in different seasons of the year, so as to enhance the ecological validity of the studies. Apart from these commonalities, some aspects of the data collection process were adapted to the specific circumstances of each project, as described in the following sections.

4.1. The Appearing Rooms

Over the course of three years, observations, notes and photographs of the installation site were collected and analysed, both in the winter season – when the Appearing Rooms was not installed – and especially in the summer, when the installation was running. In the latter case, the data collection took place in August and September of 2015 and 2016, in which period time-lapse photography was employed (in addition to the aforementioned methods) to capture the urban context and the various interactions taking place both within the Appearing Rooms and in the immediate surroundings of the installation. The sessions of time-lapse photography lasted a minimum of 30 minutes and employed a small action camera, which was set to take photographs at regular intervals of 30 seconds. Eventually, the series of still images captured on each session were assembled into time-lapse videos.

The data collection was primarily conducted from the Level 5 balcony of the Royal Festival Hall, a high and inconspicuous position affording bird's-eye views of the study site – the Riverside Terrace – and its neighbourhoods. This position matched the large-scale, complex and dynamic setting of the Southbank Centre, which called for an expanded perspective, wide enough to observe and capture not only the site of the Appearing Rooms, but also its broader urban context.

4.2. Mirror Pool

Since the Mirror Pool is a permanent urban facility, the fieldworks were distributed across various seasons, from November 2016 to November 2017. This was an important methodological decision because the use of open, outdoor spaces like the Mirror Pool is highly contingent on factors like temperature, rain, wind and light conditions – and one of the core objectives of our study is to clarify whether, and to what extent, the interactive and playful features of the Mirror Pool were able to attract and retain people under different weather conditions.

Altogether, the data collection of the Mirror Pool involved 33 recording sessions using time-lapse photography, following the same methodological procedure adopted in the study of The Appearing Rooms. In addition to time-lapse photography, field notes and high-resolution photographs were also used throughout the study as subsidiary methods, especially to record fleeting, unusual and/or revealing moments of interactions in the Mirror Pool. Two opposite locations overlooking the Mirror Pool were used at different times to position the camera and to observe the social activities: the terrace on the roof of The Pavilion Café (in the southern approach to the City Park) and the third floor of the City Hall building, in the north side of the park.

5. Case studies – analysis

This section presents the two case studies separately, following the same order: we begin by outlining the urban context of each project, then we zoom in and describe its interactive and playful elements, followed by the results of each case study.

5.1. Case Study I: The Appearing Rooms

5.1.1. Urban context

The installation Appearing Rooms is located in the Southbank Centre, a major complex of artistic and cultural venues in Central London. The installation occupies a prominent area of the Southbank Centre, known as the Riverside Terrace – a broad, continuous, open area overlooking the river Thames and stretching alongside the principal landmarks of the Southbank Centre: two performance venues (the Royal Festival Hall and the Queen Elizabeth Hall) and an art gallery (the Hayward Gallery). This central position of the Riverside Terrace, in addition to the various connections it offers for pedestrian circulation, makes the installation site a highly used urban space on an everyday basis (Figure 3).

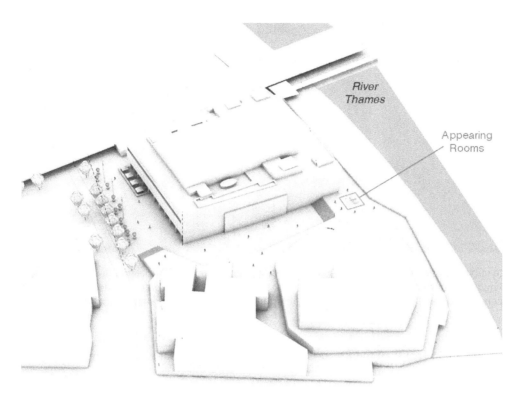

Figure 3. Urban context of the Appearing Rooms: perspective of the Southbank Centre with the Royal Festival Hall on the top, the Hayward Gallery on the bottom left and the Queen Elizabeth Hall on the bottom right. Image adapted from Ivers 2018 (with permission).

In normal conditions, i.e. when the installation Appearing Rooms is not present, or it is switched off, the study site does not offer many props or facilities for people to stay or socialise. These are limited to a few concrete benches and wooden tables placed at the borders of the study site, where, in mild and warm days, some people can be observed engaged in activities like chatting, smoking, reading, using the mobile phone, taking a nap or simply sunbathing. Apart from these benches and tables, the study site stands as an empty outdoor space; an area in which, on an everyday basis – and especially during cold seasons – static activities or social encounters are rather low and incidental.

5.1.2. Project overview

The Appearing Rooms is an installation that has participated in several exhibitions across the world since 2004. In London, the Appearing Rooms has been installed every summer since 2007, at the same site in Southbank Centre, as part of the annual Summer Festival. Designed by Danish artist Jeppe Hein, the Appearing Rooms is a water-based interactive installation with a dynamic character. The artwork consists of four inner spaces – the 'rooms' – that seem to constantly appear and disappear as a series of computer-programmed, 2.30-metre-high water jets come up and down (Hein 2019) (Figure 4).

At regular intervals of 10 seconds, the water choreography changes in some parts of the installation; yet such changes do not respect a clear or predictable sequence and, as a result, players can only guess which water jets will raise and which will fall within the next few seconds. The visual effect is that of watery walls coming up and down, defining inner spaces that become momentarily more or less accessible. From an interactional perspective, the Appearing Rooms can be described as a challenging 'water pavilion' or 'aquatic sculpture', in which the interactions are mainly driven by surprise, risk and chance. In fact, the key playful character of the installation consists of encouraging people to enter, to move across and to leave the 'appearing rooms' without getting wet. Being trapped inside one of the 'rooms' or soaking parts of the body while moving in or out of the installation is all part of the playful experience proposed by the artist.

5.1.3. Results

We begin by presenting the results of a macro-scale socio-spatial analysis of the installation site. Firstly, we observed and mapped the pedestrian flows in the Riverside Terrace when the Appearing Rooms was installed and operating. Two main axis of circulation were identified: the first across the full extension of the terrace,

Figure 4. Sequence of pictures showing people's interactions and the behaviour of the Appearing Rooms. Each one of the four 'rooms' measures 3.5 × 3.5 m; the platform beneath them measures 12 × 12 m and conceals the pipes and nozzles of the installation, while the computing machinery that gives life to the installation is stored in a metallic shed, located beside the platform (not shown in the pictures).

running parallel to the main facade of the Royal Festival Hall (i.e. the facade facing the river); and the second axis perpendicular to the first one, stretching through the adjoining area known as Festival Terrace, adjacent to the south-western facade of the Royal Festival Hall (Figure 5). These main routes of pedestrian circulation remained the same after the removal of the Appearing Rooms. The changes we observed, in this case, were related to the secondary, less used routes, since the installation functioned as a target point or a temporary destination, introducing additional local-scale pedestrian flows (short-range flows towards the

installation) that would disappear in ordinary conditions (Figure 5, right).

Looking at the stationary activities, we mapped three main zones of occupation: the spatial vicinities of the installation Appearing Rooms; the narrow linear space adjacent to the main facade of the Royal Festival Hall; and the space that includes the central area of the Riverside Terrace and extends alongside its north-western border (Figure 5, left). Once the installation was removed, the only noticeable change in the spatial distribution of static activities occurred on the area formerly occupied by the installation (Figure 5, right). This is

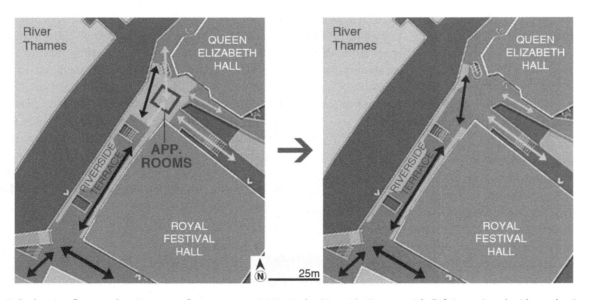

Figure 5. Pedestrian flows and main zones of stationary activities in the Riverside Terrace with (left image) and without the Appearing Rooms (right image). The grey rectangle in the left image represents the position and approximate size of the installation. The arrows indicate the pedestrian flows in the area: black arrows for main flows and grey arrows for secondary flows. The areas shaded in light grey represent the main zones occupied by stationary activities.

unsurprising: as explained earlier, that part of the Riverside Terrace lacks further facilities for people to stay or socialise (apart from a few concrete benches and tables placed at the border). Yet, such benches and tables would still attract occasional static activities throughout the year, even in the cold seasons – for example at times when the sun reached the benches.

Zooming in to the micro-scale aspects of the interactions, the case study reveals that the playful and bodily interactions with the Appearing Rooms is as much about space as it is about *time*: as people approach the installation, they feel enticed to observe the water jets' dynamic behaviour from the outside, for at least a few seconds. The ten-second timing of the water choreography gives the installation a sense of vitality while encouraging people to take quick decisions: *spectators* (Reeves 2011) should decide between stepping forward to join the inner rooms (and becoming players) or to keep watching the interactions from the outside (and stay as spectators). Here, spectating represents an interactional activity, which is continuously ordered and temporally coordinated (Tekin and Reeves 2017), where spectators potentially support players with continuous 'scaffolding'; critique players' techniques during and between moments of play; or recognize and praise competent players' conduct. Likewise, *players* (O'Hara, Glancy, and Robertshaw 2008) should decide between staying in their specific position within the installation, moving to another 'room' or leaving the play area. Failing to synchronising one's movements to the set pace of the watery

walls often results in players being 'hit' by a fair amount of cold water that will certainly soak their clothes and shoes. For children players this situation is easier to cope with, as many of them were observed in swimwear around the installation area – which indicates that numerous families were acquainted with the Appearing Rooms and made a planned visit to the site. For teenagers and adult players, on the contrary, who were observed engaging with the installation wearing everyday clothes – some of them in suits and carrying bags or backpacks – the ever immediate risk of missing the timing of the watery walls and soaking themselves seems to furnish their experience with an extra amount of thrill.

Such sense of challenge and thrill has long been described by literature as *vertigo*, one of the key typologies of play, originally classified by Roger Caillois in the 1960s (Caillois 2001) and further discussed in the context of playful activities in urban spaces by Stevens (2007). Vertigo relates to the pursuit of a 'special disorder or sudden panic' (Caillois 2001, 26); the deliberate escape from normal bodily experiences and self-control, which 'negates instrumental benefit and embraces risk for its own sake and the affirmation of human bodily experience' (Stevens 2007, 43). Common actions and behaviours observed among players in the Appearing Rooms, such as laughing, shouting and hesitating as to which direction to move, all reflect the vertiginous character of the interactions with the installation. The design of the Appearing Rooms explores *time* as the basis for vertigo: time, in this case, is the pressing element that

Figure 6. Social encounters around the Appearing Rooms. The installation area (highlighted in dark grey) is primarily used by players engaged in whole-body interactions with the water features, while the surroundings of the installation (highlighted in clear grey) are mainly occupied by people engaged in other activities, like observing, waiting, photographing, and chatting.

calls players to immediate action, in response to the ever-changing spatial configuration of the appearing and disappearing rooms.

Arguably, the social gathering observed around the Appearing Rooms, as shown in Figure 6, would also take place if the fountain's behaviour were not digitally controlled. The mere presence and easy access to clear water jets situated in an open, outdoor urban space – especially on a sunny, warm day – is certainly a powerful attractor in itself of passers-by and visitors to the area. Furthermore, the architectural and urban qualities of the Riverside Terrace, site of the Appearing Rooms, helps to create an atmosphere of livelihood and relaxation, suitable for social encounters. The site is large enough to accommodate numerous visitors at once, and people are free to choose where to stay, how to settle their bodies (e.g. sitting on the floor, leaning against the railings or simply standing), and how to group themselves, since the space is flat, fully pedestrianised and mostly devoid of urban furniture. In fact, the site of the Appearing Rooms provides a micro version of an urban beach: apart from the water squirting on the fountain itself, this character is reinforced by the cultural buzz and the leisure facilities spread across the premises (the Southbank Centre), in addition to the panoramic vistas of the flowing waters of the River Thames.

In spite of the aspects outlined above, our observations found that, in the case of the Appearing Rooms, the recourse to digital technology does make a difference in the way the fountain is approached and experienced. The computer-controlled random movements of the water jets create a sense of surprise and unpredictability that is fundamental in attracting passers-by and making them stop, observe and potentially play with the fountain. This unpredictable character of the fountain is especially important to attract adults, who are not as predisposed as children to engage with flowing water in urban spaces, as our initial exploratory studies of splash facilities revealed (Table 1).

From an urban and social perspective, our study also revealed that the digitally controlled behaviour of the Appearing Rooms is equally important, because the bodily, social and playful interactions observed *within* the fountain usually sparked other forms of interactions, social encounters and playfulness in the space *around* the fountain. For example, we frequently observed passers-by stopping in the vicinities of the Appearing Rooms after noticing other people playing with the fountain. The presence of these spectators usually attracted more people to the area, causing the so-called 'honey pot effect' (Fischer and Hornecker 2012). Once spectators gathered in the surroundings of the fountain, various types of interactions and encounters took place; these included: photographing or filming the fountain, talking to other people, observing people playing, walking around the fountain and stepping on the Appearing Rooms to play (Figure 7).

5.2. Case Study II: The Mirror Pool

5.2.1. Urban context

The water feature known as 'Mirror Pool' is the centrepiece of the City Park, a large-scale project of urban regeneration situated in central Bradford, UK, which opened to the public in 2012. Costing £24.4 million, the project of the City Park was intended to be a 'catalyst for regeneration', a milestone initiative aimed at boosting the economy of Bradford, fostering the civic pride and restoring a sense of belonging to its inhabitants (Barker, Manning, and Sirriyeh 2014). The City Park occupies a historically significant area in the centre of Bradford,

Figure 7. A sequence of playful and social interactions in the Appearing Rooms: a group of friends play with the fountain, moving into different 'rooms', while another member of the group (the grey person outlined) photographs their experience from different positions on and around the fountain.

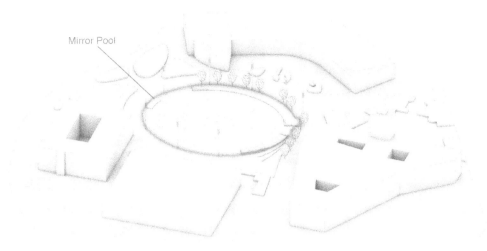

Figure 8. Urban context of the Mirror Pool: perspective of Bradford's City Park with the City Hall building on the right, the commercial centre on the top and the Magistrate's Court on the bottom. Image adapted from Ivers 2018 (with permission).

home to the Grade I listed Victorian building of the City Hall (Figure 8).

From an urban perspective, the City Park sits in a focal point which links together a diverse commercial area, a cultural and educational neighbourhood, and a major transport hub. From a spatial standpoint, such urban position gives the City Park area a transitional character, a place where people coming and going from the mixed neighbouring areas pass through and meet each other. Apart from these passing pedestrians, the area also attracts a steady number of people who come to work on or visit the urban facilities at the City Park – especially the City Hall, the Magistrates' Court, the local library and a few eateries concentrated in the North side of the park.

5.2.2. Project overview

The Mirror Pool is a project jointly designed by the teams of The Fountains Workshop, Gillespies (2019), Haque Design + Research and the artist Wolfgang Buttress. It consists of three independent pools whose geometrical arrangement, in addition to the coordinating behaviour of its water jets, defines a single, dynamic interactive space, which is perceived and experienced as a coherent

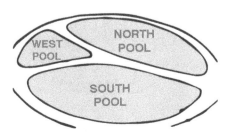

Figure 9. The Mirror Pool's three independent pools.

whole. Two elliptical pools are symmetrically positioned in the north and south portions of the area, while the third pool, triangular and smaller than the others, is located at the west (Figure 9). In technical terms, each one of the three pools constitutes a splash pad in itself: three separate tanks supply and collect the water flowing on each pool, while the system allows the water effects within each pool to be controlled independently. Normally, though, the animations of the water jets are programmed to operate in concert across all three pools, reinforcing the sense of unity of the Mirror Pool.

Three pre-programmed modes define the water level on each pool at any time: the 'drain' mode, which, as the name indicates, drains all the water and transforms the pool's space into a dry plaza; the 'partial' mode, which limits the water to puddles around the fountains; and the 'full' mode, which floods the entire surface of the pool. Distinct spaces and affordances arise from these modes; the 'drain' mode operates daily, from midnight to 7.00am, in order to save power, allow for routine cleaning and maintenance, and also to make room for the especially commissioned urban media artwork *Another Life* (Haque Design + Research 2012) – dynamic and interactive laser lights projected on the floor of the site every night (Figure 10, right). The 'drain' mode is also enabled when the space of the Mirror Pool hosts special events, such as Christmas and civic celebrations, performance festivals and fairs. The 'partial' mode can be set to varying levels, from small puddles concentrated alongside the edges of the pool, leaving a broad dry surface that can be used as a crossing area, to large ponds covering most of the pool and defining narrow causeways. The name *Mirror Pool* stems from the visual effect sparked when the 'full' mode is enabled in all three pools. As the water fills the 3600 square metres

Figure 10. Day and night views: two markedly different configurations of the Mirror Pool, seen from the City Hall building: the full mode turning the space into a massive watery mirror (left), and the nocturnal dry mode with the dynamic laser projections and illuminated fountains (right).

of the fountains, the causeways gradually disappear and a continuous, urban-scale 'watery mirror' takes over, reflecting the surrounding architecture and the sky. In spite of its massive dimensions, the Mirror Pool is a very shallow water feature, with a maximum depth of 25 cm that makes it a safe and accessible area, even for little children.

The Mirror Pool also features a variety of fountains that are fitted with LED lights and can be observed in action at different times of the day. The most frequently operating fountains are the *perimeter fountains* (distributed around the edge of the Mirror Pool and programmed to run different choreographies); the *play jets* (low pressure, playful fountains especially suitable for children, situated in the west pool); and the *arching jets* (located between the south and west pools and forming a watery tunnel that playfully invites people to walk through). Other water effects of the Mirror Pool are activated less often, and are not usually seen on an everyday basis: the *geysers* (special fountains able to produce steam and fog effects) and the so-called *Bradford Blast*, a powerful central fountain capable of blasting water up to thirty metres in the air (Figure 11).

The Mirror Pool can be described as an interactive space, both in a loose and in the more strict sense of the term 'interactive'. Firstly, because the water features and the surrounding built elements of the Mirror Pool encourage people to engage in different activities – or 'interact' – either with the environment (for example by observing, sitting, relaxing or playing with the water jets), or with other people, for example by chatting or meeting friends or strangers. Secondly, the Mirror Pool also features some properly interactive technologies, if we take HCI's view of interaction as a process based on a feedback loop, whereby a user provides some sort of input to a system, which processes the information and then provides the person with an output, in a contingent, undetermined and dynamic process (Preece, Rogers, and Sharp 2002; Dubberly, Haque, and Pangaro 2009). Following this notion of interaction, the Mirror Pool features one of Europe's largest permanent interactive artworks, named 'Another Life' and designed by the practice Haque Design + Research. The interactive features of the artwork Another Life include dynamic light projections on the water and ground of the Mirror Pool that respond to the movements of visitors. As the design team describes it:

> We created a software engine and 'urban operating system' that choreographs and coordinates the activity of various elements within and around the pool,

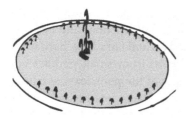 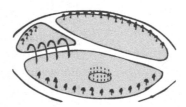 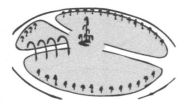

Figure 11. A few samples of the multiple layouts and water effects performed by the Mirror Pool. Left: the full mode with central and perimeter fountains and play jets; middle: the partial mode revealing clear causeways, with the arching jets and mist effect activated; right: the partial mode with the central fountain flooding part of the causeways.

determining what happens when, and how the projections and fountains respond to visitors. The system continually adjusts its outputs in response to various environmental and infrared camera sensors, as well as external factors and community requirements [...]. Another Life gives the City Park development an adaptive and distinctive 'personality', which changes over time and according to varying conditions. The richness of the interactions (created by the choreographies and the sensors and outputs) will gradually develop as visitors and the local community engage with the artwork over the course of several years (Haque Design + Research 2012).

5.2.3. Results

This section begins with the results of our macro-scale socio-spatial analysis of Bradford's City Park, site of the Mirror Pool. Then we zoom in and look at the bodily, social and playful encounters that emerged within and immediately around the Mirror Pool.

As outlined earlier, the City Park occupies a privileged position in central Bradford, connecting diverse neighbourhoods and communities. This favourable position is reflected in the high levels of pedestrian flows observed across the City Park. As shown in Figure 12, we identified a main axis of circulation stretching through the open space to the north of the Mirror Pool and extending towards the street crossings located at either side of the City Park. The central and southern areas of the study site registered lower levels of pedestrian flows, and the same occurred at the spatial vicinities of the Mirror Pool (not including its northern surroundings).

We also mapped the stationary activities in the City Park's public outdoor spaces.[6] After observing and registering the social activities across various times, days and seasons, we identified two main zones of occupation: the first is the boardwalk of the Mirror Pool, including its internal and external borders as well as the benches. The second preferred zone is not a single, continuous area; it rather consists of several spots: the sitting surfaces located at the borders of the garden beds scattered through the City Park (Figure 12). Gardens located in close proximity to the main pedestrian flow were the most used for static activities, and the garden borders facing the inner spaces of the City Park were even more popular than those facing outwards.

With regard to the space of the Mirror Pool itself – the fountains and its surrounding boardwalk –, the case study reveals that, on an everyday basis, this area is used as a multi-functional urban space. The gradual yet constant change of the water level, in addition to the dynamic behaviour of the many fountains across the entire space, provides people with ever-changing affordances for interactions, social encounters and playful behaviours.

Overall, the most frequent setup of the Mirror Pool observed during our study was the 'partial' mode, which was running in 16 out of the 33 sessions of data collection. The common feature of the partial mode is the presence of causeways, although the size of such causeways, as well as the behaviour of the surrounding fountains, did change significantly from one session to another. This is a natural result of the dynamic character of the Mirror Pool, which is digitally set to change its water effects gradually throughout the day. Most important to our discussion, though, is the fact that even subtle changes in the setup of the water features did cause noticeable alterations in how the space was used, shared and experienced. According to our observations, one of the most dramatic features that influenced the everyday

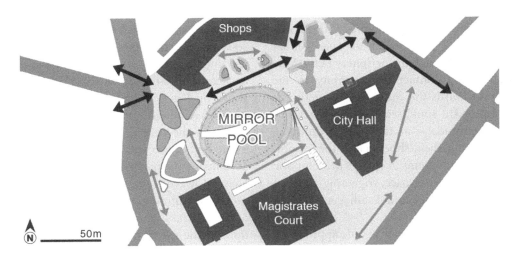

Figure 12. Pedestrian flows and main zones of stationary activities in the City Park. The arrows indicate the pedestrian flows in the area: black arrows for main flows and grey arrows for secondary flows. The areas shaded in light grey represent the main zones occupied by stationary activities.

Figure 13. Two contrasting affordances of the Mirror Pool: clear and dry causeways creating alternative pedestrian routes (left); central fountains activated in the middle of the causeways, turning these utilitarian routes into spaces for play (right).

use of the Mirror Pool was the activation of the group of central water jets. During six sessions of the study, the central jets were off while the partial mode was running, meaning that the causeways offered a clear, unobstructed route to pedestrians across the Mirror Pool (Figure 13, left). With such configuration, the space of the fountain acquired an important utilitarian urban purpose: it became a thoroughfare between different areas of Central Bradford. In another six sessions, the partial mode was running while the central jets were also activated – a setup that caused a whole new approach and perception of the Mirror Pool: instead of a functional place to be traversed, the central area of the fountain was turned into a non-functional place to be contemplated, enjoyed, challenged and played with (Figure 13, right).

Because the central fountains occupy the area in which the causeways intercept each other, pedestrians were hardly indifferent to these fountains. From a distance people decided how to approach the space, either following their journey through the periphery of the Mirror Pool (avoiding any contact or proximity to the water), or heading towards the causeways to enjoy the scenic vistas and pleasant soundscape of the water jets, in a more playful attitude – at the risk of dumping their clothes or soaking their shoes. Here the combination of lights and sounds seems to change the temporal dimension of the experienced space, triggering an extra layer of curiosity (Petrusevski and Fatah gen. Schieck 2017).

The substantial change in the way people approached the Mirror Pool – i.e. from a non-playful to a playful arena and vice-versa – was evident in the four remaining sessions of the study in which the Mirror Pool was set to

the partial mode. In these sessions, we were able to observe the transition between the two contrasting situations illustrated in Figure 13. The presence of the central fountains created a target point, an area of interest that, on the one hand, attracted people to the centre of the Mirror Pool (mainly visitors in groups and children), who either stood near the water jets to observe or to photograph them, or approached even further so as to feel the water or engage through playful actions amid the jets. On the other hand, it was clear that the crossing traffic of pedestrians decreased when the central fountains were running, indicating that the playful character brought about by those fountains came at the expense of the utilitarian, non-playful use of the Mirror Pool as a thoroughfare.

The second most frequent configuration of the Mirror Pool was the 'full' mode, i.e. the entire floor surface covered with water, which was observed in 12 out of the 33 sessions. In such situation, there was a slight variation in the fountains setup: the perimeter fountains ran evenly and constantly during all the 12 'full pool' sessions (as shown in Figure 10, left), while the setup of the central fountains changed from one session to another – the power of the central water jet varied from around 2-metre high up to approximately 15-metre high, with its accompanying barrier fountains changing proportionately. However, our study reveals that, when the full mode was running, the variations in the water pressure of the central fountains did not cause important alterations in the use of the Mirror Pool. On such occasions, external factors – like the time of the day, the day of the week and the weather conditions – were much more determinant of the use and attendance levels than the behaviour displayed by the water features. With this regard, our findings confirm what is expected from open, outdoor water-based leisure facilities: weekends tend to see higher attendance than weekdays; afternoons are more popular than mornings and, above all that, the atmospheric conditions play a crucial role in the use of the space and the time people spend there.

The five remaining sessions of this case study took place at night, when the Mirror Pool was set to the dry mode and the laser light projections were running (Figure 10, right). An interesting situation was observed throughout these nocturnal sessions: despite the spectacular, eye-catching visual effects afforded by the animated light projections surrounded by the coloured perimeter fountains, little social activity and almost no playful behaviour were recorded on the site. In only one occasion a group of youngsters briefly played with the laser projections, while no individuals were recorded playing with the illuminated fountains whatsoever. Even though this virtual absence of players may be partially attributed to the method applied in the study (time-lapse photography with 30 seconds of interval between shootings, which means that fleeting actions performed within these intervals were not captured and therefore are not available for analysis), the in loco observations reinforce the results drawn from the series of photographs. Furthermore, the five nocturnal sessions of the study were distributed across different seasons (in March, July, August and two sessions in November), and across various days of the week, during which the weather conditions oscillated between clear sky with mild temperature and rainy, cold and windy nights. Thus, the general absence of players and the low levels of social encounters on the site during the night cannot be solely attributed to unfavourable external circumstances.

From the observations above, we argue that the digital technology embedded in the Mirror Pool is more effective to bring people together and to promote playful behaviours during the day. The varying layouts and multiple water effects displayed throughout the day help to create a space that is able to accommodate numerous forms of social encounters and bodily interactions, not only for children but all age groups. In this regard, the digital layer of the fountains truly supports the social life of the site and helps transform the experience of its visitors. In several sessions of the study, we observed a diverse community of users sharing the Mirror Pool and its surrounding facilities: some visitors sitting on benches, others on the boardwalk, others standing or playing; in mild afternoons or sunny weekends there were families and friends spending a long time on the place, and under much worse weather conditions we could still see children braving the cold water of the fountains, and a few adults enjoying a brief moment of playfulness on their commute (Figure 14).

Figure 14. The playful experience of walking under the watery tunnel of the arching jets (top) and diverse types of bodily interactions and social encounters on the boardwalk and inner space of the Mirror Pool (bottom).

During the night-time, though, the digital components of the Mirror Pool – particularly the laser projections on the floor – did not animate the space as the fountains did in the daytime. In our analysis, this situation is likely due to some characteristics of the project and its urban context: firstly, the laser projections have been running every night on the site for years, which eliminates the so-called 'novelty effect' (Bianchi-Berthouze 2013) that could attract people to interact and play; secondly, the area of study is primarily frequented by residents of Bradford, who are accustomed to the visually striking features of the Mirror Pool; thirdly, part of these residents may not perceive the City Park as a safe space to stay during the night precisely because they do not usually see many people there – 'people attract people' (Whyte 1980); and finally, the local weather is rarely pleasant enough to encourage people to stay around the Mirror Pool at night, even in the summer.

6. Discussion

In this section, we discuss findings that emerged from the observation of social behaviours and embodied interactions with the Appearing Rooms and the Mirror Pool. To help inform the discussion, we will take the Granary Square fountains, in London, as a baseline for comparison.

Much can be learned through a comparative study of the same fundamental socio-spatial phenomenon – in our case, playful outdoor water features supported by digital technologies – arising from and manifested through markedly different design paradigms. In this respect, it is possible to identify a set of key differences between the two urban interfaces, and compare them with the Granary Square fountains, according to a range of design qualities, as follows:

(1) *Context*: while the Appearing Rooms was conceived as a piece of installation art (Bishop 2005), the Mirror Pool was built as part of an urban design regeneration project. Significant differences result from these two distinct approaches. On the one hand, the Appearing Rooms stand as an independent, self-contained artwork possessing a plug-in, add-on character (Aurigi 2017) – an installation that can be placed on virtually any physical space, provided that the basic spatial and infrastructural requirements are met, such as sufficient floor space and height, a flat horizontal surface at ground level, and the presence of power and water supplies to run the installation. On the other hand, the Mirror Pool project is essentially contextual: the whole rationale of its design derives from a larger project of urban design within which the Mirror Pool is embedded. In this case, a complex set of spatial, cultural, social, political and economic factors that are unique to the city of Bradford, and particularly to its central area, played a crucial role in the design and construction processes of the Mirror Pool.

The Granary Square fountains were, like the Mirror Pool, built as the centrepiece of a greater scheme of urban redevelopment (Ivers 2018). However, while the Mirror Pool sits in a location highly connected to pre-existent neighbourhoods and mixed functions, Granary Square's urban surroundings consist mostly of whole new districts, buildings and services, therefore subject to movement flows that are 'constructed, rather than following 'natural movement' in cities' (Hillier 1996b). Moreover, Granary Square and King's Cross as a whole, despite its appearance of public space, is in fact a private property, where the presence or circulation of 'different types' of people/communities may be restricted or banned. Recently, King's Cross development became one of the first property companies in Britain to acknowledge deploying facial recognition software, able to capture images of people without their consent.[7]

(2) *Temporality*: the Appearing Rooms consist of a temporary installation, which has participated in several exhibitions across the world since its first appearance, in 2004. In London, the artwork has been installed every summer (from May or June until September, depending on the year) since 2007, in the same area of the Southbank Centre, as part of the Summer Festival. In contrast, both the Mirror Pool, in Bradford, and the Granary Square fountains, in London, are installed on a permanent basis, and thus possess an infrastructural character – even though the Mirror Pool's controlling software is programmed to switch off the water and light effects of the facility daily from midnight to 7.00am for maintenance, security and energy-saving reasons.

(3) *Scale*: the two splash facilities of our case studies differ greatly in terms of their physical dimensions: while the water jets of the Appearing Rooms are installed on a square platform measuring approximately 7×7 metres (hence totalling around 50 square metres), the wet surface of the Mirror Pool covers an extensive oval area (maximum dimensions of 75 metres long and 58 metres across), totalling approximately 3600 square metres – which makes the Mirror Pool the largest urban water feature in the UK (Landezine 2014; City Park 2019). Since we believe

that the physical and spatial properties of playful urban interfaces perform a crucial role in shaping the lived experiences around them, further insights may potentially be gained by analysing two projects with such a dramatic difference in scale.

(4) *Technological mediation and access*: as situated media, the case studies also differ in the way they employ digital technologies to mediate the players' experiences. The computer that controls the Appearing Rooms remains in the 'backstage' of the playful arena, hidden inside a metallic shed near the installation, its sole function being controlling the water jets choreography. This characterises a *back end* technological approach to the mediation of the interactions. In contrast, the digital components employed in the Mirror Pool – such as motion sensors, laser projections and especially the site-specific media artwork *Another Life* – tend to take centre stage and drive the urban experience, characterising an urban situation where the situated technology is both *back end* and *front end*. For the sake of illustration and comparison, the *Snake* game at the Granary Square fountains points to yet another model of mediated experience: in this case, the digital interactive technology is not directly accessible, as people need (a) an internet-enabled mobile device; (b) a pre-installed mobile app (the *Granary Squirt*); and (c) access to the local Wi-Fi network.

6.1. Urban fountains in the digital turn: from contemplative to playful interfaces

From a bodily and sensory standpoint (considering, of course, favourable weather conditions), traditional, contemplative water fountains tend to subtly induce people to find a comfortable place nearby – ideally a place to sit – and, once settled in that place with their bodies relaxed, people can spend time chatting with others or enjoying the moment on their own, while observing the flow of water in the fountain and the flow of other people around it. Depending on the urban context and the design of the fountain itself, listening to the water jets can become a significant part of the experience. Going even further into the sensory realm, certain circumstances, like people's position around the fountain and the local atmospheric conditions, may render the encounter an also tactile and olfactory experience; for example, the wind can carry droplets of water towards people nearby, or may equally disperse intangible elements of the fountain across the environment, such as the odour of the chemicals used to treat the water. At any rate, such traditional typology of urban fountains usually does not encourage an active, physical and playful encounter between people and the water features. In fact, many mechanisms have been developed to keep people away from the water, ranging from design decisions (built structures that hinder direct access to the fountain) up to more or less explicit forms of law enforcement, such as warning signs, security guards and surveillance cameras.

The design of the emergent generation of playful, interactive urban water features, such as the Appearing Rooms, the Mirror Pool and the Granary Square fountains, increasingly relies on digital technologies to disrupt or augment the ways people use their own bodies to approach and engage with the water and with other people in outdoor urban spaces. Instead of the bodily-detached onlookers found around conventional fountains, this new generation of playful, technologically enhanced fountains encourages individuals to assume a 'physically' active and participatory role. The sense of presence is reinforced and acquires a new meaning through a complex web of material, bodily-kinaesthetic and social encounters that unfold on and around the fountain over time. We may characterise this emergent typology of interactive water features as platforms for multi-layered bodily, spatial and social encounters, since the fountain defines an interaction space (Fischer and Hornecker 2012) that potentially enables a multitude of shared encounters and spatial negotiations – not only between players acquainted with each other but, most interestingly, encounters between people who happen to meet for the first time during the very act of play.

Playing with an interactive fountain is hardly a solely individual experience: as urban facilities located in shared, open spaces of the city, the fountains create an opportunity for citizens to engage in a variety of activities, ranging from explicit playful behaviours, with a sheer *performative* character (Rico and Brewster 2010; Reeves 2011) – for example moving in and out of the spaces defined by the water jets – up to more implicit forms of play, such as observing or photographing from a distance the players amid the water features. Importantly, these bodily and playful interactions with the fountain may also stimulate other forms of social interaction among nearby people who are not physically engaged with the water features, for example through the so-called 'triangulation' (Whyte 1980), in which an interface (in this case, the fountains) prompts strangers to talk to each other, or through 'shared encounters', where a sense of performative co-presence arises from the 'mutual recognition of spatial or social proximity' (Willis et al. 2010). In the selected studies we found that, when

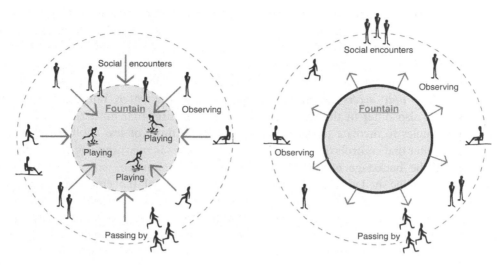

Figure 15. Diagrams of two contrasting design affordances: a playful fountain with a centripetal socio-spatial character (left) and a contemplative fountain with a centrifugal character (right). The grey arrows represent, in each case, the typical socio-spatial and bodily forces at play that either draw people to the space of the fountain, on a convergent fashion (left) or keep people away from the fountain, on a divergent fashion (right). Whereas the centripetal model (left) features porous socio-spatial boundaries (represented by the dashed inner circle), in the centrifugal model (right) these boundaries are clearly demarcated and define a secluded space.

visiting the Appearing Rooms or the Mirror Pool in pairs or groups, at least one person of the party often stayed outside, at the close vicinities of the fountain, while other members of the group engaged with the water features. In such situations, the person(s) who remained outside the fountain usually took up impromptu social roles, such as photographing or filming the players, looking after their personal belongings or engaging in a conversation with someone else – not rarely a member of another social group. At times of high attendance, the opportunities of social encounters and informal contacts between strangers around interactive fountains are naturally multiplied.

From a socio-spatial perspective, interactive fountains may be contrasted with their non-interactive counterparts by applying the analogy of centripetal and centrifugal forces. Accessible urban fountains designed to encourage playful behaviours – as those investigated in this article – usually possess what we call a *centripetal* socio-spatial character: these fountains tend to draw people towards their inner interaction space (Fischer and Hornecker 2012), offering players the possibility to engage through whole-body interactions with the materiality of both the water and the built environment (Figure 15, left). Contemplative, non-interactive fountains, on the contrary, tend to possess what we call a *centrifugal* socio-spatial character: they encourage people to assume the role of spectators by keeping some distance from the water (Figure 15, right). Centrifugal fountains function as pure landscaping elements, whose scenic or topological qualities tend to overshadow any sense of bodily-kinaesthetic experience or playful interactions.

Importantly, both centripetal and centrifugal fountains have the potential to trigger a web of social encounters, for both typologies define a place where a sense of co-presence is experienced. Though, while centripetal fountains stand as porous, accessible urban interfaces in which players are protagonists and playing is always a possibility for those in the spatial surroundings, in the case of centrifugal fountains spectators dominate the scene, and accessing or playing with the fountain itself is not possible and/or not allowed. Since contemplative fountains are not supposed to be physically accessed or played with (see, for example, Trafalgar Square in Figure 1), the spatial quality of its urban surroundings – expressed in amenities such as seating spaces, green and shaded areas, and protection from the weather – becomes an ever more important factor for a number of reasons: bringing people together, making them stay longer in the area, fostering casual encounters and person-to-person interactions.

6.2. Broadening the scope: living and playing in the 'smart city' – concluding remarks

In this paper, we have argued for rethinking the notion of 'smart cities' as playable cities. We presented two case studies of playful urban media installations that enable 'unplanned' encounters in the city: the Appearing Rooms and the Mirror Pool. These installations share some important characteristics:

(1) They are situated and fixed interactive interfaces, therefore embedded in the urban fabric;

(2) They are water-based installations;
(3) They encourage playful and whole-body interactions.

We analysed emergent playful interactions at different levels and scales: from the micro scale of the bodily engagement to the macro scale of the spatial and social configurations. The Appearing Rooms and the Mirror Pool were then contrasted with a third example of water-based interface (the Granary Square fountains) that shares similarities but also essential differences. These three cases illustrate an emergent use of situated technologies coupling urban design, computing resources, hydraulic engineering and interaction design to create conditions for playful experiences in urban outdoor settings. As such, these interfaces redefine the very notions of 'urban play' and 'urban fountains' regarded as infrastructure: what they mean and how we should approach, share and experience them. More than simply interactive water features or splash facilities, urban structures like the Appearing Rooms and the Mirror Pool – and unlike the Granary Square fountains – are more faithfully characterised as situated urban media interfaces, able to cater to a wide range of bodily and playful interactions, often combined with equally diverse forms of social encounters and spatial negotiations. Our case studies suggest that the digital should be coupled with a careful consideration of the spatial, physical, material and bodily aspects of interactions, which are fundamental to our lived experience of the city.

Addressing the *lived experience* entails a due consideration of the spatial, material and bodily dimensions that ultimately define how we interact with the world. By exploiting the sheer materiality of water, the Appearing Rooms and the Mirror Pool succeed in heightening such a sense of lived experience. Both interfaces subtly invite urban inhabitants to (re)discover their own spaces through a palpable, corporeal, dynamic encounter with the water – an element whose sensory richness and playful possibilities can be experienced in many forms. At the same time, and particularly important in the context of *smart cities*, is the fact that the Appearing Rooms and the Mirror Pool make use of computing technologies to encourage a wide range of potential experiences and encounters in public outdoor settings. Building on the concept of 'smart spaces' set out in the Introduction, we argue that situated urban media interfaces like the Appearing Rooms and the Mirror Pool are potential enablers of real smart spaces: by transcending the conventional, data-driven notion of 'smart cities' and incorporating the idea of play through bodily interactions and social encounters, these interfaces help create the conditions for meaningful urban experiences to emerge.

We have argued, in the Background section, that urban interactive installations – including those enhanced by media technologies – are far from being an automatic or ultimate solution for the activation or 'creation' of lively and socially thriving places. On a broader historical perspective, urban spaces are resilient settings: over time, they stage new forms of social encounters while accommodating new types of conflicts and negotiations. These processes tend to reflect and respond to manifold contextual aspects, including trends, fads and fashions brought about by emerging technologies. Naturally, any spatial element (for example, a media installation encouraging playful interactions) that prevails over the others is not necessarily the most suitable alternative for a socially diverse and rich urban setting. However, our case studies suggest that permanent, site-specific installations, like Bradford's Mirror Pool, which are planned and designed as part of a broader urban design scheme (i.e. taking into account the manifold factors that are unique to their urban settings), have better chances to become embedded elements of their environment, bringing the social and civic benefits associated with lively places. Playful interactions become, in this context, a rich and multi-layered design paradigm. Play turns itself into the trigger for people's deeper involvement with their surroundings, considered both from the corporeal, social and spatial perspectives. On the contrary, plug-in, self-contained installations, like the Appearing Rooms, despite their potential to enable smart spaces, risk not being able to sustain social life after the 'novelty effect' has passed.

Coupling the conceived space with the lived space, or more specifically a playful interface with interactions and play, is hardly an automatic or clear-cut process. This seems even more evident in the case of situated media technologies, as illustrated by the game in Granary Square. Continuing efforts and investments must be made in planning, commissioning, curating, advertising and managing urban media initiatives, particularly those installed on a permanent or long-term basis. A good example is the large urban screen installed at Federation Square, Melbourne, which is considered a successful application of urban media: this success is partly due to an active public programme of local activities and events devised to encourage social diversity and participation on the site (Papastergiadis et al. 2013). Likewise, some British towns have adopted a more playful approach to the use of urban screens (O'Hara, Glancy, and Robertshaw 2008).

With the rise of 'smart cities' phenomena, and as the scope of urban interaction design and research changes to respond to the city scale and context, we believe that city managers and practitioners involved in design decisions of urban spaces need to explore an additional level of knowledge that relates to the material, temporal and embodied aspects of interactions, in addition to the other important aspects that have informed their decisions so far – for example the social, spatial, political, cultural and economic dimensions of urban spaces.

Building on our case studies and discussions on urban play in the context of smart cities, we also believe that re-imagining and reinforcing the notion of *play* in cities, through digital or non-digital interfaces (such as the Appearing Rooms and the Mirror Pool), can offer a community-oriented and place-based approach to smart cities. In this regard, our exploratory research offers material that can help inform design decisions for smart cities by a range of stakeholders, including city managers, urban designers, architects, artists and interaction designers.

Notes

1. Hillier (1996a).
2. Back-end refers to the use of digital technologies only to control the installation's behaviour.
3. Back-end and front-end refer to the use of digital technologies on both ends of the installation; 1) tocontrol the installation's behaviour (behind the scene) and 2) as a mediator for interactions among people (as part of the main interaction scene).
4. See, for example: Borden (1996). *Strangely familiar: narratives of architecture in the city*; Borden (2001). Another pavement, another beach: skateboarding and the performative critique of architecture. In I. Borden et al (Eds.), *The unknown city: contesting architecture and social space: a Strangely Familiar project*; Borden (2014). The role of risk in urban design. In Carmona, M. (Ed.). *Explorations in Urban Design: An Urban Design Research Primer*.
5. Developed by The Fountain Workshop (2019) (the same team responsible for the Mirror Pool, one of our case studies).
6. By "public outdoor spaces" we mean all open spaces in the City Park, with the exception of commercial or institutional precincts that occupy the area, such as the outdoor designated space with tables for customers of the local pub and café.
7. https://www.theguardian.com/uk-news/2019/aug/12/regulator-looking-at-use-of-facial-recognition-at-kings-cross-site
8. Up to eight people can play the game simultaneously. The game is activated in Granary Square daily, normally during a one-hour time slot, which varies according to the season. Further details on: https://www.kingscross.co.uk/granary-squirt

Disclosure statement

No potential conflict of interest was reported by the authors.

Funding

This work is partially supported by Conselho Nacional de Desenvolvimento Científico e Tecnológico: [grant number 204379/ 2014-8].

References

Ackermann, J., A. Rauscher, and D. Stein. 2016. "Introductions: PLAYIN' THE CITY: Artistic and Scientific Approaches to Playful Urban Arts." *Navigationen: Playin' the City, Jg* 16 (1): 16.

Afonso, A., E. Ergin, and A. Fatah gen. Schieck. 2019. "Flowing Bodies: Exploring the Micro and Macro Scales of Bodily Interactions with Urban Media Installations." In *Proceedings of the Designing Interactive Systems Conference (DIS '19)*, 1183–1193. San Diego, CA: ACM.

Argent St. George. 2001. *Principles for a Human City*. A document prepared by Argent St George, the selected developer for King's Cross Central, and the landowners, London and Continental Railways and Exel. 3rd Edition, July 2001. Accessed 24.09.2019. https://www.kingscross.co.uk/media/Principles_for_a_Human_City.pdf.

Aurigi, A. 2017, April 18–19. "Space is Not a Platform – Foregrounding Place in Smart Urban Design." In *Enhancing Places Through Technologies: Proceedings from the ICiTy Conference*, edited by A. Zammit and T. Kenna, 7–18. Valletta: University of Malta.

Barker, A., N. Manning, and A. Sirriyeh. 2014. *The Great Meeting Place: A Study of Bradford's City Park*. Report. University of Bradford.

Behrens, M., A. Fatah gen. Schieck, E. Kostopoulou, S. North, W. Motta, L. Ye, and H. Schnadelbach. 2013. "Exploring the Effect of Spatial Layout on Mediated Urban Interactions." In *Proceedings: 2nd ACM International Symposium on Pervasive Displays 2013*, edited by B. Schilit, R. Want, and T. Ojala, 79–84. Mountain View, CA: ACM.

Behrens, M., A. Fatah gen. Schieck, and D. P. Brumby. 2015. "Designing Media Architectural Interfaces for Interactions in Urban Spaces." In *Citizen's Right to the Digital City*, edited by M. Foth, M. Brynskov, and T. Ojala, 55–77. Singapore: Springer.

Benford, S., and G. Giannachi. 2011. *Performing Mixed Reality*. Cambridge, MA: The MIT Press.

Bianchi-Berthouze, N. 2013. "Understanding the Role of Body Movement in Player Engagement." *Human–Computer Interaction* 28: 40–75.

Bishop, C. 2005. *Installation Art: A Critical History*. London: Tate.

Borden, I. 1996. *Strangely Familiar: Narratives of Architecture in the City*. London: Routledge.

Borden, I. 2001. "Another Pavement, Another Beach: Skateboarding and the Performative Critique of Architecture." In *The Unknown City: Contesting Architecture and Social Space: A Strangely Familiar Project*, edited by I. Borden, 178–199. Cambridge, MA: MIT Press.

Borden, I. 2014. "The Role of Risk in Urban Design." In *Explorations in Urban Design: An Urban Design Research Primer*, edited by M. Carmona, 15–24. London: Routledge.

Caillois, R. 2001. *Man, Play, and Games*. Urbana: University of Illinois Press.

Caldwell, G. A., and M. Foth. 2014. "DIY Media Architecture: Open and Participatory Approaches to Community Engagement." In *Proceedings of the 2nd Media*

Architecture Biennale Conference: World Cities (MAB '14), edited by M. Brynskov, P. Dalsgaard, and A. Fatah gen. Schieck, 1–10. New York, NY: ACM.

Carvalho, L. 2015. "Smart Cities from Scratch? A Socio-Technical Perspective." *Cambridge Journal of Regions, Economy and Society* 8 (1): 43–60. March 2015. Accessed 02.08.2019 at https://doi.org/10.1093/cjres/rsu010.

Catapult Future Cities. 2017. "Smart City Strategies. A Global Review." Accessed 30.07.2019. https://futurecities.catapult.org.uk/wp-content/uploads/2017/11/GRSCS-Final-Report.pdf.

City Park. 2019. City Park Mirror Pool. Accessed 11.02.2019. http://www.cityparkbradford.com/mirror-pool/.

de Lange, M., and M. de Waal. 2019. *The Hackable City: Digital Media and Collaborative City-Making in the Network Society*. Singapore: Springer.

de Waal, M. 2014. *The City as Interface: How New Media Are Changing the City*. Rotterdam: Nai010.

Digital Water Pavilion. 2008. "Carlorattiassocciati." Accessed 15.03.2019. https://carloratti.com/project/digital-water-pavilion/.

Dubberly, H., U. Haque, and P. Pangaro. 2009. "What is Interaction? Are There Different Types?" *Interactions* 16 (1): 69–75.

Fatah gen. Schieck, A., C. Briones, and C. Mottram. 2008. "The Urban Screen as a Socialising Platform: Exploring the Role of Place Within the Urban Space." In *MEDIACITY. Situations, Practices and Encounters*, edited by F. Eckardt, J. Geelhaar, L. Colini, K. S. Willis, K. Chorianopoulos, and R. Hennig, 285–307. Berlin: Frank & Timme GmbH.

Fischer, P. T., and E. Hornecker. 2012. "Urban HCI: Spatial Aspects in the Design of Shared Encounters for Media Facades." In CHI 2012. ACM, New York, NY, USA.

Fritsch, J., M. Brynskov. 2011. "Between Experience, Affect, and Information: Experimental Urban Interfaces in the Climate Change Debate." In *From Social Butterfly to Engaged Citizen*, edited by M. Foth, L. Forlano, C. Satchell, and M. Gibbs, 115–134. Cambridge, MA: MITP.

Gillespies. 2019. "Bradford City Park." Accessed 01.02.2019. https://www.gillespies.co.uk/projects/bradford-city-park.

Haque Design + Research. 2012. "Another Life." Accessed 12.02.2019. http://www.haque.co.uk/anotherlife.php.

Hein, J. 2019. "Appearing Rooms." Accessed 11.02.2019. http://www.jeppehein.net/pages/project_id.php?path=works&id=127.

Hillier, B. 1996a. *Space is the Machine: A Configurational Theory of Architecture*. Cambridge: Cambridge University Press.

Hillier, B. 1996b. "Cities as Movement Economies." *Urban Design International* 1 (1): 41–60.

Hillier, B., and J. Hanson. 1984. *The Social Logic of Space*. Cambridge: Cambridge University Press.

Huizinga, J. 1955. *Homo Ludens: A Study of the Play-Element in Culture*. Boston: Beacon Press.

Innocent, T. 2016. "Play and Placemaking in Urban art Environments." In *Proceedings of the 3rd Conference on Media Architecture Biennale. MAB16*, edited by M. Tomitsch, H. Haeusler, P. Dalsgaard, and A. Fatah gen. Schieck, 11–14. Sydney: ACM.

Innocent, T. 2019. "Citizens of Play: Revisiting the Relationship Between Playable and Smart Cities." In *Making Smart Cities More Playable: Exploring Playable Cities*, edited by A. Nijholt, 25–49. Singapore: Springer.

Ivers, C. 2018. *Staging Urban Landscapes: The Activation and Curation of Flexible Public Spaces*. Basel: Birkhauser.

Kitchin, R. 2014. "The Real-Time City? Big Data and Smart Urbanism." *GeoJournal* 79: 1–14.

Kitchin, R. 2015. "The Promise and Perils of Smart Cities." *Computers & Law* 26: 2.

Kress, G., and K. Cowan. 2017. "From Making Meaning to Meaning-Making with Writing: Reflecting on Four-Year-Olds at Play." In *Literacy and Learning in Primary School*, edited by D. Østergren-Olsen and K. Friis Larsen, 1–15. Copenhagen: Dafolo.

Kwastek, K. 2013. *Aesthetics of Interaction in Digital Art*. Cambridge, MA: MIT Press.

Landezine. 2014. "Bradford's City Park." Accessed 11.02.2019. http://www.landezine.com/index.php/2014/08/bradfords-city-park-by-gillespies/.

Larssen, A. T., T. Robertson, and J. Edwards. 2007. "Experiential Bodily Knowing as a Design (Sens)-Ability in Interaction Design." In *Proceedings of the 3rd European Conference on Design and Semantics of Form and Movement (DeSForM '07)*, 1–15. Newcastle upon Tyne: Koninklijke Philips Electronics N.V.

Lefebvre, H. 1991. *The Production of Space*. Oxford: Blackwell.

Lennard, S. H. C., and H. L. Lennard. 1984. *Public Life in Urban Places: Social and Architectural Characteristics Conducive to Public Life in European Cities*. Southampton, N.Y.: Gondolier Press.

Levisohn, A., and T. Schiphorst. 2011. "Embodied Engagement: Supporting Movement Awareness in Ubiquitous Computing Systems." *Ubiquit. Learn. Int. J* 3 (4): 97–112.

Luke, R. 2005. "The Phoneur: Mobile Commerce and the Digital Pedagogies of the Wireless Web." In *Communities of Difference*, edited by P. P. Trifonas, 185–204. London: Palgrave Macmillan.

Müller, J., F. Alt, D. Michelis, and A. Schmidt. 2010. "Requirements and Design Space for Interactive Public Displays." In *Proceedings of the International Conference on Multimedia*, edited by A. del Bimbo and S.-F. Chang, 1285–1294. Firenze: ACM.

Niederland, W. G. 1989. "River Symbolism, Part I." In *Maps from the Mind: Readings in Psychogeography*, edited by Howard F. Stein and William G. Niederland, 15–45. Norman, OK: University of Oklahoma Press.

Nijholt, A. 2017. "Towards Playful and Playable Cities." In *Playable Cities: The City as a Digital Playground*, edited by A. Nijholt, 1–20. Singapore: Springer.

Nijholt, A. 2019. *Making Smart Cities More Playable. Exploring Playable Cities*. Singapore: Springer.

O'Hara, K., M. Glancy, and S. Robertshaw. 2008. "Understanding Collective Play in an Urban Screen Game." In *Proceedings of CSCW 08*, edited by B. Begole and D. W. McDonald, 67–76. San Diego, CA: ACM.

Papastergiadis, N., S. McQuire, X. Gu, A. Barikin, R. Gibson, A. Yue, S. Jung, C. Cmielewski, S. Yeong Roh, and M. Jones. 2013. "Mega Screens for Mega Cities." *Theory, Culture & Society* 30 (7/8): 325–341.

Pérez de Arce, R. 2018. *City of Play: An Architectural and Urban History of Recreation and Leisure*. London: Bloomsbury.

Petrusevski, I., and A. Fatah gen. Schieck. 2017. "Enhancing Interaction Within Urban Settings Using Light and Sound Stimuli." In *The Virtual and the Real in Planning and Urban Design Perspectives, Practices and Applications*, edited by C. Yamu, A. Poplin, O. Devish, and G. de Roo, 252–266. London: Routledge.

Playable City. 2019. Accessed 01.08.2019. https://www.playablecity.com.

Pop, S., T. Toft, N. Calvillo, and M. Wright. 2016. *What Urban Media Art Can Do: Why When Where & How*. Stuttgart: avedition.

Preece, J., Y. Rogers, and H. Sharp. 2002. *Interaction Design: Beyond Human-Computer Interaction*. Chichester: John Wiley & Sons.

Reeves, S. 2011. *Designing Interfaces in Public Settings: Understanding the Role of the Spectator in Human-Computer Interaction*. London: Springer.

Rico, J., and S. Brewster. "Usable Gestures for Mobile Interfaces: Evaluating Social Acceptability." In CHI 2010.

Saker, M., and L. Evans. 2016. "Everyday Life and Locative Play: an Exploration of Foursquare and Playful Engagements with Space and Place." *Media, Culture & Society* 38 (8): 1169–1183.

Sicart, M. 2016. "Play and the City." In *Introductions*: PLAYIN' THE CITY: Artistic and Scientific Approaches to Playful Urban Arts. *Navigationen: Playin' the city*, Jg. 16.

Stevens, Q. 2007. *The Ludic City: Exploring the Potential of Public Spaces*. London: Routledge.

Tekin, B., and S. Reeves. 2017. "Ways of Spectating: Unravelling Spectator Participation in Kinect Play." CHI 2017, Denver, CO. doi:10.1145/3025453.

The Fountain Workshop. 2019. "Bradford City Park." Accessed 01.02.2019. https://www.fountains.co.uk/project/bradford-mirror-pool.

The Guardian. 2019. "Pink Seesaws Reach Across the Divide at US-Mexico Border." Accessed 01.08.2019. https://www.theguardian.com/us-news/2019/jul/30/pink-seesaws-reach-across-divide-us-mexico-border.

Urbanowicz, K., and N. Lucyna. 2012. "Media Architecture – Participation Through the Senses." In *Proceedings of the Media Architecture Biennale (MAB '12)*, edited by M. Brynskov, P. Dalsgaard, and A. Fatah gen. Schieck, 51–54. New York, NY: ACM.

van Vleet, M., and B. C. Feeney. 2015. "Play Behavior and Playfulness in Adulthood." *Social and Personality Psychology Compass* 9 (11): 630–643.

Verhoeff, N. 2015. "Mobile Media Architecture: Between Infrastructure, Interface, and Intervention." *Observatorio (OBS*)* 9: 71–84.

Whyte, W. 1980. *The Social Life of Small Urban Spaces*. Washington, DC: Conservation Foundation.

Willis, K. S., G. Roussos, K. Chorianopoulos, and M. Struppek (Eds). 2010. *Shared Encounters*. London: Springer.

Zielinska-Dabkowska, K. 2019. "Urban Lighting Masterplan: Origins, Definitions, Methodologies and Collaborations." In *Urban Lighting for People: Evidence-Based Lighting Design for the Built Environment*, edited by A. Davoudian, 18–41. London: RIBA.

Smart data at play: improving accessibility in the urban transport system

Paloma Cáceres [ID], Carlos E. Cuesta [ID], Belén Vela, José María Cavero and Almudena Sierra

ABSTRACT

Human mobility is **one of** the most important concerns in smart **city** initiatives and is especially relevant when **combined** with accessibility issues. This **paper** describes work in the context of the Access@City Research Project**,** which seeks to improve the accessibility in the public transport system by using available information (open data, semantic-aware knowledge) provided by transport organisations. However, these organisations provide partial data**,** and a lot of information is **still available only on their websites**, or simply does not exist. This absence can be tackled using a playful approach – the use of gaming apps to obtain and update accessibility information. In this paper, we describe the use of a hybrid reality game (HRG) to enrich information **regarding** the accessibility of subway stations. In turn, the player improves her score, which is included as part of the game. The correlation between these observations is able to provide, in a relatively short time, an accurate description of the accessibility of these stations. In summary, this playful approach makes **it** possible to recover a set of accessibility data **that** ultimately provide **these** smart capabilities, **which are** the core of this 'accessible city' **endeavour**.

1. Introduction

Smart cities **have been** conceived as the next step in the evolution of the adaptation of physical space to human needs. Their purpose is to use information technologies to improve everyday life in urban environments by obtaining and processing data **concerning behaviour** in the city and applying this additional intelligence **in order** to overcome the limitations imposed by their traditional static structure. Human mobility is among the most important concerns in these initiatives, particularly when it is integrated **into** the main infrastructure **that** cities **provide** to support **it**, namely the urban transport system (Kapenekakis and Chorianopoulos 2017).

This is especially relevant when it is **combined** with *accessibility* issues: **although** the public transport system is critical for **all citizens**, it is of vital importance for groups with restricted mobility. **These encompass not only the obvious groups of** disabled people, but also citizens with any kind of special mobility needs, such as parents with a pushchair, or an injured person using a crutch.

Our research is, **therefore**, focused on improving the accessibility in **increasingly smarter** cities, using the urban transport system as the mainstay of this initiative. The basic idea is to obtain and compile all the information **available** about the transport system, rephrase it in the form of linked data, and provide the semantic

annotations **required** to transform this structure into knowledge. By processing these *smart data*, citizens are now able to plan and schedule their mobility in the urban transport system. In general terms, this will **immediately** improve its efficiency**, and** in **this** specific case **it will** also **improve** accessibility, as **it will provide the** groups **of interest with prior knowledge regarding** whether **or not** a certain route is accessible.

However, most of the data sources **concerning** public transport are *static* in nature, and this limits their usefulness. **One** of the biggest **initial** issues when compiling this information was that it was often incomplete**,** a lot of effort had to be **made**, and many sources had to be combined to achieve a thorough description of the transport system in several representative cities. Accessibility data were among the most difficult to obtain; even IFOPT (CEN/TC278 2012), the working standard **employed** to describe nodes in the transport network (i.e. stations and other 'fixed objects'), provides only a part of the relevant information, while many accessibility features are not clearly represented.

But this incompleteness is not the only problem; an additional issue is that these data do not evolve easily, but the actual city does. Even a well-studied subway station, **at which** every line is defined, every platform has been listed, and even accessibility-related elements (i.e. lifts, escalators) have been described, can change without notice, **thus** affecting both the **topology of the** transport network **and** the accessibility **of the node**. In general, **all the elements** in the system can be affected by several *incidences*, which could mean a blocked bus line, a closed subway station, or **simply** a broken escalator.

The solution **as regards** both **filling** the gaps in the network description and **reacting** to many potential incidences is **the** use **of** *smart devices* in the connected city. The idea is to involve the citizens themselves in the process of capturing and providing the required information, by using their own smartphones in a *crowdsourcing* process. **Partial** data, as provided by open data sources, will, **therefore,** not only be checked but also *completed* by **the** users themselves. This **signifies that** accessibility elements (i.e. lifts, escalators) will not be considered until they **have been** confirmed by a significant number of citizens. **Furthermore**, incidences can easily be reported using the same mobile app.

However, crowdsourcing requires a motivation: in this model, **the** users themselves provide the system with the information **required**, **by making** a cumulative effort and dividing the job; but they should receive something in return. With respect to accessibility in urban mobility, the related groups of interest (**and** disabled people, in particular) may have an obvious incentive, and some people among the general public might consider their participation as a contribution to the greater good. But previous experience shows that **it** is difficult to build a community on top of this foundation; and when the group of users does not reach a critical mass, crowdsourcing **results** in failure.

In this **paper, we suggest exploring** another option: **that of defining** the application as a *serious game* to be played by citizens for their own amusement. The idea is **to design** the mobile app as a videogame, in which the users **will** provide the required data as the means to advance in the game dynamics. **Each** user **will** have the relevant pieces of information as their goal within the game, **and their** interaction with these elements **will, therefore,** serve either to discover new data or to confirm previously captured information. This is the same smart data referred to above, **and each** record **will** have a definite meaning, even within the game, thus becoming *smart data at play*.

2. Related work

Crowdsourcing takes advantage of the Internet, thus allowing large numbers of people to contribute to some kind of common objective, and many organisations and initiatives have employed it as part of their strategies (Morschheuser, Hamari, and Maedche 2019). One of the definitions of crowdsourcing states that it is 'the act of taking a job traditionally performed by **employees** and outsourcing it to an undefined, generally large group of people in the form of an open call' (Howe 2008, p. backcover). Crowdsourcing is a 'multifaceted phenomenon and appears in many different forms' (Morschheuser, Hamari, and Maedche 2019, 8), or is 'just a rubric for a wide range of activities' (Howe 2008, 18). In fact, the growth and expansion of the Internet and mobile phones has also expanded the possibilities of crowdsourcing. The flexibility of the crowdsourcing model makes it possible to apply to a broad range of activities (Prandi et al. 2018), and some of its initiatives have achieved major results when large groups of crowdsourcees have taken part in the process (Wikipedia, Open Street Maps, Waze …)(Morschheuser, Hamari, and Maedche 2019).

The users' participation is a relevant factor in this kind of applications and others, such as health or gambling areas, and can determine the success or failure of a proposal. Moreover, the users' continuous intention is not always guaranteed. There are consequently some interesting proposals (Lehto and Oinas-Kukkonen 2015; Mohadis, Mohamad Ali, and Smeaton 2016) based on the Persuasive System Design (PSD) model (Oinas-Kukkonen and Harjumaa 2009), which offers systematic means of understanding and analysing the persuasion context and enlists persuasive design principles. The research core of persuasive technologies are behaviour change support systems (Lehto and Oinas-Kukkonen 2015), which provide their users with many benefits. However, when used for this purpose, they need to guarantee the success of the systems in order to retain their users.

Expanding on this, a playful approach would also appear to be a good incentive by which to stimulate participation. The crowdsourcing approach fits very well with the gamification philosophy (Hamari, Koivisto, and Sarsa 2014). Gamification is 'the use of game design elements in non-game contexts' (Deterding et al. 2011, 10) and can motivate users and, therefore, help to increase the number of the crowdsourcees. Gamification techniques have expanded from start-ups to traditional companies (Hamari, Koivisto, and Sarsa 2014). When applying gamification to some applications, it is necessary to take into account certain principles. For example, developers should enhance activities through gamification while maintaining the focus on the activities themselves; developers should, therefore, also consider the playful aspects that will be emulated by means of gamification (Knaving and Staffan 2013).

Several works deal with the use of gamification in urban mobility and smart cities, an example of which is one that implements a game that motivates users to stand up on very crowded public transport (Kuramoto et al. 2013). Other examples are, on the one hand, a service-based gamification framework that can be used to develop games on top of existing systems in a Smart City (Kazhamiakin et al. 2015) and, on the other, the personalisation of urban paths across heritage sites in **the** sharing of multimedia resources (Prandi et al. 2018). Others are related to seeking an improvement in the use of bicycles, thus improving public transportation (Vieira et al. 2012; Weber et al. 2018). Yet another focuses on obtaining a pedestrian cartography in cities through mobile gamification, given that digital maps usually focus principally on routes followed when using vehicles (Kapenekakis and Chorianopoulos 2017). **However, to the best of our knowledge, there are currently no software applications dealing with public transport and its accessibility features, while also using crowdsourcing and gamification techniques to update their data.**

3. Motivation and context

This work is developed in the context of a research project denominated as Access@City (Vela et al. 2017a). It is a coordinated project that defines a technological framework in which to process, manage and use open data concerning public transport with the goal of promoting accessible mobility. In this **respect**, we have **produced** some previous works. The Regional Consortium for Public Transport in Madrid (CRTM 2019), the Madrid public bus company (EMT Madrid 2019) and the Spanish National Society for the Blind (ONCE 2019) have all expressed an interest in the results of our Access@City project.

One of its subprojects is Multiply@City (Vela et al. 2017b), which focuses on processing and harmonising public transport accessibility data in a semantic manner by means of an ontology, taking into account that data are provided by different sources and have different formats. Figure 1 provides a general depiction of this latter project.

The public transport infrastructure and its accessibility elements (lifts, escalators, etc.) are obtained from open data by means of web scraping. This infrastructure does not usually change, and neither does its open data. However, the working state of the accessibility elements (ACEs) can frequently change (i.e. whether or not a lift or an escalator works) and consequently, ACEs data have to be updated. **We, therefore,** collect these data via crowdsourcing techniques.

Crowdsourcing initiatives involve groups of people in order to solve distributed problems (Morschheuser, Hamari, and Maedche 2019) and are a correct way in which to classify and mark content (Geiger and Schader 2014). These studies are interesting for our purpose because it is necessary to annotate the working state **of ACEs.** But we also need to motivate people to participate as crowdsources and **we,** therefore, define our proposal according to a gamification strategy.

The principal objective of gamification is to design features with which to produce feelings similar to those experienced when playing games. Several research works have shown that gamification could be an effective means to increase motivations and influence behaviour (Hamari, Koivisto, and Sarsa 2014). Our intention is, therefore, to use a game in order to involve a significant number of people in the process of capturing and confirming existing information concerning accessibility in the transport network and, by extension, in the city itself. This crowdsourcing process should provide sufficient data to allow informed decisions to be made regarding mobility and life in the city. These data assist when making smart decisions about these issues, signifying that these smart data are helping to build our smart city.

In this context, we have developed an Android app for smart devices (denominated as Access 'n' Go!) with which to enrich the accessibility information concerning the public transport network through the use of crowdsourcing and gamification, thus improving accessibility in increasingly smarter cities, even within the game, and consequently making the data *smart data at play.*

4. Our proposal: access 'n' Go!

As mentioned previously, the eventual objective of the Access@City project (Vela et al. 2017a) is to support new social accessibility services, such as calculating public transport routes, which will be made accessible to all, by taking into account the users' needs (i.e. someone moving with a twin baby carriage or who has a phobia **about** escalators). These routes must be based on stable data regarding the infrastructure of the transport network (i.e. stations, lines and stops) and on continuously updated data related to accessibility features (i.e. whether or not a lift or an escalator works).

The need to consider these last features has led us to develop the proposal presented herein, which also includes information concerning the current working state of the public transport network. This has been done using a gamification and crowdsourcing approach. The relevant aspect of this work is that of identifying the working state of each existing ACE in the public transport network, along with capturing new ACEs that are not registered within the current information that we have previously collected from different open sources.

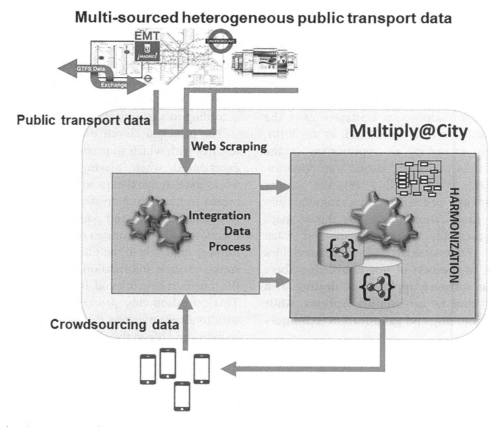

Figure 1. Multiply@City project architecture.

Access 'n' Go!, a game for Android smartphones, makes it possible to update all the accessibility features of public transport (its working state) using crowdsourcing and gamification techniques.

In this section, we first introduce the game design, after which we describe the fine details and decisions **made**. Finally, we present the technological infrastructure and the architecture developed.

4.1. Game design: strategy and workflow

Having made the decision to design a crowdsourcing and gamification solution, we **then** had to select the most appropriate strategies for this proposal.

Motivated and active crowd operators of crowdsourcing approaches must also continually attract new participants in order to compensate for crowdsourcee churn (Morschheuser, Hamari, and Maedche 2019). It is, therefore, important for active users to invite others to participate in the system. Crowdsourcees benefit from an increasing number of supporters and these reciprocal benefits may motivate people to invite others to participate in crowdsourcing. We consequently decided that the game would permit the creation of teams and that more players would be allowed to join it.

Some works on gamification design address the question of whether it is better to use competition-based or cooperation-based designs. One of the individualistic strategies of the competitive game design is 'when individual actions obstruct the actions of others (negative interdependence; e.g. competitions in which player compete with each other)', while the cooperative strategy is 'when individual actions promote the goals of others (positive interdependence; e.g. shared challenges for a team of players)' (Liu, Li, and Santhanam 2013, 22). Moreover, being part of a team that works together towards a shared goal has been identified as motivational gratification for players of online games with cooperative features (Rigby and Ryan 2011). Cooperative play allows players to overcome challenges that it would be impossible to meet when playing alone. We are, therefore, of the opinion that the inter-team competition design is probably best for our purposes, because 'inter-group competitions may be particularly effective for supporting intrinsic motivation and behaviour in crowdsourcing, compared to pure cooperative or competitive gamification designs' (Morschheuser et al. 2018, 11). This kind of design is: (a) collaborative between the team members, providing specific aims in groups and (b) competitive between groups, creating clear barriers between groups. We have consequently decided to follow an inter-team competition strategy in this work.

The main objective of the game is to update information related to the ACEs in the public transport network. The complete dynamics of Access 'n' Go! is the following: the app shows the ACEs on a map and checks the player's proximity to an ACE; if the player is close to the ACE, s/he can capture it and must then indicate its working state. The app then verifies whether a level has been achieved. A level is achieved when a station and/or line **in** the public transport network is completed. The app subsequently awards the corresponding points and/or badges to the player and to his/her team (a badge is awarded to a team if the badge is new for the team; a team will never have duplicated badges; however, a player can accumulate duplicated badges and exchange them later).

Figure 2 shows the game workflow employed to capture an ACE by means of a UML (UML 2019) activity diagram.

4.2. Fine details and decision making

In this subsection, we describe the game elements, the screen design and the Access 'n' Go! functionality.

First, we introduce the details of the game elements according to an inter-team competitive strategy:

- There is a set of 12 badges. Each badge has a different colour. The badge icon is represented as the Access 'n' Go! logo (a train).

- Each player can collect points, levels and badges. These elements make up the player and team score. A player collects points when s/he captures an ACE. A player collects a badge when s/he attains a specific number of points. A player reaches a level when s/he completes a station, that is, when s/he attains the whole set of ACEs associated with a station. A player also achieves a level when s/he completes a line, that is, when s/he attains the whole set of stations associated with a line. In both cases, the player obtains special points.

- A player can attain duplicated badges, a team cannot. The player can exchange a duplicated badge for a new one. New badges will automatically be awarded to the player and the team score.

- There is a ranking only between teams. This ranking shows the team score, that is, the number of points, levels and badges associated with each team. However, there is no ranking between players.

- A team comprises more than 2 people. A team receives points when an individual player joins it. A team is complete when it has 5 players, in which case it also receives a badge.

In Table 1, we describe the game score.

With regard to the screen design, three different ones are presented in this paper. The first shows the ACEs on a map. ACEs are the entrances to a station (lifts, escalators, stairs or ramps) and have geographical coordinates (latitude and longitude), thus enabling their

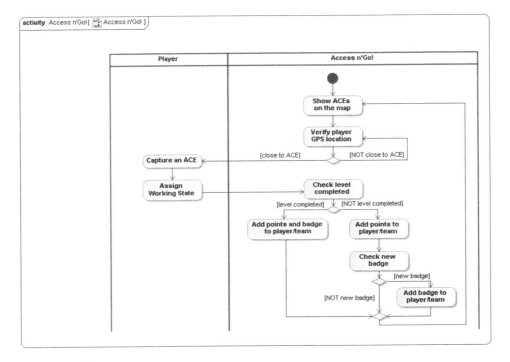

Figure 2. Capture an ACE! workflow.

Table 1. Scores in the game.

Event	Points	Badges
Capture an ACE	points + = 25	N/A
Establish a NEW ACE	points + = 500	Award a badge
Join a player	points + = 50	N/A
Complete the team (5 players)	points + = 100	Award a badge
Exchange a badge	points + = 75	N/A
New badge	points + = 50	N/A
Reach 6 different badges	points + = 100	N/A
Reach all badges	points + = 500	N/A
Complete a station	points + = 100	N/A
Complete a line	points + = 250	Award a badge
Reach 10.000 points	N/A	Award a badge

representation on a map. A player can capture an ACE when s/he is close to it. We consequently represent ACEs and the player's current position on the map with different colours: the player's current position is a red pin, the ACEs captured are grey and the ACEs that have not yet been captured are green. The scores (points, levels and badges) are shown at the top of screen. Figure 3(a) depicts the screen employed to capture ACEs.

The second screen presents the game ranking. As our proposal follows an inter-team competition strategy, we have created a ranking only between teams. This represents a list of teams and their scores (points, levels and badges achieved). Figure 3(b) shows the game ranking screen.

In order to revitalise the game, a player can exchange his/her duplicated badges with other players. The screen presents two lists of badges, as is shown in Figure 3(c): the list on the left presents the badges offered by the player, while that on the right presents the badges required.

Finally, we describe the Access 'n' Go! functionality. The objective of the game is to conquer a means of transport by capturing all the ACEs on it. The functionality is supported by a dataset containing public transport information. In previous works (Cáceres et al. 2017), (Cáceres et al. 2019), we designed a public transport network dataset (*infrastructure dataset*) of the metro (MetroMadrid 2019) in Madrid, Spain. This dataset resides in our server (Coruscant server) and contains information about stations, which includes stops and accessibility elements, and lines and their corresponding stops. Each element in the dataset has geographic coordinates (latitude and longitude), thus allowing them to be represented on a map. As mentioned **previously**, ACEs are lifts, escalators, ramps and stairs. **In order t**o identify **all** the ACEs **in** any public transport network, we have carefully studied the Identification of Fixed Objects in Public Transport (IFOPT) reference datamodel (CEN/TC278 2012), a standard **that** defines a model for the main *fixed objects* related to the access to Public Transport (e.g. stop points, stations, entrances, etc.). Moreover, IFOPT includes specific structures with which to describe accessibility data concerning the equipment **at** stations, among others. **The a**ccessibility elements of a public transport network make **it** possible **for** any user with a special need to move through that network (i.e. someone who has a phobia **about** escalators, **or** is able **only** to use stairs, ramps or lifts).

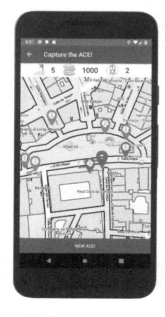

(a) Capture anACE!   (b) Team ranking   (c) Exchange badges

Figure 3. Access 'n' Go! Screens.

We have established the correspondence between ACEs in public transport and users' needs, and we summarise them in Table 2. **We have, therefore,** identified the kinds of ACEs **that must be taken** into account in this **paper.**

In this game, we work solely with the ACEs. We periodically update this *infrastructure dataset*, but it is possible that some new accessibility elements (lifts, escalators, etc.) were incorporated into the network after the dataset was updated. **It is for this reason that** Access 'n' Go! **makes it** possible to add new ACEs and to modify the working state of the existing ones.

When the app starts, it queries the *infrastructure dataset* in the Coruscant server. Access 'n' Go!, **therefore,** extracts the existing ACEs from this dataset and represents them on a map. However, the information about new ACEs and the working state of each of the ACEs captured will be incorporated **into** a different dataset (the *event dataset*), which will be sent to the server to be integrated.

The dynamics and complete behaviour of the game **have** been structured into the following use cases:

- *Capture an ACE!* This use case represents the main game functionality (the associated workflow has been previously described by means of the UML activity diagram shown in Figure 2 in section 4.1). The player has to indicate the working state of the ACE captured. Access 'n' Go! should then determine whether a station or line has been completed and add points to the team and player's score, while randomly awarding badges to the player. It is for this reason that a player may have duplicated badges. A badge will be added to the team if the ACE is new for the team. The working state of the captured ACE represents an event in the public transport network and Access 'n' Go! should, therefore, send this event to the Coruscant actor.
- *Establish a new ACE!* This use case permits a player to add a new ACE. This situation occurs when the player finds an ACE on the street that is not shown on the map. In this case, the app asks the player to take a picture of the ACE (with the aim of establishing its

geographic coordinates) and to establish its working state. This occurrence also represents an event in the public transport network and **has** the same behaviour as that of the previous use case.

- *Exchange badges.* This use case permits a player to exchange duplicated badges, thus allowing the player to attain new badges for the team.
- *View team ranking.* This use case makes it possible to see the ranking between teams, showing the points, levels and badges attained by each team.
- *Create a team.* This use case permits a player to create a team if s/he does not yet belong to one.
- *Join a player.* This use case allows a player to join a team. Access 'n' Go! adds points to the score, and when the team is completed (5 players), it adds extra points.
- *Chat.* This use case permits a player to enter the game chat. Access 'n' Go! incorporates a chat in which players can chat with each other.
- *Register.* This use case permits a user to register in Access 'n' Go! The app requests an email address and a password.
- *Login.* This use case permits a player to log into the game.
- *Recover password.* This use case allows players to recover their passwords.

In order to support these use cases, we had to develop a specific backend for Access 'n' Go! On the one hand, it was necessary to manage the game elements (players, points, levels and badges), and we consequently selected Firebase to manage this information, signifying that Access 'n' Go! has to interact with the Firebase actor. On the other hand, it is necessary to send the events concerning the working state of the ACEs, generated by the players when capturing them, and we have, therefore, developed a specific system in a server (named Coruscant). Access 'n' Go! must, therefore, interact with the Coruscant actor.

Figure 4 represents the **most** representative use cases of Access 'n' Go! by means of a UML use case diagram.

A more detailed description of the backend of this game is provided in the following subsection.

4.3. Technological infrastructure and architecture

As mentioned above, our framework implements a client-server architecture with some additional features.

This proposal applies a client-server architectural style, with features akin to the microservices approach. On the client side, our software is able to update the accessibility information and send it to the server. On the server side, we have developed and deployed a

Table 2. Relationship between ACEs and Users' Needs.

ACEs of public transport (based on IFOPT)	Users' accessibility needs			
	Auditory and visual	Mobility	Phobia about lifts	Phobia about escalators
Lift	✓	✓	X	✓
Escalator	✓	X	✓	X
Ramp	✓	✓	✓	✓
Stairs	✓	X	✓	✓

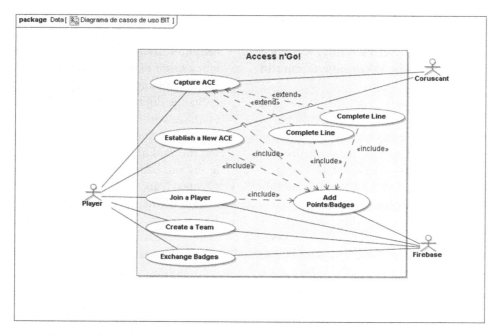

Figure 4. UML Use case diagram of **Access 'n' Go!**

datastore, which holds the relevant information about the transport network and its accessibility features, listens to and processes different notifications from our client software (and other **software** clients and returns to them any data which is requested by the same client).

The client is an Android app denominated as Access 'n' Go! that offers crowdsourcing software with which to capture the accessibility elements of public transport and to update their working state (for example, whether or not a lift is working).

At the backend, we use two different infrastructures. The first of these supports the game management by means of Firebase technology in the cloud. Firebase provides authentication in a simple and **secure** manner, hosting, cloud storage and a real-time database. We, therefore, use this technology to manage the players' registration and authentication, along with the storage of the game elements, such as the players' scores, points, badges, etc. The second is implemented in our own on-premise server (**denominated as** Coruscant) and supports the management of the different public transport accessibility elements and their working state. In this server, we have deployed an architecture based on microservices in order to serve the public transport infrastructure (dataset for the transport network) to the Access 'n' Go! App and to send new accessibility elements or the updated state of the existing accessibility elements (event dataset) from the app to the server. In order to store these data in the server, we have developed a Jena semantic repository (SR) (Apache Jena n.d.) with two different datasets. Moreover, so as to attend to the

requests from the client side, we have implemented an application server (AppServer), implemented with Spring Boot (SpringBoot 2019). **In** order to communicate the updated data (events) collected by the players, it is also necessary to send these incidents to the server, which should simultaneously listen to the (potentially many) notifications of events about the accessibility features that are –or are not- available for the public transport network at that moment. We have, therefore, implemented an Apache Kakfa server (Apache Kafka n.d.) as a queuing manager (QM). The QM gathers the different events notified from the crowdsourcees, i.e. the players (through their smart devices). This information, once processed, must be stored in the semantic repository, signifying that the AppServer also manages and controls the communication between the QM and the SR.

Figure 5 depicts the main elements and data exchanges in the proposed architecture.

In summary, we have implemented the following elements in the server (Coruscant, an HP multicore high-performance server, with a direct high-speed Internet connection): a Spring Boot as the application server (AppServer), an Apache Kakfa server as a queuing manager (QM) and a Jena semantic repository (SR). The Jena repository maintains two separate data collections, one of which provides the (mostly static) data concerning stations, lines and stops, denominated as the *infrastructure collection* (i), and the other of which provides the (dynamic) data related to the state of the network as regards its accessibility features, denominated as the *events collection* (ii).

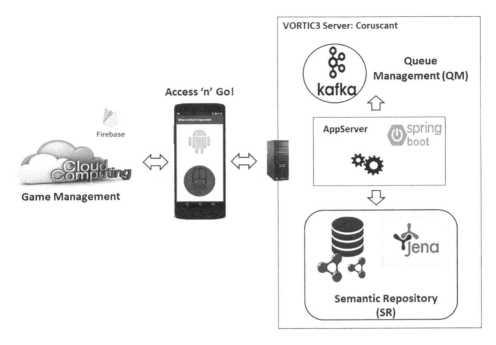

Figure 5. Proposed architecture (smart client-semantic server).

5. Empirical validation

In order to validate this proposal, we had two different, while related, validation targets. Our final goal was to check the proposal itself, that is, the efficiency of the game as a method to capture information about accessibility elements, and to involve people in that task; the intermediate target was simply to test the applicability of the mobile app, which is instrumental **to** the success of the global approach.

The validation of the proposal was**, therefore,** designed as two separate stages, each one of **which was** conceived for these two targets. Specifically:

- In the first stage, the purpose was **merely** to capture a specific Metro line. Players merely had to traverse the stations **on** the line, capturing every ACE **on** them. **Each** player '**won**' at this stage **by** simply capturing the whole line. The purpose of this stage was to define the game dynamics and to test the mobile app. Indeed, the app interface was still evolving during this stage, and different versions of **the** interface were tested in this phase.
- In the second stage, once the app was considered **to be sufficiently** satisfactory (while not definitive), the whole game, with its complete set of rules, was completely unfolded, and the app was deployed to be tested in a real competition.

In both stages, the validation was performed by a group of volunteers, selected **from** among the students on the second year of our Bachelor**'s** degree in Mathematics. **Each** student had the opportunity to join this group; but only willing volunteers were selected. **The activity was never considered mandatory; the idea was that the only incentives for participation were to encourage solidarity and the social relevance of the study.** While participation in the initial stage had some minor benefits, we explicitly avoided **providing** further stimuli in a later stage. The idea was that the game should be sufficiently addictive, **thus encouraging** the students **to** choose to continue playing it once they became familiar with it, even when they thought that the experiment had ended.

Our test group was initially limited to 20 people; the reason **for limiting** this number was to maintain the first tests within a manageable size, and also **to** use scarcity as a minor incentive (i.e. we noticed that if only some students were included in the experiment, it became more desirable to be chosen for it). These students were used during the first stage to refine the mobile app (as already noted), and became familiar with the interface, the purpose of the game and group dynamics. This initial stage lasted approximately one month; students were assigned a Metro line close to their home address and were tasked with capturing every identified ACE in this line. By the second week, they were allowed to begin the formation of teams – mostly chosen by personal affinity, by geographical closeness, or both. By then end of the month, most of the students had completed their assignment, but only 17 decided to continue in the experiment. As a significant note, only the students who had become part of a team continued in the game.

Therefore, in the second stage, the remaining players were already grouped in stable teams. The size of a team was designed to be within the rank of 3–5 people (again, to have manageable teams). In the final stage, there were four teams, namely Team 1 (a team of 5 people), Team 2 (4 members), Team 3 (5 members) and the smaller, but still committed Team 4 (composed of just 3 people).

Metro Madrid has 12 lines (there are, **in fact,** 13 lines, but the remaining one has a particular design and was not considered). With regard to distance, the longest ones are probably Line 7 (Orange) and 10 (Blue), which have 30 and 31 stations, **respectively**; but Line 1 (Cyan) has **the most** stations, **with a total of** 33. Not surprisingly, most of the teams chose the most centric lines as their playground. The most popular choices were Line 2 (Red, 20 stations), Line 3 (Yellow, 18 stations), Line 6 (Circular, 28 stations) and Line 12 (South, 28 stations). The first two are basically confined to the city centre and **provide access to** some of the **most** popular places in the city. The third surrounds the central area in the city and provides easy **connections** between different locations, and the last was geographically convenient for most of the students.

During the first stage, the students had to capture the ACEs **at** the stations **on** Metro Line 1 (which is also centric and convenient). **All** 33 stations **on** Line 1 were, therefore, captured during this stage. However, not every volunteer was able to complete this challenge; in fact, those who did not finish this stage were the three people **who left** the game. The remaining players had, **simultaneously,** already formed groups, even **though** groups were not relevant at this stage. This led us to **confirm our initial belief**; that is, that belonging to a team is a powerful motivation. At the beginning of the second stage, everybody was **now** a member of a group, and **we** thus had a **fully**-fledged inter-team strategy. We intended to take advantage of this, and **in order** to test the actual impact of stimulating participation by presenting a competition, we decided to use two different approaches in the design of the second stage of our game.

- In the first approach, two Lines (the aforementioned 3 and also Line 4, Brown, 23 stations) were selected as the playground. The team **that** was able to capture all the ACEs first would be considered the winner. In this case, all the teams completed every station and ACEs **on** the Yellow Line, but only three of them were able to complete the stations **on** Line 4. Once **a** team (Team 1) **had been** proclaimed as the winner, the rest of the teams decided to stop. The experience was **nonetheless** a great success: we

were able **to** achieve independent confirmation of every known ACE **on** Line 3 from every team, and about 80% of the elements **on** Line 4 had at least 3 confirmations. This phase of the experiment lasted almost two weeks (14 days).

- In the second approach, which defined our final stage, every Line in the Metro network was considered as part of the game board; but **we** now **decided** to limit the time. Essentially, the team **that** was able to achieve **the highest** score before the time ended was considered the winner. This phase of the game lasted one month, and in this stage, every rule in the game **had now been** applied.

In this (last) part of the experiment, the players had **now** become accustomed to **capturing** ACEs as part of their routine, independently of the game itself. For instance, several players captured stations **on** lines **that** were never completed, but which were close to their home address. However, competition became the main driver for them to remain in the game. **Team** loyalty was **also** important – several members remained in the game to support their team, and conversely, Team 3 was the first to abandon the game, after it became clear that they were not **attaining** the same scores as their rivals. The remaining teams began to compete to complete Line 6 (Circular), which **they chose** by themselves: we did not need to intervene in this part of the process. The last stations **on** this Line were captured in a matter of hours, **despite the fact that** several of the **teams' members were** geographically distant **from it,** and this Line was completed by the three remaining teams, **thus** providing a significant amount of information and proving that the motivation was **now** the game itself.

Table 3 **provides a summary of** some of the figures in our experiment, showing some details **regarding** Phase 1, when the app was still evolving; and more information about Phase 2, which describes the actual validation process. The first row summarises the number of different elements captured in **each** phase – for instance, only 4 Metro lines were fully identified in Phase 2, but 148 different stations were, **nevertheless,** confirmed, including many that were not a part of these four lines. **Our** 17 players combined **simultaneously** captured 1529 stations in this Phase, **signifying that there were obviously many confirmations for each ACE and station.** This was the desired effect, **and** the approach **was, therefore,** a clear success –even considering that at least 5 players left the game before the end, **meaning that** their figures distort the statistics, particularly the mean values.

Finally, **please** note that in the final version of our game, the outcome that defines a 'victory' is assigned

SMART CITIES AT PLAY

Table 3. Global results in the two phases of the experiment.

	Phase 1	#stations	Phase 2	#stations	#lines	#ACEs	Points
# Players' Gender	20	33	17	148	4	544	206.450
Male	11	355	10	776	31	848	114.025
Female	9	272	7	753	24	610	92.425
Age	Mean	SD	Mean	SD	–	–	–
	19	0,45	19	0,22			
Avg time (days)	Phase	Station	Phase	Station	Line	–	–
1st half	23,45	20,32	14	11,50	12,7		
2nd half	–	–	30	14,64	20,8		

to the team **that** achieves all the possible badges. This **avoids** the negative effects of having a limited playground (as in Phase 1) or a limited duration of the game (which could discourage competition). With badges, the rules and their dynamics define the duration of the game. However, this approach was not included in our experiment (badges were already present during Phase 2, but they did not define the duration, **and** we have not yet, **therefore,** validated this particular feature.

We would also like to note that nobody **managed** to *establish a new ACE* during the validation phase; this is **owing simply** to the fact that the infrastructure dataset was sufficiently updated, and there were, **therefore,** no new ACEs to establish. This is not, **of course,** a problem: it was simply not necessary.

6. Conclusions and future work

One of the major challenges of smart **city** initiatives is to achieve an inclusive society for all citizens, including those with special needs, such as mobility issues. For this challenge to be met, more thorough information about the means of transport and their accessibility features is required, with the aim **of arranging and providing** accessible routes for everybody. **Although** a great effort **has recently been made** to publish accessibility information about transport networks, a careful examination reveals that this information is still scarce. Specifically, these recent efforts have **done** good work **as regards** describing the stable elements in the infrastructure, but information about the most recent updates and the working state of these elements is often difficult to find. However, these data are critical for everyday mobility, **and** even more so for people with special needs.

Our previous work, in the context of the Access@City Research Project (funded by the Spanish National R&D Program), has been focused **on** improving mobility and accessibility in the urban environment, and particularly in the public transport system, by capturing **the** information **available** about these issues. **Citizens are provided with these data** by means of smart adequately processed **devices** in order to facilitate urban mobility

and to serve accessible routes in a dynamic **manner,** with the goal **of achieving** a smarter city.

However, the scarcity of information about the working state of accessibility elements (our ACEs) hinders **this** purpose. Even **when** dynamically created, an accessible route is useless when a crucial ACE (e.g. the only lift **that** could help a citizen to reach the surface in the final station **on** the route) is not working properly (e.g. **it** is broken). **Moreover,** when the infrastructure information is not quickly updated, there might be alternative routes **that** are, in fact, possible in the real world, but are never computed because the relevant information has not yet been captured.

We soon realised that the only way **in which** to obtain this information was by means of crowdsourcing: citizens themselves are the best source of information about ACEs and their working state. However, even in the context of social needs such as this, it is not easy to involve people **who wish** to assist in the process. **It was for this** reason that we considered using a playful approach: not only the process, but **also** the tool will be a game, **and** people will **provide** the required information by playing this game.

We have, therefore, developed an Android gaming app, **denominated as** *Access 'n' Go!,* **which we specifically describe** as a hybrid reality game (HRG) openly designed to acquire information about the accessibility of subway stations. The game **consists of identifying** (and geolocating) accessible spots (i.e. ACEs), and **using** them to feed a description of the station. In turn, every time that the player provides some information, her score in the game is improved. The correlation between many independent observations makes **it** possible to provide an accurate description of the accessibility of these stations **in a relatively short amount of time**. In this **paper,** we have **provided a detailed explanation of** both the design of the game itself and the implementation of the gaming app, including the design of its most relevant screens and features. The preliminary results are even better than expected: we have been successful in involving a significant amount of people (with no need for external incentives once the process **had been** bootstrapped), and we have been able to confirm the information contained in our pre-existing dataset (the *infrastructure dataset*), **thus** illustrating its accuracy (at least for a substantial subset).

We have defined the game on **the basis of** an inter-team competitive strategy, as most of the existing literature suggests that this approach is able to achieve the **best** results. Our own validation process **appears** to substantiate these claims. In the first stage, when we had individual players, they nonetheless tended to group into teams once they were given the opportunity. **It is very significant that** those who never became involved in a team were precisely those who decided to leave the experiment. On the contrary, those belonging to a group were highly motivated: players are glad to cooperate with their teammates **in order to meet** a challenge and are even more compelled to compete with other teams in a constant effort to surpass them. The final stage of our second phase clearly **shows** that competition serves as an excellent incentive. In summary, it seems clear that the inter-team strategy, as expected, increases the intrinsic motivation and improves the desired behaviour in a crowdsourcing process.

In order to support this process, **we not only developed** the design of the game and produced the mobile app, but we also had to provide the sustaining infrastructure. Indeed, the game itself would be useless without the underlying architecture; our purpose was really to feed this architecture with updated information.

The architecture defines a set **of** semantic datastores and combines the information **from** available datastreams. This results in a complex data processing system, which is made available to the users of the public transport by using smart devices – most frequently, their own smartphones. This processing system **also** has to be complemented with the elements designed to capture new information (a new crowdsourced datastream of ACE data and working states) and to support the game management (players and scores) itself. With respect to this, we used the Firebase technology to manage **both the** players' registration and authentication **and** the storage of game elements. The information captured by crowdsourcing (ACE data and working states) is supported by a Jena semantic repository (SR) (Apache Jena n.d.) with two different datasets, an Application Server based on Spring Boot, and a microservices architecture **that** is able to serve the information **from** the infrastructure dataset to the the Access 'n' Go! App. **Moreover**, in order to achieve a better scalability, we have implemented an Apache Kakfa server (Apache Kafka n.d.) as a queuing manager (QM). The QM gathers the different events notified by the players (through their smart devices), and this information, once processed, must be stored in the semantic repository, **signifying that** the AppServer

also manages and controls the communication between the QM and the SR. Our experiments **to date** show that this infrastructure is able to **function perfectly** correctly **when confronted with** a significant workload.

We have already planned **to make** some **extensions to** Access 'n' Go! **as** future work. One of the most relevant modifications **is related to** the capability to adapt the application and the dynamics of the game to the specific needs of our experiments and to focus **on** the hunt for specific information. **We, therefore, intend** to provide a new version, which can be configured according to different challenges in order to win the game. For instance, we **could** decide that a team **will win** when the whole set of 12 badges is acquired (i.e. the current behaviour), but we **could** also choose other options, such as conquering a concrete sub-network or even the whole network, or **attaining** a specific number of transport lines, **limiting** the time or the geographical area, etc. Our actual goal is to enrich the accessibility information dataset, **and** we should, **therefore,** be able to adapt the game strategy to our specific needs by defining specific challenges. **Another relevant modification is that of improving our app in order to engage and retain the users, following behaviour change proposals** (Lehto and Oinas-Kukkonen 2015; Mohadis, Mohamad Ali, and Smeaton 2016). **As mentioned in Section 2, the Persuasive System Design (PSD) model** (Oinas-Kukkonen and Harjumaa 2009) **is supported by different proposals, and offers systematic ways in which to understand and analyse the persuasion context. Finally, we also plan to perform an additional validation step, which will be carried out by people from different backgrounds, thus avoiding the population being restricted to our student cohort.**

As **a** final conclusion, we are very satisfied with the results of this experiment. Our previous work made **it** clear that **it** is very difficult to complement information about the stable infrastructure with updated data and working states. Some previous initiatives with other crowdsourcing approaches **were not** able to **provoke** significant interest; **this,** however, changed when we decided to use a playful approach. We not only **captured** a much **greater** amount of information, **but** it was quickly obtained and integrated, very easily confirmed, and it was also of better quality. In this regard, the experiment has been a total success.

In summary, smart data are better when they are also at play.

Acknowledgements

This work is supported by the Multiply@City and the Access@City projects (TIN2016-78103-C2-1-R), funded by the Spanish Ministry of Science, Innovation and Universities. We want to thank Isaac Lozano Osorio for his support.

Disclosure statement

No potential conflict of interest was reported by the authors.

Funding

This work was supported by Spanish Ministry of Science, Innovation and Universities: [Grant Number TIN2016-78103-C2-1-R].

ORCID

Paloma Cáceres http://orcid.org/0000-0002-2722-2434
Carlos E. Cuesta http://orcid.org/0000-0003-0286-4219

References

Apache Jena. n.d. Jena. https://jena.apache.org/index.html.
Apache Kafka. n.d. Kafka. https://kafka.apache.org/intro.
Cáceres, Paloma, Carlos E. Cuesta, Almudena Sierra-Alonso, Belén Vela, José María Cavero, and Miguel A. Garrido. 2019. "Even Smarter Data: Using Crowdsourcing to Improve Accessibility in Real-Time." In *Proceedings on the Fourth International Conference on Universal Accessibility in the Internet of Things and Smart Environments (SMART ACCESSIBILITY 2019)*.
Cáceres, Paloma, Almudena Sierra-Alonso, Paloma Cáceres, Belén Vela, José María Cavero, and Carlos E. Cuesta. 2017. "Towards Smart Public Transport Data: A Specific Process to Generate Datasets Containing Public Transport Accessibility Information." In *Proceedings on the Third International Conference on Universal Accessibility in the Internet of Things and Smart Environments (SMART ACCESSIBILITY 2018)*, 66–71.
CEN/TC278. 2012. Intelligent transport systems - Public transport - Identification of Fixed Objects In Public Transport (IFOPT), EN 28701.
CRTM. 2019. Regional Consortium for Public Transport. http://datos.crtm.es/.
Deterding, S., D. Dixon, R. Khaled, and L. Nacke. 2011. "From Game Design Elements to Gamefulness: Defining Gamification." In *Proceedings of the 15th International Academic MindTrek Conference: Envisioning Future Media Environments, MindTrek* 2011 (Vol. 11, pp. 9–15). doi:10.1145/2181037.2181040.
EMT Madrid, E. M. de T. de M. 2019. Municipal Company of Transport of Madrid. http://www.emtmadrid.es/Index.aspx?lang=en-GB.
Geiger, D., and M. Schader. 2014. "Personalized Task Recommendation in Crowdsourcing Information Systems — Current State of the art." *Decision Support Systems* 65 (C): 3–16. doi:10.1016/j.dss.2014.05.007.
Hamari, J., J. Koivisto, and H. Sarsa. 2014. "Does Gamification Work? – A Literature Review of Empirical Studies on Gamification." 2014 *47th Hawaii International Conference on System Sciences*, 3025–3034.

Howe, J. 2008. *Crowdsourcing: Why the Power of the Crowd Is Driving the Future of Business.* 1st ed. New York, NY, USA: Crown Publishing Group.
Kapenekakis, I., and K. Chorianopoulos. 2017. "Citizen Science for Pedestrian Cartography: Collection and Moderation of Walkable Routes in Cities Through Mobile Gamification." *Human-Centric Computing and Information Sciences* 7 (1): 10. doi:10.1186/s13673-017-0090-9.
Kazhamiakin, R., A. Marconi, M. Perillo, M. Pistore, L. Piras, F. Avesani, and G. Valetto. 2015. Using Gamification to Incentivize Sustainable Urban Mobility. doi:10.13140/RG.2.1.2622.2166.
Knaving, K., and B. Staffan. 2013. "Designing for fun and play: exploring possibilities in design for gamification." In *e First International Conference on Gameful Design, Research, and Applications Gamification*, 131–134.
Kuramoto, I., T. Ishibashi, K. Yamamoto, and Y. Tsujino. 2013. "Stand Up, Heroes!: Gamification for Standing People on Crowded Public Transportation." In *Design, User Experience, and Usability. Health, Learning, Playing, Cultural, and Cross-Cultural User Experience*, edited by A. Marcus, 538–547. Berlin, Heidelberg: Springer Berlin Heidelberg.
Lehto, T., and H. Oinas-Kukkonen. 2015. "Explaining and Predicting Perceived Effectiveness and use Continuance Intention of a Behaviour Change Support System for Weight Loss." *Behaviour & Information Technology* 34 (2): 176–189.
Liu, D., X. Li, and R. Santhanam. 2013. "Digital Games and Beyond: What Happens When Players Compete?" *MIS Quarterly* 37 (1): 111–124. doi:10.25300/MISQ/2013/37.1.05.
MetroMadrid. 2019. Metro. http://www.metromadrid.es/en/.
Mohadis, H. M., N. Mohamad Ali, and A. F. Smeaton. 2016. "Designing a Persuasive Physical Activity Application for Older Workers: Understanding end-User Perceptions." *Behaviour & Information Technology* 35 (12): 1102–1114.
Morschheuser, B., J. Hamari, and A. Maedche. 2019. "Cooperation or Competition – When do People Contribute More? A Field Experiment on Gamification of Crowdsourcing." *International Journal of Human-Computer Studies* 127: 7–24. doi:10.1016/j.ijhcs.2018.10.001.
Oinas-Kukkonen, H., and M. Harjumaa. 2009. "Persuasive Systems Design: Key Issues." *Process Model, and System Features. Communication Association Information System* 24: 1.
ONCE, O. N. de C. de E. 2019. Spanish National Society of Blind People. http://www.once.es/new/otras-webs/english.
Prandi, C., A. Melis, M. Prandini, G. Delnevo, L. Monti, S. Mirri, and P. Salomoni. 2018. "Gamifying Cultural Experiences Across the Urban Environment." *Multimedia Tools and Applications*. doi:10.1007/s11042-018-6513-4.
Rigby, S., and R. M. Ryan. 2011. *Glued to Games: How Video Games Draw us in and Hold us Spellbound.Glued to Games: How Video Games Draw us in and Hold us Spellbound.* Santa Barbara, CA, US: Praeger/ABC-CLIO.
SpringBoot. 2019. Spring Boot. http://spring.io/projects/spring-boot.
UML. 2019. Unified Modeling Languaje. http://www.uml.org/.

Vela, Belén, Paloma Cáceres, José María Cavero, Almudena Sierra-Alonso, and Carlos E. Cuesta. 2017a. "Access@City Project (TIN2016-78103-C2-1-R).".

Vela, Belén, Paloma Cáceres, José María Cavero, Almudena Sierra-Alonso, and Carlos E. Cuesta. 2017b. "Multiply@City Project (TIN2016-78103-C2-1-R).".

Vieira, V., A. Fialho, V. Martinez, J. Brito, L. Brito, and A. Duran. 2012. "An Exploratory Study on the Use of Collaborative Riding Based on Gamification as a Support to Public Transportation." 2012 *Brazilian Symposium on Collaborative Systems*, 84–93.

Weber, J., M. Azad, W. Riggs, and C. R. Cherry. 2018. "The Convergence of Smartphone Apps, Gamification and Competition to Increase Cycling." *Transportation Research Part F: Traffic Psychology and Behaviour* 56: 333–343. doi:10.1016/j.trf.2018.04.025.

Serious gaming as a means of facilitating truly smart cities: a narrative review

M. Cavada and C. D. F. Rogers ⓘ

ABSTRACT

The term 'smart cities' is contested: its interpretation is becoming ever broader, often to accommodate commercial interests. Since cities are made up of individuals, all of whom are guided by their own world views and attitudes, the residual question is not 'what should we do?' but 'how should we do it and how should we encourage and enable everyone to join in?' By exploring the ways that gamification can be used to understand the effects of 'smart initiatives' on cities and their operation, it was concluded that gaming has considerable potential to affect individual and societal practices by profoundly influencing the gamers themselves, while technology and the game design itself play a central role to how gamification is implemented and used. This paper proposes one way of both creating cities to which citizens aspire and delivering a beneficial change in attitudes and behaviours to make such cities work. We propose that way-finding games should be developed as the most appropriate tools for participation. Designing such serious games with sustainability, resilience and liveability agendas in mind, encouraging widespread citizen participation as gamers, and taking cognisance of the outcomes would lead to both smarter citizens and smarter cities.

1. Introduction: the smart cities context

Often, 'smart' is used in relation to technological efficiencies in urban systems, yet if these efficiencies perpetuate short-term, unsustainable ways of life then their claim to 'smartness' is hardly appropriate. The growing evidence base on what we should be aiming for in cities – sustainability, resilience, liveability, adaptability, nimbleness of thinking in the face of contextual change – is now comprehensive and compelling. Serious gaming provides a potential means of citizen engagement in which the consequences of actions are made explicit, and has thus it has been explored via a review of the published literature. This was achieved using a narrative review due to considerable divergence on the concept of 'liveability' and interpretations of the term 'smart'. Moreover, playing an appropriately-designed (truly) smart city game has the effect of drawing the gamer into the role of citizen co-creator, or at least shaper, of cities and their systems. This participative, bottom-up approach to the development of smarter cities combines with the top-down approach provided by those who govern the city, hence enabling both citizens' and the city's aspirations to be met. Defining liveability as a combination of individual, societal and planetary wellbeing – features of a city that are highly interdependent – the review showed that smart city initiatives tended to place less emphasis on planetary wellbeing. Therefore when considering serious gaming to develop smart cities, actions that enhance planetary wellbeing should feature strongly in game design.

Despite the positive claims of 'smart cities', the term is still unclear and contested because the academic approach to 'smart' is ever-changing and commercial interests have appropriated the term both loosely and pervasively. All too often, the term 'smart' is used to describe the delivery of efficiencies in urban systems, and yet if the systems perpetuate short-term, unsustainable ways of life then 'smart' could be regarded as a contradiction in terms. As the authors have argued repeatedly: actions towards 'smart' are only 'truly smart' if they lead to more sustainable, resilient and liveable cities (Cavada 2019; Cavada, Rogers, and Hunt 2014). This requires a positive focus on individual and societal health and wellbeing, and planetary wellbeing. More specifically, these criteria should be embraced in any assessment of city performance and therefore lie at the heart of the decision-making process when attempting to create 'smart cities'.

This change of mindset amongst decision-makers requires a compelling case for change to founded upon a comprehensive evidence base. This has been created over the past 20–30 years or more in the case of sustainability and resilience, and more recently in the case of liveability (Leach et al. 2016; Leach, Lee, Boyko et al.

2017; Leach, Lee, Hunt, et al. 2017; Leach, Rogers et al. 2019; Liveable Cities 2019). It has to be anchored in the local context of the city in question and must follow a deep analysis of the city's current challenges (Leach, Rogers, et al. 2019) alongside its current performance (Leach, Lee, Boyko et al. 2017; Leach, Lee, Hunt, et al. 2017). Crucially, any form of intervention in a city – whether via a policy, a change of operational practice, or the adaptation of an existing or construction of a new artefact or infrastructure system – should be co-created with the citizens who form the 'end users' of the outcome. The question is: 'how can this be achieved?'

The starting point is the recognition that citizens should have the chance to be part of the decision-making processes when it comes to improving the smartness of their city, and therefore part of the decision-making surrounding smart initiatives (Cavada 2019). To achieve this, they should be empowered to combine with those who govern the city, and other city stakeholders, to help create 'the narrative' for the city's future and be instrumental in delivering it (Rogers et al. 2014). An enabler of this was created by the authors in partnership with the UK Government Foresight Future of Cities project, which aimed to advise government ministers of the potential benefits of taking a far-future perspective of cities in policy development (GoFS 2019a, 2019b). Rogers and Hunt (2019) describe an aspirational futures methodology that combines the aspirations of citizens and sectors (bottom-up) with the aspirations of those who govern (top-down).

While this provides the evidence, visualising the impact remains a challenge and one that potentially inhibits citizen engagement. UK action in this area includes the creation of the Centre for Digital Built Britain (www.cdbb.cam.ac.uk), which focuses on the so-called 'digital twin' approach. Valuable though this is, at the citizen level it is gaming that brings such ideas to life, and it is the potential for 'gamification of smart cities' that is explored in this paper. This provides the basis of a hypothesis to be tested when addressing the primary research question: not 'what should we do?' – there is ample evidence for this – but 'how should we do it and how should we encourage and enable everyone to join in?'

Interestingly, uncertainty in smartness can be harnessed in the interplay of different concepts that are embedded the 'gamification of smart' – a term used herein to mean the use of serious gaming to deliver 'truly smart' outcomes. Given that this will throw new light on the situation, the research question was extended to: '...and might this lead to further innovations in implementing true smartness alongside technologies that aim to engage users in more sustainable, resilient and liveable practices?'. This research aims to make the case for the adoption of gamification methods in delivering truly smart cities. Attempting to achieve this using a systematic review methodology failed, primarily due to the contested nature of the term 'smart' and the diverse languages used (especially around the concept of liveability), the universality of claims made and the multiple literatures in which the answer sits (Cavada, Rogers, and Hunt 2014). The authors therefore conducted a narrative review – a standard engineering approach – to address the research question.

In any specific urban context, actions towards liveability should be included in real-life scenarios alongside the demand for high-tech (supposedly smart) solutions to problems in cites. Smart city gamification provides evidence of the conceptualisation of liveability as it advances, and reinforces the truism that city decision-makers need to acknowledge societal, environmental, economic, and governance interdependencies when devising and implementing civil interventions. It should make explicit the consequences of alternative actions in terms of sustainability and resilience, as well as liveability (Rogers 2018). In short, serious gaming for citizen 'players' dealing with real scenarios in urban contexts is a powerful potential enabler of delivery of city futures incorporating 'truly smart' interventions. Alignment with citizen aspirations and co-creation of the interventions with citizens would ensure that they would be embraced by citizens and society, and therefore work effectively.

Any analysis of future cities needs a context, and this research has consequently considered 'Location Based Games' (LBGs) since context is crucial to true smartness. The authors aim to provide a foundation for future research in serious gaming, allowing urban interventions to be understood in relation to sustainability, resilience and liveability and become widely accessible using gaming methodologies (Rogers et al. 2012). These concepts are now widely accepted. Smartness, on the contrary, is a term not fully capturing its potential, given the multiple interpretations of its meaning (Cavada, Rogers, and Hunt 2014; Yigitcanlar 2015; Yigitcanlar, Kamruzzaman, et al. 2019). Figure 1 shows a simple illustration of

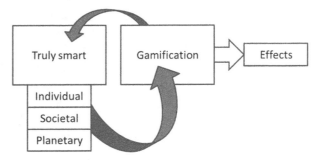

Figure 1. A simplified structure to explore true smartness via gamification.

the structure of this paper: the three elements of truly smart cities (individual, societal, and planetary health & wellbeing) that underpin true smartness are explored iteratively using gamification (for example, applying technologies, policies or practices) such that positive effects are generated in the urban context in question.

While arguments for, and means of delivery of, sustainability and resilience are well rehearsed, more attention needs to be paid to the smart city concept in terms of liveability. Smartness therefore needs to be seen through the lens of liveability, without which a smart initiative is in danger of falling into the realm of a digital service provision (Cavada, Rogers, and Hunt 2014; Cavada, Tight, and Rogers 2019). Liveability was captured in a 5-year study entitled 'Liveable Cities: Transforming the Engineering of Cities to Deliver Societal and Planetary Wellbeing' (Liveable Cities 2019). This major research programme explored the fundamental city engineering needed for the betterment of living in urban areas across disciplines including engineering, economics, architecture, geography, environmental science and social science. It used methodologies that crossed these disciplines, manifestly advancing towards transdisciplinarity, to address cities as holistic systems. For convenience, the research team viewed its assessment of city performance through Societal, Environmental, Economic, and Governance Lenses (Leach, Lee, Hunt, et al. 2017, Liveable Cities 2019), yet acknowledging that these perspectives are all highly interdependent.

However, truly smart cities are not just visionary; it is practical implementation of engineering interventions that leads to the betterment of urban living. A good example is sharing schemes (which might or might not benefit from digitalisation) to support the four lenses of liveability in city living at a local scale (Boyko et al. 2017; Yigitcanlar et al. 2018; Yigitcanlar, Foth et al. 2019). Whatever the scale of the intervention, its implementation should generate value and this value needs to be captured in one or more (alternative) business models (Bouch et al. 2018). Engineered solutions (or in the smart city realm, city initiatives) should be seen as holistic – cutting across different sectors – and resilient – ensuring that they are equally effective in future cities under different circumstances or contexts (Cavada, Hunt, and Rogers 2017a; Lombardi et al. 2012). This paper explores the literature on smart cities in relation to both liveability and gamification as a methodology that has the potential to be an effective delivery mechanism.

2. Methodology for the gamification for truly smart cities

Previous research on smart cities has aimed to assess the meaning of smartness, for which a rigorous review of the ever-changing morph was required (Anthopoulos 2017; Cavada, Hunt, and Rogers 2014; Yigitcanlar 2018). This paper focuses on exploring cities that are truly smart and the practices that aim to make them so, and how future research in serious gaming might help (Cavada, Tight, and Rogers 2019). Several review methodologies have explored the subject as a combination of research components, seeking to consider the opportunities for gaming in a rigorous manner by considering it in context, using approaches such as 'mapping', 'qualitative evidence synthesis', or 'umbrella', all of which can be exploited once the research has matured (Grant and Booth 2009; Xiao and Watson 2019). Similarly, an 'integrative' or 'systematic' review would be appropriate when the proposed combination of the components being addressed in this paper (cities, liveability, true smartness and serious gaming) are grounded, and data can be extracted and analysed thematically to provide a comprehensive approach (Tranfield, Denyer, and Smart 2003; Whittermore and Knafl 2005). However, for reasons articulated above this is not yet possible.

Accordingly, this paper provides a solid foundation on which to translate tangible true smartness into city contexts using gamification technologies. To do this, it adopts a 'narrative' review of the literature to describe the baseline fundamentals required for story-telling of this concept (Angelidou and Psaltoglou 2017; Grant and Booth 2009). Building upon the combination of the two primary research elements (truly smart cities and gamification), it provides narrative evidence to formulate future synthesis and appropriate data interpretations. To understand the combination of the two, the structure of this paper captures this narrative in three steps:

(1) Set the context of 'true smartness' (achieved in the Introduction)
(2) Conduct a narrative review and describe the findings of the research (in terms of the outcomes from Location Based Games)
(3) Draw lessons from the findings (achieved in the Discussion and Conclusions)

The objectives of this research are to understand the beneficial impacts of Location Based Games (LBGs) explore these impacts and then use this understanding to support the gamification of truly smart cities. To meet these objectives, the methodology follows two steps: explore the literature on LBGs, and evaluate the gamification process in relation to the creation of truly smart cities. The literature was initially extracted using the Web of Sciences platform and employing the terms 'smart cities gamification' and 'location based technologies smart cities', and highly-cited publications were reviewed. An initial selection was made according to 'individual, societal, and planetary' impacts of gamification referred to in the abstract and conclusions of each academic, peer-reviewed publication. This was done to avoid general findings on smartness or digitalisations, and to specifically focus on the effects matching the 'truly smart cities' conceptualisation. This provided the leads to other essential aspects of the narrative where different uses of language might have rendered papers being overlooked.

3. Impacts of location based games (LBGs)

3.1. Types of LBGs

A widely-accepted interpretation of the term 'game' is that it explains the experience of an individual or member of a team, and thus gaming has been observed to be a positive participation strategy (Fasce 2014). With the support of contemporary technology, the gaming industry has been able to expand in terms of multimedia, types of games, and ways of participation and interaction. Innovative technologies have been integrated in digital networks – for example, the Location Based Services Network (LBSN) has provided the foundation for social media and online location games connecting the geo-location of the user/gamer to the virtual (online) location. This becomes a part of the 'online existence' of the gamer's spatial exploration (Saker and Evans 2016a, 2016b). An initial characterisation of such games would classify them into three main groups: (i) unfolding stories, (ii) social media, and (iii) replication of the real world (Imbellone, Botte1, and Medaglia 2015).

In the first category, for example, PokemonGO, an online gaming app, develops a storyline depending on geo-location, requiring players to chase and catch computer-generated mythical creatures which appear on their smartphone screens (Clark and Clark 2016). This blends the story with the physical environment, theoretically enhancing social interaction and way-finding in the urban context, and has been shown to enhance social ties between players and the game context (Garrido et al. 2017; Saker and Evans 2018). Papangelis et al. (2017a, 2017b) developed a mobile game named 'Conquering the City', an application that tests the location for its qualities. Here gamers can post online their own interpretation of the given city context ('claim it' from other gamers), which offers the ability to analyse the communication – mostly path exploration and communication between players.

In the second category, Foursquare (similar to Twitter and Facebook) allows participants to digitally inscribe their geo-location along with other users, using information, commentary, or images of the place (Saker 2016; Leighton and Saker 2018). This information is transcribed onto a digital map and could be used to analyse contextual information on a micro-scale (due to the brief, shared information). Often this is a complex matter of distinguishing the kind of information that is valuable (Likhyani et al. 2015; Vasconcelos, Almeida, and Gonçalves 2015; Zhou and Zhang 2016).

The third category includes city simulation games (with SimCity being far the most played), which Adams (1997, 385, 391) consider to be 'abstract notions of urban development built into the simulation and its response patterns … a visual vocabulary' and not to require different skills to other games. It involves a digital topographical space where the player combines systems (of infrastructure services and the built environment) to construct and develop an imaginary urban context (White 1992). Often, the urban context mimics the reality of car-dependency, which is a mainstream urban perception and one that is far from the contemporary thinking on more sustainable, resilient and liveable modes of transport. Including radical transformations of people movement in cities would be a valuable advancement for city simulation games (Bereitschaft 2016; Cecchini and Rizzi 2001; Sukhov 2016).

According to Woessner (2015), city simulation gaming is not a collaborative process, but one that turns the individual gamer into a mayoral figure. Gamers thus follow their own decision-making strategy without political influences, based on either their personal opinions (which might or might not have any basis in education or skill) or an obscured image which they wish to portray whilst playing (Atkinson and Willis 2009; Wohn and Wash 2013).

City gaming in general offers the experience of the positive effects of a game and realisation of city complexity. It delivers a sense accomplishment and develops a better understanding of city governance and the human implications of city living (Lin and Lin 2017; Leach, Mulhall et al. 2019). City simulation uses LBG technologies, similar to those used in commercial sectors to deliver cost and time efficiencies, and sometimes to predict potential risk in projects (Bangert 2013).

3.2. Way-finding technology for LBGs

LBGs mostly use Geographic Information Systems (GIS), a computer system which collects and displays geographical data. GIS has been used extensively as a tool to show real time datasets from the built environment, for example to assess energy use (Li et al. 2016;

Monika, Srinivasan, and Reindl 2015; Togawa et al. 2016), and thereby to ground city decision-making. The possibilities offered by GIS are enormous, considering the 'big data' now available (and the potential for combination of datasets to reach conclusions), and this is particularly true in relation to shared infrastructures offering a novel understanding how cities operate (Tao 2013; Virrantaus et al. 2002; Yue et al. 2015; Zhao et al. 2016). GIS has offered urban reasoning for strategic decision-making in fields ranging from military purposes (one can relate this to strategy games) to counteracting air pollution. It has also featured in theoretical implementations, such as the Filomena, Verstegena, and Manley (2019) qualitative approach to the (urban) Lynch study, which describes urban nodes with the aim of urban digitalisation. This is, of course, part of and adds to way-finding gaming technology (Ahlqvist et al. 2012; Ahlqvist, Khodke, and Rammath 2018; Kose, Erbas, and Ersen 2017; Khan et al. 2019).

Almost two decades ago, Batty (1997) perceived the future urban context as a single digital entity, which opened up a new dimension for seeing all varieties of opportunities way before the smart city movement was widely popular. Today, however, this happens sporadically. For example, private organisations (Arcadis's Digital Twins; Gupte 2019), city municipalities and some individuals (gamers, perhaps, some of them) are able to access parts of the digital city (Shennan 2018). This leaves a huge unexplored opportunity for citizens' participation in the public realm, not only as clients of real-time data geo-location, but by seizing the opportunity (or alternatively, their civic right) to experience, understand and explore the city as a whole and become part of the decision-making process (Medaglia 2007).

More specifically, GIS technology has advanced the deployment of sensors into cities' systems, making these systems easier to manage (Hancke, Silva, and Hancke 2013) and less susceptible to risk, and reducing costs for those who manage them. In the next section, the impacts of city gamification are explored, both in terms of envisaging the challenges of and revealing the opportunities for the (truly) smart city.

3.3. Societal, individual, and technological impacts of LBGs

We see PokemonGO as the most representative example of city simulation mixed with realistic contexts: it involves physical activity and at the same time enables socialising with other players. This fosters both collaboration and learning about the urban environment (Nigaglioni 2017), and is in contrast with physical activity known as the 'Pikachu effect' (Kaczmarek et al. 2017).

Within such a system, new interaction methods among individuals (or teams) can potentially lead to further exploration and development of learning environments. This is especially relevant in generating interest in innovative technologies in younger generations (Nigaglioni 2017).

Along with the opportunities, way-finding presents challenges, as happens with many innovative technologies. Way-finding games' challenges include numerous game (or device) updates and economic prerequisites for continuing the excitement of the game, even when the initial enthusiasm fades or where continuation of success cannot be sustained (Althoff, White, and Horvitz 2016). Despite parents' distress at the risks that augmented reality games pose (where kids could focus on their screens, rather on the physical environment, and might get injured as a result), family interactions seem to benefit from joint PokemonGO hunting. In addition, it can provide contextual exploration, a practice that could offer multiple benefits in future cities (Lindqvist et al. 2018). On a personal level, challenges relate to age and gender limitations, and/or even local disruption at popular locations, along with the siloed approach (and compromised value?) that is often adopted by private organisations and those who manage the system (Yue et al. 2015).

3.4. Societal effects

Recent research points to positive societal effects of gamification in terms of health where outdoor activity is required while playing, in contrast to the playing of Virtual Reality (VR) video-games indoors. Lucas, Shrager, and Winograd (2017) consider the new type of Augmented Reality (AR) gaming, which motivates contextual interaction and connections with fellow gamers. Although it cannot solely be responsible for behavioural change, due to the temporal character of almost every AR game (Nigg, Mateo, and An 2017), it will undoubtedly help. However, the positive effects of gamification at a city-scale are not yet fully explored – can a VR or AR game affect the city entity? Currently, some elements can be considered to play a societal role. A 'good city', according to Amin (2006), considers social value to play a central role in local governance. It is certainly true that citizens are usually connected emotionally to cities – at the very least, by what they experience through their senses – and this can lead to more sustainable and smart attitudes (Belanche, Casaló, and Orús 2016). However smart city products have not always addressed the citizenry as a whole: many of them (*smart cards*, for example) are not used by everyone and thus do not provide benefits to all individuals (Belanche, Casaló, and Flavián 2014).

As an example, Ahas and Mark (2005) refer to the 'Social Positioning Method (SPM)' – a place- and real-time-specific method that is used for social observations, which can affect decision-making and have an input into urban planning policy. Poplin (2012) describes 'Next-Campus', a game approach to evaluate stakeholders' views on a proposed campus relocation (in Hamburg, Germany). It explores views on potential scenarios in terms of cost, building use and other more general influences. While the views thus solicited were never intended to dictate final decisions, the game was introduced as part of a process of encouraging participation and iterative evaluation, and thus has some influence on the final decisions on the campus move. Another example concerns gamifying diagnostics ('QuesTInSitu: The Game'), a game that has helped to present data to support self-assessment in education. This uses visualisations to 'interact trends with students' (Melero et al. 2015).

These digital tools could provide a contemporary way for individual expression of the complex city environment, in contrast to Proshansky's (1978, 165) view that digitalisation has a negative connotation of one's existence in the city. The urban context, he believes, is a complex urban system in which citizens are characterised by a *nexus* of city senses. As we see today, digital technologies have shifted the route of cities in time and the current automation of city systems is a reality. However, digital systems have a huge energy footprint and this brings its own adverse consequences, at least to the climate change challenge (Batty and Xie 1999). Furthermore, paediatricians have called for guiding principles on safety, specifically in relation to physical or criminal actions (Serino et al. 2016). Jung, Jo, and Park (2015) suggest that safety procedures should be implemented in the existing infrastructure of location-based services and games.

The gamification of cities might therefore introduce current urban challenges at a digital level, or in terms of locations of conflict and/or groups or individuals who associate with urban cultural territories, while innovative technologies might yield problems that are not yet envisaged. However, innovative technologies also offer opportunities for understanding, and forecasting, and provide solutions for both the city as a whole and the individual gamer.

3.5. Individual effects (and self-identity in gamification)

Location-based technologies offer the user the opportunity to represent themselves and their choices online as individuals – game identity here is related to the locational context of the game (Papangelis et al. 2017c; Saker 2016). These participants communicate and make personal decisions based on the visual representation of space: they can claim special knowledge of space (twitter 'mayorship') and they can see where their peers are at a certain moment in time, and this in turn can bring an element of accomplishment in the game (Saker and Frith 2018). Schwartz and Halegoua (2015) suggest that such a digital self-paradigm is the reflection of one's aspirational online self; one that relates its existence according to its location and provides traceable historical evidence. They note that this can be an accurate representation in terms of context (map, images, or opinions). However, as Schwartz and Halegoua (2015) notes, the user's intentions might differ from reality. Often participants (similar to internet and social media behaviour) represent themselves in the virtual world of gaming in a different way to one that reflects their real-life behaviour. In this case, their online persona fits their aspirations or the rules of the game they are playing, and does not necessarily help in providing a view on how a city might become truly smart in reality, and indeed might hinder it.

This is an attitude that has been expressed also in online purchases and payment (Kim, Chan, and Kankanhalli 2012) i.e. an individual uses virtual purchases which fit their online persona. Although this is a private action, such individual transactions are nevertheless part of the wider digitalisation agenda – in terms of governance, the digital system is still very much a top-down decision-making process. In the case for the gamification of smart cities, therefore, there are lessons to be drawn from governance and control of the banking system model (Au and Kauffman 2008). This further reinforces the observation that similar to the individual use of the internet, online action is personalised rather than a collective shift to digitalisation (Brunsting and Postmes 2002).

When digital solutions are addressing matters at a personal level and applied in life scenarios (for example applications in health), they show an increased level of worth, thereby building stronger ties between participants and offering the opportunity to measure participant attitudes in pertinent (e.g. health emergency) situations (Schmitz et al. 2015). An interesting example here concerns the use of a virtual application ('Route Mate'), which was developed to support in real-time those with disabilities, offering alternative travelling choices that can change the expected collective behaviour and ultimately improve liveability for an otherwise potentially disenfranchised section of the citizenry (Brown et al. 2011). Similarly, technologies can be used to improve memory using senses, for example sound (Vemuri et al. 2004), which can have further implications for the use of sensescapes in the city and their selective enhancement.

It has been observed that the way that a gamer senses the context or their online selves does not equal representation of the real world. There is a perception that playing might bring personal online risk and gamers want to protect their identity. In order to support privacy (and mitigate the risks), non-realistic characters can be integrated by the system, thereby changing the parameters, or players can appear at non-existent locations. This can be viewed as protection of the individual gamer, or any other personal data (Liu et al. 2013), but it alters the outcome of the game. This means that altered elements are part of the game dataset, leading to outcomes that are not realistic.

A pretend virtual location can easily change, and indeed can also become more detailed due to the constant improvement in game features and wearable technology (Bedford et al. 2004). Additionally, a pretend character or location can develop a storyline which gives the individual the potential to act differently in the given scenario, meaning that this could be an educational tool if the game is morally constructive (Mariani and Spallazzo 2016).

Research on personal context showed that the public is likely to use way-finding technologies (say, in transport scenarios) since they ground the activity, although it seems that younger generations are mostly at ease with digital skills (Ho 2012). These required skills, however, are not yet part of a recognised curriculum (at least in city engineering education), but it is evident that they could provide encouragement, especially to younger generations, to engage in serious gaming to produce valuable societal outcomes (Giedd 2012; Minsung and Jungyeop 2016). The effects of gamification, Giedd continues, are not yet fully understood and we are not entirely sure how it will unfold in the future. Other authors, however, report that individual gaming responses can lead to accurate estimations behaviours, for example group dynamics and behavioural patterns using rewards and predictive actions (Avrahami, Guth, and Kareev 2005; Morschheuser et al. 2017).

3.6. Gamification technology for current smart cities

Game exploration for advancing smart cities could prove challenging, or perhaps less effective than anticipated, because we are neither fully aware of smart city 'limitations' nor of the full range of possibilities that technology offers. Looking at the current technological trends influencing the city provide clues, of course, but the fields of sensing, monitoring and application of AI are developing rapidly and the future technological applications are as yet unknown in their entirety and

potential. This suggests that 'smart initiatives' should be nimble, i.e. continually reviewed and adapted to latest developments in technology and contextual change.

Boulos et al. (2017) suggest that technological implementations can provide a basis for the smart city in the form of a sharing platform that supports local governance (or indeed, large organisations). This would also benefit citizens (social, health, safety, even data interrogation are some of the possibilities) provided that participants are skill-literate and willing to share personal information (L'Heureux 2015; L'Heureux et al. 2017). Looking beyond the analytical possibilities for smartness using existing and emerging data, technology needs to respond to higher-level conceptualisation challenges and requirements of the skillset to 'play the game' or their continuous advancement (Zica, Ionica, and Leba 2017).

This discussion raises the question: how will technology lead future developments? In this respect, a collective system of interoperable technologies should be holistically integrated in terms of their infrastructure and governance (Delmastro, Arnaboldi, and Conti 2016). It is likely that once such a system is in place to support the development of a (truly) smart city, it can support a joint citizen-city decision making procedure that delivers on the aspirations of both (i.e. marrying both top-down and bottom-up aspirations, see Rogers and Hunt 2019) and possibly one that is visualised in real-time (Raper et al. 2007).

At a smaller scale, smart city initiatives have developed solutions that (intentionally, or not) adopted gamification methods; for example, car-sharing schemes which claim to reduce CO_2 levels (Olszewski, Pałka, and Turek 2018). Virtual Reality (VR) is a strong tool because it visually influences people, and thus should be used for issues that have a positive effect in society (Sakamoto, Alexandrova, and Nakajima 2015). Various technologies that are associated with VR (and other software systems used in spatial representation) align with the technical requirements of the stakeholder – for example planners, engineers, and local authorities – but these are not integrated into a single system that supports social ties and real-time communication, and one that is available for use by individuals (Saker and Frith 2019).

Therefore, although VR has been used by professionals to recreate contexts since the 1980s, mostly for clients or services, the more relevant term now is 'serious games' since they go farther in helping communication with clients and complex decision-making (Jamei et al. 2017). The relevance to the technologies of what is considered smart is highly relevant, because digital technology supports the idea of becoming 'smart' mostly because things can now be quantified and built into a system that is faster and more efficient than traditional processes (Anthopoulos 2017). However, this narrow thinking presents unforeseen challenges, both for the system itself but mostly for those are affected by it (Miorandi et al. 2012). GIS offers smart city possibilities to geo-locate and quantify smart city parameters: for example, to minimise adverse consequences (urban areas that demand attention due to criminal or anti-social activity) or enhance positive consequences (providing opportunities for low-carbon transportation; Togawa et al. 2016). To improve this situation further, if a city that aspires to be smarter adopts elements of gamification, citizens, as gamers, could make decisions based on their positive experience and influenced by their personal sensation of the city (Opromolla et al. 2014).

The above review shows that the literature exhibits many discrete individual, societal, and technological features relevant to the gamification sphere. As Table 1 demonstrates, there are positive aspects in each of these three domains that relate to true smartness on some level. For example, energy and low-carbon aspects contribute directly to the planetary wellbeing agenda, while others (e.g. car sharing schemes) support both the individual & societal and planetary wellbeing agendas. Nevertheless it is evident that gamification primarily tends to operate in an individual context 'looking out towards society' rather that providing holistic

benefits for planetary wellbeing unless the 'game' is specifically directed towards planetary wellbeing outcomes (i.e. seeking to change behaviours to deliver environmentally-beneficial outcomes). The technology features in general provide the enabler of benefit delivery (Cavada, Hunt, and Rogers 2016).

However, useful though Table 1 is in crystallising arguments in the literature, the goal of gamification should reach beyond the siloed categorisation employed in Table 1 towards a holistic approach, one that strategically integrates individual, societal and planetary wellbeing. For this to happen, these three strands of wellbeing need to shape the development of the enabling technology, ensuring that smart city initiatives offer the potential of aspects such as civic rights and environmental respect to underpin the *genius loci* of the urban space.

4. Discussion

4.1. Gamification in truly smart cities

The literature has clearly demonstrated that the practicalities inherent in geo-location games can have an (often profound) impact on individual and group attitudes. With the help of VR and AR technologies, the impact of interventions included in serious gaming can address wider urban challenges at both a societal and an individual level. Specifically, entailing game elements into any interaction with citizens on the creation of smarter cities would entice participants to the game (and the topic area requiring attention) and support citizens in developing skills to be able to use the smart cities systems (Carrasco-Sáez, Butter, and Badilla-Quintana 2017). As argued above, implementing smartness with gamification should extend to city interventions that are truly smart – those aiming to deliver on liveability and overlapping (resilience and sustainability) city agendas, and not solely efficiency due to the use of technology; the latter would be just 'intelligent' (Cavada 2019; Rogers 2018). In addition to a theoretical approach of smartness, a practical approach is required to provide a truly smart foundation in the research agenda for the gamification of truly smart cities.

The authors of this paper suggest that this is best achieved by the use of scenarios. For example, recent research on technologies to support engineering interventions in cities relating to buried utility service provision (conducted at the University of Birmingham, UK) concerned the use of ground-penetrating radar (GPR) and other geophysical devices to detect and map the buried utility infrastructure that lies beneath city streets, current records often being incomplete and/or inaccurate. At first glance, this might seem an

Table 1. Individual, societal, and technology features relevant to gamification.

Individual	Societal	Technology
Self-representation	Health Implications	Potential
Game identity	Contextual interaction	Basis for smart city
Personal decisions	Connect fellow gamers	Sharing platform
Self-accomplishment	Temporal awareness	Local governance
Shaping of the context	Senses experience	Share personal information
Online persona	Urban planning policy	Continuous advancement
Virtual payments	Urban scenarios	Interoperable, Integrated
Real life health scenarios	Encouraging participation	Citizen-city decision-making
Real-time travelling with disabilities	Gamifying diagnostics	Car sharing schemes
Improve memory	Self-assessment	Virtual reality
Personal online risk	Expression of complex city environment	Technical requirement
Non-realistic elements	City automation	Real time communication
Wearable technology	Digital energy footprint	Recreate context
Educational tool	Criminal / anti-social activity	Complex decision-making
Transport scenarios	Digital urban challenges	Quantifiable system
Digital skills	Forecasting	Unforeseen challenges
Behavioural patterns		Identify illegal activity
Rewards		Low-carbon transport
Predictive actions		Sensing and monitoring
Personal sensation of the city		Application of AI

unusual example and yet it has much potential to introduce serious gaming to help in delivering truly smart cities (i.e. improving sustainability, resilience and liveability). This application of serious gaming places the gamer into the role of the city engineer, the person responsible for ensuring the city continues to function effectively in spite of the need for some form of intervention in the buried infrastructure – installing a new utility, or repairing, maintaining or upgrading an existing pipeline or cable.

The gamer is offered alternative opportunities of interventions, including traditional open cut excavations (trenching) and several different types of 'trenchless technologies' that require minimal or zero excavation and occupation of the road space. [Trenchless technologies are far less disruptive and far less damaging than open cut excavations, their direct cost of deployment can be significantly greater, and yet the adverse consequences – in terms of social costs, environmental costs and indirect economic costs – far outweigh the additional direct economic costs. The problem arises in terms of 'who pays and who benefits (directly and indirectly)?'.] The technological developments occurred in the Mapping the Underworld (MTU 2012) and Assessing the Underworld (ATU 2018) projects, and it is in the latter of these that the potential of gamification for behavioural change, participation and sharing has been explored in terms of using remote sensors (and big data) to enhance the resiliency of city systems – knowing where the existing buried infrastructure lies in the urban subsurface, and its physical condition, enables more sustainable and resilient engineering operations to be deployed. This in turn raises the question of the value of the infrastructure assets from an overall perspective (serving society) rather than a single monetary assessment that serves only the interests of the utility service provider (Hojjati et al. 2018). The gamer is exposed to the tensions between industrial organisations that are mandated to make a profit for their shareholders *while providing a public service* and the consequences of their actions to society and on the environment – tensions that exist in very many spheres of business.

This research underpins forthcoming high-level decisions on how we should maintain and upgrade a city's buried utility systems in the face of growing traffic congestion, worsening air quality, seriously deteriorating roads (leading to potholes, damage to vehicles, compromised road safety for cyclists and drivers), and so on – it impacts on the quality of living above ground (there are individual, societal and planetary benefits and disbenefits to balance; see Rogers 2015). Such a feature of a smart city game (e.g. one that aims to achieve people movement with the minimum of harm to citizens,

society and the planet) could result in social, and political, attitudes being turned against unsuitable practices that serve only to save money for private organisations. Superficially counterintuitively perhaps, this is an example of a truly smart city initiative, and one that would complement a suite of other initiatives to improve air quality, reduce traffic congestion and accidents, facilitate active transport (walking and cycling), and so on.

In the engineering context, gamification is seen as a civic model that builds a narrative for city collaboration at a lower level from which ideas emerge 'bottom-up', rather than the default top-down governance which has been typically dictating city systems so far (Rogers et al. 2014). A conceptual framework for a bottom-up approach would evaluate the current operational systems (and heritage) context, and explore beneficial changes to them, by placing the people – that is the users, or gamers – at the core of these systems. Their experiences would help to inform future decisions. However, this can happen only if they are aware of the opportunities (these need to be designed into the game), or even able to engage digitally (for which they require the skills). Yet if serious gaming is thus enabled, the overall societal, and individual, effects of future engineering could be explored (Papangelis, Chamberlain, and Liang 2016; Rogers 2018).

We consider this type of action to be a 'smart initiative', a move towards integration of better services and urban systems by enhancing public participation in their creation and operation (Cavada, Hunt, and Rogers 2017b). Engineers need to think and act truly smart, i.e. in a way that prioritises individual, societal and planetary wellbeing alongside the service that they are seeking to deliver. Truly smart initiatives are those that deliver positive impacts to liveability lenses referred to earlier (Leach et al., 2017; Liveable Cities 2019). These have been specifically assessed in the development of the Smart Model Assessment Resilient Tool (SMART) for true smartness (Cavada 2019; Hargreaves, Cavada, and Rogers 2019) and are discussed hereafter.

4.2. True smartness

Cities have been developing smart agendas as part of their local governance systems for many years. Recent examples can be found in *Smarter London Together* (London, UK; MoL 2018) and Digital Birmingham's *Smart City Roadmap* (Birmingham, UK; DB 2014). Although smart agendas are dynamic (influenced by funding, political cycles, and timeframes), there is sporadic public participation, at least as an objective, in most of them. In a truly smart context, a holistic approach would provide citizen articulation and clarification of the liveability agenda and put people at the centre of city system co-creation (Cavada, Hunt, and Rogers 2017b). Given that the goals of liveability are based strongly on community and individual wellbeing, improved citizen health, meeting citizens' aspirations and cultural benefits would naturally flow from this approach (Liveable Cities 2019).

It can be argued that the foremost effects of smart cities' gamification are societal. These should naturally focus on fairness (equity, inclusivity, etc.), and indeed when they address issues such environmental sustainability they will positively impact on cities to the benefit of all. The point here is that a positive impact on one of the trilogy of individual, societal and planetary wellbeing almost always yields benefits to the others – they are highly interdependent. This in turn means that influencing the city as a result of gamification (the outcome of the game) and at the same time influencing the gamer (changing attitudes and behaviours for the better) would likely provide guidance on how to move towards a truly smarter city.

For example, Birmingham's strategic agenda aimed at life improvement in the city – the *Smart City Roadmap* (DB 2014) – includes several smart city initiatives. Selecting two citizen-centric initiatives: the *Eastern Green Corridor* combines skills, health and investment to improve city living locally (BCC 2018), while the *Birmingham Development Plan* supports urban and population growth, and includes requirements for sustainable living (BCC 2012). Both have features that would appear to advance the liveability agenda in the city, yet both could potentially be enhanced (or otherwise confirmed to be optimal) by the experience of individuals engaged in serious gaming to explore their outcomes from a citizen (gamer) perspective. An initiative with a focus on environmental considerations is found in the Birmingham's *Eastern Growth Corridor* (DB 2019a), and this likewise would benefit from the outcomes of serious gaming. Furthermore, any gamification approach that links to the environmental considerations of cities could (and should) also combine considerations of individual and societal wellbeing, and moreover should provide opportunities to overlap with the Sustainable Development Goals (SGDs; UN 2015).

Similarly, in London, UK, actions such as *London's Smart Park Sustainable Districts* to expand the sustainable capabilities of the Queen Elizabeth Olympic Park (MoL 2015a), *Sensing London* that involves the deployment of sensor technologies to assess air quality (MoL 2015b), London's *Living Lab* employing technologies to enable environmental evaluation of a particular site (MoL 2014a), and *Hyde Park Sensing* that uses yet another set of sensing technologies to test environmental qualities of the ground, air, and water conditions with the aim of enhancing the quality of living that city parks offer (Mol 2014b) would all benefit from the experiences of individuals engaged in context-dependent gaming (LBGs).

There is a further consideration that has deliberately been overlooked in the discussions so far. This is the third pillar of sustainability: economy. Societal and environmental considerations affect the economy, both generally in a city-wide context and in terms of individual business development that can support the shift towards a truly smart city. For this, financial goals should target sustainable financing, i.e. financing that supports 'green' solutions separately from economic growth. Copenhagen is an example of a smart city that has developed a system of green economy (CoC 2018). Some UK examples from smart agendas seek to develop financial support to local businesses, such as the *Greater Birmingham Digital Academy* that aims to provide acceleration for local businesses (DB 2019b), the *Small Business Digital Capability Challenge Fund* given to local business for upgrading their digital systems (DB 2019c) and the *Birmingham Smart City Alliance*, a group of local businesses set up for the purposes of collaboration and development of data (IA 2018). These would appear superficially to sit far from the liveability agenda; yet devising a serious game around influencing the local economy could yield unexpected benefits by changing the initiative's design or operation. Likewise *Energy Smart City Opportunities for London*, an energy strategy developed by Arup (Buscher, Doody, and Dimireva 2016) to foster collaborations between local business and universities, and the *Singapore Networked Trade Platform*, an on online system to support business to develop solutions in the energy market (GovTech 2019a), could benefit from gamification.

Finally, governance is one of the pillars of liveability (Liveable Cities 2019) and the basis for developing truly smart agendas. In order to implement solutions that are truly smart, cities need to enhance governmental systems that ensure fair governance and support public participation (Granier and Kudo 2016; Simonofski et al. 2017). Often, a city gets funding from national or European reserves, which means that smart initiatives are developed according to a competition between cities (EC 2018a, 2018b). This paper proposes the consideration of truly smart practices that ensure governance systems going beyond established political agendas and their timescales: a gamification approach that amplifies public participation to help shape policy.

One of the latest updates in the smart agenda that supports public participation is the *New London Plan*, the updated version addressing urban development challenges and regulating solutions (MoL 2019). However, governance examples vary in their effectiveness and reach. Good examples include Singapore's *Whole of Government 'Ask Jamie'* online service to enable citizen participation in governance (GovTech 2019b), while *Singapore Personal Access (SingPass)* gives citizens the ability to access government information online (Gov-Tech 2019c). While these initiatives are laudable, practices are needed to support a bottom-up approach to influence governance rather than simply providing a collective citizens' data system (Cavada, Tight, and Rogers 2019). Serious gaming could undoubtedly help here.

5. Conclusions

To answer the research question of how gamification can realise truly smart cities, this paper has explored the literature on gamification. While the review process started with the use of keywords ('smart cities gamification' and 'location based technologies smart cities'), a narrative review was conducted to extend the reach and enrich the picture of opportunities and challenges associated with the multi-dimensional complexity of city engineering. While the outcomes of gamification will necessarily need to integrate with other approaches to city engineering and governance (e.g. digital twins of cities and policy development), both of these domains would benefit from a gamification approach to explore the individual, societal, and planetary wellbeing effects of interventions from the perspective of the individual – the gamer. Most importantly, this personalised approach to digitalisation and smart cities has the effect of educating, and thereby almost certainly changing attitudes and behaviours, of the individual. This in turn will shape the outcomes of the game and has the potential to shape city engineering interventions and policy development and implementation.

This paper adds to existing literature of city gamification by exploring the benefits for truly smart cities. It is a narrative exploration of gamification in truly smart cities. It explored the ways that gamification (and related recreational technologies) can be used to understand the effects of 'smart initiatives' on cities and their operation. It was found that gamification has considerable potential to affect individual and societal practices, while technology and the game design itself play a central role to how gamification is implemented and used. When using digital geo-location systems, gamers interact with each other and the context where the game takes place. In this space, users can develop an advanced level of personality, often with educational enhancement, supporting real-time societal actions. This gives the opportunity for further exploration and implementation of (truly) smart actions, drawing the gamer into the role of citizen co-creator of

cities and their systems. In particular, way-finding technologies can be used in combination with civil interventions to make systems self-explanatory and accessible to all.

The literature showed that when considering serious gaming to develop smart cities, there is less appreciation of the need for actions that enhance planetary wellbeing. This should be consciously addressed to provide holistic benefits for true smartness. The reporting and discussion of the narrative review therefore provides an answer to the 'how should we do it?' question posed in this paper. Gamification methods (and the technology that supports it) provides the enabling step to develop opportunities for citizen co-creation of urban systems and provides an answer to the 'and how should we encourage and enable everyone to join in?'

The paper has demonstrated that using digital technologies (or simply playing the games) has the potential to positively influence both individual and societal wellbeing. Way-finding games, in particular, have positive impacts due to local context exploration and strengthening family (and friends') ties, and can provide additional educational benefits (Lindqvist et al. 2018). However, the full potential of way-finding games and the extent of their effects are not clear, even if there is currently substantial evidence that they are beneficial. Game-like technologies in health or mobility, which are likewise undoubtedly beneficial at some level, have yet to explore in detail the scalability potential for the truly smart city.

In exploring some of the actions in certain city's smart agendas that promise ethically constructive outcomes, it was evident these could provide some shared benefits across the trilogy of individual, societal and planetary wellbeing, and yet serious gaming could help to widen and deepen these benefits. The conclusion here is that gamification in tandem with true smartness should aim to overlap all liveability lenses and wellbeing benefits.

We propose that way-finding games should be developed as tools for participation (and enjoyment) in helping to bring about truly smart cities. They should be designed, and their outcomes utilised, to shape smart initiatives and actions that benefit the societal, environmental, economic and governance goals that all cities have. This approach to gamification should lead to a combination of actions (smart initiatives) that place people at the core, enabling exploration of the complexity of what it means to be truly smart, and providing educational and participatory benefits to the gamers. Taking this argument farther, serious gaming provides a means of citizen co-creation of (truly) smarter cities by providing a bottom-up approach to combine with the top-down approach necessarily provided by those who govern the city. This addresses the final part of the research question: ' … and might this lead to further innovations in implementing true smartness alongside technologies that aim to engage users in more sustainable, resilient and liveable practices?'. A scenario to illustrate this drawn from research into buried utility service provision has been used to illustrate the power of serious gaming in introducing the gamer to the tensions between industrial imperatives and societal and environmental protection when considering public service provision. By designing serious games with sustainability, resilience and liveability agendas in mind, encouraging widespread citizen participation as gamers, and taking cognisance of the outcomes, both (truly) smarter citizens and (truly) smarter cities would result.

Acknowledgements

The authors gratefully acknowledge the financial support of the UK Engineering and Physical Sciences Research Council under grant numbers EP/F065965 (*Mapping The Underworld*), EP/F007426 (*Designing Resilient Cities–Urban Futures*), EP/K012398 (*iBUILD*), EP/K021699 (*Assessing The Underworld*), EP/J017698 (*Liveable Cities–Transforming the Engineering of Cities to Deliver Societal and Planetary Wellbeing*), EP/N010523 (*Self-Repairing Cities–Balancing the impact of City Infrastructure Engineering on Natural Systems using Robots*), and EP/P002021 (*Urban Living Birmingham*), and the University of Birmingham for funding the *Policy Commission on Future Urban Living*.

Disclosure statement

No potential conflict of interest was reported by the authors.

Funding

This work was supported by Assessing The Underworld [grant number EP/K021699]; Mapping The Underworld [grant number EP/F065965]; iBUILD [grant number EP/K012398]; UKCRIC Coordination Node [grant number EP/R017727]; Self-Repairing Cities [grant number EP/N010523]; Liveable Cities [grant number EP/J017698].

ORCID

C. D. F. Rogers ⓘ http://orcid.org/0000-0002-1693-1999

References

Adams, P. C. 1997. "Software Review: SimCity." *Cities (london, England)* 14 (6): 383–392. PIh S0264-2751 (97)00030-9. Pergamon.

Ahas, R., and U. Mark. 2005. "Location Based Services—New Challenges for Planning and Public Administration?" *Futures* 37: 547–561.

Ahlqvist, O., N. Khodke, and R. Ramnath. 2018. "GeoGame Analytics – A Cyber-Enabled Petri Dish for Geographic Modeling and Simulation." *Computers, Environment and Urban Systems* 67: 1–8.

Ahlqvist, O., J. Ramanathan, T. Loffing, and A. Kocher. 2012. "Geospatial Human-Environment Simulation Through Integration of Massive Multiplayer Online Games and Geographic Information Systems." *Transactions in GIS* 16 (3): 331–350.

Althoff, T., R. W. White, and E. Horvitz. 2016. "Influence of Pokémon Go on Physical Activity: Study and Implications." *Journal of Medical Internet Research* 18 (12): e315. http://www.jmir.org/2016/12/e315/.

Amin, A. 2006. "The Good City." *Urban Studies* 43 (5–6): 1009–1023. doi:10.1080/00420980600676717.

Angelidou, M., and A. Psaltoglou. 2017. "An Empirical Investigation of Social Innovation Initiatives for Sustainable Urban Development." *Sustainable Cities and Society* 33: 113–125.

Anthopoulos, L. 2017. "Understanding Smart Cities – A tool for Smart Government or an Industrial Trick?" *Public Administration and Information Technology*, Vol. 22. New York: Springer Science and Business Media. ISBN: 978-3-319-57014-3 (Print) 978-3-319-57015-0 (Online). https://link.springer.com/book/10.1007%2F978-3-319-57015-0.

Atkinson, R., and P. Willis. 2009. "Transparent Cities: Re-Shaping the Urban Experience Through Interactive Video Game Simulation." *City* 13 (4): 403–417.

ATU. 2018. "Assessing the Underworld." Accessed September 25, 2019. www.assessingtheunderworld.org.

Au, Y. A., and R. J. Kauffman. 2008. "The Economics of Mobile Payments: Understanding Stakeholder Issues for an Emerging Financial Technology Application." *Electronic Commerce Research and Applications* 7 (2): 141–164.

Avrahami, J., W. Guth, and Y. Kareev. 2005. "Games of Competition in a Stochastic Environment." *Theory and Decision* 59: 255–294.

Bangert, M. 2013. "'Simulation City' Software and Analysis." *Quality Magazine* 038-QM0813-FT-software.indd.

Batty, M. 1997. "The Computable City." *International Planning Studies* 2 (2): 155–173.

Batty, M., and Y. Xie. 1999. "Self-organized Criticality and Urban Development." *Discrete Dynamics in Nature and Society* 3: 109–124.

BCC. 2018. *Eastern Corridor Smart Demonstrator.* Birmingham City Council. Accessed January 19, 2019. http://digitalbirmingham.co.uk/project/east-birmingham-smart-city-demontrator/.

BCC (Birmingham City Council). 2012. *Birmingham Development Plan. Planning for Birmingham's Growing Population*. Birmingham Plan 2031.

Bedford, S., W. Seager, M. Flintham, R. Anastasi, D. Rowland, J. Humble, D. Stanton, et al. 2004. "The Error of Our Ways: The Experience of Self-Reported Position in a Location-Based Game." In '*UbiComp 2004: Ubiquitous Computing' 6th International Conference Nottingham, UK, Proceedings*, edited by N. Davies, Mynatt El, and I. Siio, 70–87.

Belanche, D., L. V. Casaló, and C. Flavián. 2014. "The Role of Place Identity in Smart Card Adoption." *Public Management Review* 16 (8): 1205–1228.

Belanche, D., L. V. Casaló, and C. Orús. 2016. "City Attachment and Use of Urban Services: Benefits for Smart Cities." *Cities (london, England)* 50: 75–81.

Bereitschaft, B. 2016. "Gods of the City? Reflecting on City Building Games as an Early Introduction to Urban Systems." *Journal of Geography* 115 (2): 51–60.

Bouch, C. J., C. D. F. Rogers, M. J. Powell, and D. A. C. Horsfall. 2018. "Developing Alternative Business Models for Smart Infrastructure: A UK Case Study." *Proceedings of the Institution of Civil Engineers – Smart Infrastructure and Construction* 171 (2): 77–87.

Boulos, M. N. K., Z. Lu, P. Guerrero, C. Jennett, and A. Steed. 2017. "From Urban Planning and Emergency Training to Pokémon Go: Applications of Virtual Reality GIS (VRGIS) and Augmented Reality GIS (ARGIS) in Personal, Public and Environmental Health." *International Journal of Health Geographics* 16: 7.

Boyko, C., S. Clune, R. Cooper, C. Coulton, N. Dunn, S. Pollastri, J. Leach, et al. 2017. "How Sharing Can Contribute to More Sustainable Cities." *Sustainability* 9 (5): 701.

Brown, D. J., D. McHugh, P. Standen, L. Evett, N. Shopland, and S. Battersby. 2011. "Designing Location-Based Learning Experiences for People with Intellectual Disabilities and Additional Sensory Impairments." *Computers and Education* 56: 11–20.

Brunsting, S., and T. Postmes. 2002. "Social Movement Participation in the Digital Age." *Small Group Research* 33 (5), 525–554.

Buscher, V., L. Doody, and I. Dimireva. 2016. *Smart City Opportunities for London.* London: Arup. Greater London Authority.

Carrasco-Sáez, J. S., M. C. Butter, and M. G. Badilla-Quintana. 2017. "The New Pyramid of Needs for the Digital Citizen: A Transition Towards Smart Human Cities." *Sustainability* 9: 2258.

Cavada, M. 2019. "Smart Model Assessment Resilient Tool (SMART): A Tool for Assessing Truly Smart Cities." Doctoral thesis, University of Birmingham, Birmingham, UK. UBIRA. E-thesis.

Cavada, M., D. V. L. Hunt, and C. D. F. Rogers. 2016. "Do Smart Cities Realise Their Potential for Lower Carbon Dioxide Emissions?" *Proceedings of the Institution of Civil Engineers – Engineering Sustainability* 169 (6): 243–252.

Cavada, M., D. V. L. Hunt, and C. D. F. Rogers. 2017a. *The Little Book of Smart Cities.* ISBN: 9780704429499.

Cavada, M., D. V. L. Hunt, and C. D. F. Rogers. 2017b. "The Role of Infrastructure in Smart Cities." In *Proceedings of the International Symposium for Next Generation Infrastructure (ISNGI)*, 72–79. London, UK.

Cavada, M., C. D. F. Rogers, and D. V. L. Hunt. 2014. "Smart Cities: Contradicting Definitions and Unclear Measures." *Forum (chicago, Ill)* 1–30. Sciforum Electronic Conference Series. Vol. 4, 2015, f004. doi:10.3390/wsf-4-f004.

Cavada, M., M. R. Tight, and C. D. F. Rogers. 2019. "A Smart City Case Study of Singapore is Singapore Truly Smart?" In *Smart City Emergence: Cases From Around the World*, 295–314. Elsevier Book Volume.

Cecchini, A., and P. Rizzi. 2001. "Is Urban Gaming Simulation Useful?" *Simulation & Gaming* 32 (4): 507–521.

Clark, A. M., and M. T. Clark. 2016. "Pokémon Go and Research: Qualitative, Mixed Methods Research, and the Supercomplexity of Interventions." *International Journal of Qualitative Methods* 15 (1): 1–3.

CoC. 2018. *Liveable Green City: The Most Liveable City.* City of Copenhagen. Accessed February 20, 2019. https://international.kk.dk/artikel/liveable-green-city.

DB. 2014. *Smart City Roadmap.* Digital Birmingham. Accessed January 9, 2019. http://digitalbirmingham.co.uk/project/the-roadmap-to-a-smarter-birmingham/.

DB. 2019a. *Eastern Corridor Smart Demonstrator.* Digital Birmingham. Accessed February 15, 2019. http://digitalbirmingham.co.uk/project/east-birmingham-smart-city-demontrator/.

DB. 2019b. *The Greater Birmingham Digital Academy.* Digital Birmingham. Accessed February 15, 2019. http://digitalbirmingham.co.uk/project/the-greater-birmingham-digital-academy/.

DB. 2019c. *Small Business Digital Capability Challenge Fund.* Digital Birmingham. Accessed February 15, 2019. http://digitalbirmingham.co.uk/project/small-business-digital-capability-challenge-fund/.

Delmastro, F., V. Arnaboldi, and M. Conti. 2016. "People-centric Computing and Communications in Smart Cities." *IEEE Communications Magazine* 54: 122–128.

EC. 2018a. "The European Capital of Innovation (iCapital) Award." *Research and Innovation Funding Opportunities Prizes.* European Commission. Accessed February 20, 2019. https://ec.europa.eu/info/research-and-innovation/funding/funding-opportunities/prizes/icapital_en.

EC. 2018b. "Horizon 2020 Overview of Funding Programmes." *Funding, Tenders, Funding Programmes.* European Commission. Accessed February 20, 2019. https://ec.europa.eu/info/funding-tenders/funding-opportunities/funding-programmes/overview-funding-programmes_en.

Fasce, F. 2014. "Beyond Serious Games: The Next Generation of Cultural Artifacts." Games and Learning Alliance GALA, 1–4. Revised Selected Papers from the Third International Conference on Games and Learning Alliance – Vol 9221.

Filomena, G., J. A. Verstegena, and E. Manley. 2019. "A Computational Approach to 'The Image of the City." *Cities (london, England)* 89: 14–25.

Garrido, E. G., L. Ferres, D. Caro, and L. Bravo. 2017. "The Effect of Pokémon Go on the Pulse of the City: a Natural Experiment." *EPJ Data Science* 6: 23.

Giedd, N. J. 2012. "The Digital Revolution and Adolescent Brain Evolution." *Journal of Adolescent Health* 51: 101–105.

GOfS. 2019a. *Future of Cities: Science of Cities.* London, UK: Government Office for Science. Accessed July 10, 2019. www.gov.uk/government/publications/future-of-cities-science-of-cities.

GOfS. 2019b. *Future of Cities: An Overview of the Evidence.* London, UK: Government Office for Science. Accessed July 10, 2019. www.gov.uk/government/publications/future-of-cities-overview-of-evidence.

GovTech. 2019a. "Singapore National Trade Platform." Accessed February 10, 2019. https://www.tech.gov.sg/products-and-services/networked-trade-platform/.

GovTech. 2019b. "Ask Jamie." Accessed February 10, 2019. https://www.tech.gov.sg/products-and-services/ask-jamie/.

GovTech. 2019c. "SingPass." *Products and Services.* Accessed February 10, 2019. https://www.tech.gov.sg/products-and-services/singpass/.

Granier, B., and H. Kudo. 2016. "How are Citizens Involved in Smart Cities? Analysing Citizen Participation in Japanese "Smart Communities"." *Information Polity* 21 (1): 61–76.

Grant, M. J., and A. Booth. 2009. "A Typology of Reviews: an Analysis of 14 Review Types and Associated Methodologies." *Health Information and Libraries Journal* 26: 91–108.

Gupte, M. 2019. "Digital Twins: Picking Up Where BIM Leaves Off—and Rushing Straight into the Future." *Arcadis*. Accessed January 24, 2019. https://www.arcadis.com/en/europe/arcadis-blog/manoj-gupte/digital-twinspicking-up-where-bim-leaves-off-and-rushing-straight-into-the-future/.

Hancke, G., B. C. Silva, and G. P. Hancke Jr. 2013. "The Role of Advanced Sensing in Smart Cities." *Sensors* 13: 393–425.

Hargreaves, A. J., M. Cavada, and C. D. F. Rogers. 2019. "Briefing: Engineering for the Far Future: Rethinking the Value Proposition." Proceedings of the Institution of Civil Engineers. Engineering Sustainability.

Ho, Y. S. 2012. "The Effects of Location Personalization on Individuals' Intention to Use Mobile Services." *Decision Support Systems* 53: 802–812.

Hojjati, A., I. Jefferson, N. Metje, and C. D. F. Rogers. 2018. "Sustainability Assessment for Urban Underground Utility Infrastructure Projects." *Proceedings of the Institution of Civil Engineers – Engineering Sustainability* 171 (2): 68–80.

IA. 2018. "Innovation Alliance for the West Midlands." *Innovation Alliance*. Accessed February 18, 2019. http://innovationwm.co.uk/.

Imbellone, A., B. Botte1, and C. M. Medaglia. 2015. "Serious Games for Mobile Devices: the InTouch Project Case Study." *International Journal of Serious Games* 2 (1): 17–27.

Jamei, E., M. Mortimer, M. Seyedmahmoudian, B. Horan, and A. Stojcevski. 2017. "Investigating the Role of Virtual Reality in Planning for Sustainable Smart Cities." *Sustainability* 9: 1–16.

Jung, K., S. Jo, and S. Park. 2015. "A Game Theoretic Approach for Collaborative Caching Techniques in Privacy Preserving Location-Based Services." Big Comp IEEE. 978-1-4799-7303-3/15/$31.00.

Kaczmarek, L. D., M. Misiak, M. Behnke, M. Dziekan, and P. Guzik. 2017. "The Pikachu Effect: Social and Health Gaming Motivations Lead to Greater Benefits of Pokémon GO Use." *Computers in Human Behavior* 75: 356–363.

Khan, J., K. Kakosimos, O. Raaschou-Nielsena, J. Brandta, S. S. Jensena, T. Ellermanna, and M. Ketzela. 2019. "Development and Performance Evaluation of New AirGIS – A GIS Based Air Pollution and Human Exposure Modelling System." *Atmospheric Environment* 198: 102–121.

Kim, H.-W., H. C. Chan, and A. Kankanhalli. 2012. "What Motivates People to Purchase Digital Items on Virtual Community Websites? The Desire for Online Self-Presentation." *INFORMS* 23 (4): 1232–1245.

Kose, E., M. Erbas, and E. Ersen. 2017. "An Integrated Approach Based on Game Theory and Geographical Information Systems to Solve Decision Problems." *Applied Mathematics and Computation* 308: 105–114.

Leach, J., P. A. Braithwaite, S. E. Lee, C. J. Bouch, D. V. L. Hunt, and C. D. F. Rogers. 2016. "Measuring Urban Sustainability and Liveability Performance: the City Analysis Methodology." *International Journal of Complexity in Applied Science and Technology* 1 (1): 86–106.

Leach, J', S. Lee, C. Boyko, C. Coulton, R. Cooper, N. Smith, H. Joffe, et al. 2017. "Dataset of the Livability Performance of the City of Birmingham, UK, as Measured by its Citizen Wellbeing, Resource Security, Resource Efficiency and Carbon Emissions." *Data in Brief*, 15, 691–695.

Leach, J., S. E. Lee, D. V. L. Hunt, and C. D. F. Rogers. 2017. "Improving City-Scale Measures of Livable Sustainability: A Study of Urban Measurement and Assessment Through Application to the City of Birmingham, UK." *Cities (london, England)* 71: 80–87.

Leach, J. M., R. Mulhall, C. D. F. Rogers, and J. R. Bryson. 2019. "Reading Cities: Developing an Urban Diagnostics Approach for Identifying Integrated Urban Problems with Application to the City of Birmingham, UK." *Cities (london, England)* 86: 136–144.

Leach, J. M., C. D. F. Rogers, A. Ortegon-Sanchez, and N. Tyler. 2019. "The Liveable Cities Method: Establishing the Case for Transformative Change." Proceedings of the Institution of Civil Engineers – Engineering Sustainability.

Leighton, E., and M. Saker. 2018. "The Player and Pokémon Go: Examining the Effects of Locative Play on Spatiality and Sociability." *Mobile Media & Communication* 38 (8): 1169–1183.

L'Heureux, A. 2015. "Gamification Framework for Sensor Data Analytics." Department of Electrical and Computer Engineering. The University of Western Ontario. Electronic Thesis and Dissertation Repository. 3200.

L'Heureux, A., K. Grolinger, H. F. Elyamany, and M. A. M. Capretz. 2017. "Machine Learning with Big Data: Challenges and Approaches." *IEEE Access* 5: 7776–7797.

Li, S., S. Dragicevic, F. A. Castro, M. Sester, S. Winter, A. Coltekin, C. Pettit, et al. 2016. "Geospatial Big Data Handling Theory and Methods: A Review and Research Challenges." *ISPRS Journal of Photogrammetry and Remote Sensing* 115: 119–133.

Likhyani, A., D. Padmanabhan, S. Bedathur, and S. Mehta. 2015. "Inferring and Exploiting Categories for Next Location Prediction." WWW 2015 Companion, Florence, Italy, May 18–22.

Lin, Y. L., and H. W. Lin. 2017. "Learning Results and Terminal Values From the Players of SimCity and the Sims." *Behaviour & Information Technology* 36 (2): 209–222.

Lindqvist, A. K., D. Castelli, J. Hallberg, and S. Rutberg. 2018. "The Praise and Price of Pokémon GO: A Qualitative Study of Children's and Parents' Experiences." *JMIR Serious Games* 6 (1): e1.

Liu, X., K. Liu, L. Guo, X. Li, and Y. Fang. 2013. "A Game-Theoretic Approach for Achieving k-Anonymity in Location Based Services." IEEE INFOCOM. 978-1-4673-5946-7/13.

Liveable Cities. 2019. "The Liveable Cities Programme." Accessed July 10, 2019. www.liveablecities.org.uk.

Lombardi, P., S. Giordano, H. Farouh, and W. Yousef. 2012. "Modelling the Smart City Performance." *Innovation: The European Journal of Social Science Research* 25 (2): 137–149.

Lucas, R., J. Shrager, and T. Winograd. 2017. "A Comparative Analysis of Augmented Reality Technologies and Their Marketability in the Consumer Electronics Segment." *Journal of Biosensor and Bioelectronics* 8: 1–19.

Mariani, I., and D. Spallazzo. 2016. "Empowering Games. Meaning Making by Designing and Playing Location Based Mobile Games." *Interaction Design and Architecture (s) Journal – IxD&A* 28: 12–33.

Medaglia, R. 2007. "The Challenged Identity of a Field: The State of the Art of eParticipation Research." *Information Polity* 12 (3): 169–181.

Melero, J., D. Hernández-Leo, J. Sun, P. Santos, and J. Blat. 2015. "How was the Activity? A Visualization Support for a Case of Location-Based Learning Design." *British Journal of Educational Technology* 46 (2): 317–329.

Minsung, K., and S. Jungyeop. 2016. "The Pedagogical Benefits OfSimCityin Urban Geography Education." *Journal of Geography* 115 (2): 39–50.

Miorandi, D., S. Sicari, F. D. Pellegrini, and I. Chlamtac. 2012. "Internet of Things: Vision, Applications and Research Challenges." *Ad Hoc Networks* 10: 1497–1516.

MoL. 2014a. *London Living Lab.* Mayor of London. Accessed February 5, 2017; Accessed February 10, 2019. http://smarterlondon.co.uk/case-studies/london-living-lab/.

MoL. 2014b. *Hyde Park Sensing.* Mayor of London. Accessed February 5, 2017. http://smarterlondon.co.uk/case-studies/hyde-park-sensing/.

MoL. 2015a. *Smart Sustainable Districts.* Queen Elizabeth Olympic Park. Mayor of London. http://www.queenelizabetholympicpark.co.uk/our-story/transforming-east-london/sustainability/smart-sustainable-districts.

MoL. 2015b. *Sensing London.* Mayor of London. Accessed February 5, 2017. http://smarterlondon.co.uk/case-studies/sensing-london/#more-1001.

MoL. 2018. *Smarter London Together: The Mayor's Roadmap to Transform London into the Smartest City in the World.* Mayor of London. Accessed February 5, 2019. https://www.london.gov.uk/sites/default/files/smarter_london_together_v1.66_-_published.pdf.

MoL. 2019. *Examination in Public for the Draft New London Plan.* Mayor of London, London Assembly. Accessed February 15, 2019. https://www.london.gov.uk/what-we-do/planning/london-plan/new-london-plan/examination-public-draft-new-london-plan#Stub-199628.

Monika, D., Srinivasan, and T. Reindl. 2015. "Real-time Display of Data from a Smart-grid on Geographical Map using a GIS Tool and its Role Inoptimization of Game Theory." 2015 IEEE Innovative Smart Grid Technologies - Asia (ISGT ASIA), Bangkok, 1–6. doi:10.1109/ISGTAsia.2015.7387161.

Morschheuser, B., M. Riar, J. Hamari, and A. Maedche. 2017. "How Games Induce Cooperation?' A Study on the Relationship between Game Features and We-Intentions in an Augmented Reality Game." *Computers in Human Behavior* 77: 169–183.

MTU. 2012. "Mapping the Underworld." Accessed September 25, 2019. http://www.mappingtheunderworld.ac.uk.

Nigaglioni, I. 2017. "Pokémon Go: An Unexpected Inspiration for Next Generation Learning Environments." *Childhood Education* 93 (4): 333–336.

Nigg, C. R., J. D. Mateo, and J. An. 2017. "Pokemon GO May Increase Physical Activity and Decrease Sedentary Behaviors." *AJPH Prespectives Editorial* 107 (1): 37–38.

Olszewski, R., P. Pałka, and A. Turek. 2018. "Solving "Smart City" Transport Problems by Designing Carpooling Gamification Schemes with Multi-Agent Systems: The Case of the So-Called "Mordor of Warsaw"." *Sensors* 18: 141.

Opromolla, A., A. Ingrosso, V. Volpi, C. M. Medaglia, M. Palatucci, and M. Pazzola. 2014. "Gamification in a Smart City Context. An Analysis and a Proposal for its Application in Co-Design Processes." In *Games and Learning Alliance, Gala 2014. Book Series: Lecture Notes in Computer Science.* Vol. 9221., edited by A. Degloria, 73–82. Bucharest, Romania: Springer-Verlag.

Papangelis, K., A. Chamberlain, and H. N. Liang. 2016. "New Directions for Preserving Intangible Cultural Heritage Through the Use of Mobile Technologies." In *MobileHCI '16 Proceedings of the 18th International Conference on Human-Computer Interaction with Mobile Devices and Services Adjunct,* 964–967.

Papangelis, K., M. Metzger, Y. Sheng, H. N. Liang, A. Chamberlain, and T. Cao. 2017a. "Conquering the City: Understanding Perceptions of Mobility and Human Territoriality in Location-Based Mobile Games." *PACM Interact. Mob. Wearable Ubiquitous Technol* 1 (3): Article 90.

Papangelis, K., M. Metzger, Y. Sheng, H.-N. Liang, A. Chamberlain, and V. J. Khan. 2017b. "Get Off My Lawn! Starting to Understand Territoriality in Location Based Mobile Games." In *CHI EA '17 Proceedings of the 2017 CHI Conference Extended Abstracts on Human Factors in Computing Systems,* 1955–1961.

Papangelis, K., Y. Sheng, H. N. Liang, A. Chamberlain, V. J. Khan, and T. Cao. 2017c. "Unfolding the Interplay of Self-Identity and Expressions of Territoriality in Location-Based Social Networks." 177–180.

Poplin, A. 2012. "Playful Public Participation in Urban Planning: A Case Study for Online Serious Games." *Computers, Environment and Urban Systems* 36: 195–206.

Proshansky, H. M. 1978. "The City and Self-Identity." *Environment and Behavior* 10 (2): 147–169.

Raper, J., G. Gartner, H. Karimi, and C. Rizos. 2007. "A Critical Evaluation of Location Based Services and Their Potential." *Journal of Location Based Services* 1 (1): 5–45.

Rogers, C. D. F. 2015. "Assessing the Underworld – Remote Sensing to Support Smart and Liveable Cities." IEE 978-1-4799-6495-6/15.

Rogers, C. D. F. 2018. "Engineering Future Liveable, Resilient, Sustainable Cities Using Foresight." *Proceedings of the Institution of Civil Engineers – Civil Engineering* 171 (6): 3–9.

Rogers, C. D. F., and D. V. L. Hunt. 2019. "Realising Visions for Future Cities: An Aspirational Futures Methodology." Proceedings of the Institution of Civil Engineers – Urban Design and Planning, in press.

Rogers, C. D. F., D. R. Lombardi, J. M. Leach, and R. F. D. Cooper. 2012. "The Urban Futures Methodology Applied to Urban Regeneration." *Proceedings of the Institution of Civil Engineers – Engineering Sustainability* 165 (1): 5–20.

Rogers, C. D. F., J. Shipley, P. Blythe, P. A. Braithwaite, C. Brown, B. S. Collins, S. Juned, et al. 2014. *Future Urban Living – A Policy Commission Investigating the Most Appropriate Means for Accommodating Changing Populations and Their Needs in the Cities of the Future.* UK: University of Birmingham. p. 60. ISBN 978-0-7044-2843-0. http://liveablecities.org.uk/outcomes/future-urban-living-policy-commission.

Sakamoto, M., T. Alexandrova, and T. Nakajima. 2015. "Enhancing Values Through Virtuality for Intelligent Artifacts That Influence Human Attitude and Behavior." *Multimedia Tools and Applications* 74: 11537–11568.

Saker, M. 2016. "Foursquare and Identity: Checking-in and Presenting the Self through Location." *New Media and Society* 19 (6): 934–949.

Saker, M., and L. Evans. 2016a. "Locative Media and Identity: Accumulative Technologies of the Self." *Sage Open* July-September: 1–10.

Saker, M., and L. Evans. 2016b. "Everyday Life and Locative Play: an Exploration of Foursquare and Playful Engagements with Space and Place." *Media, Culture & Society* 38 (8): 1169–1183.

Saker, M., and L. Evans. 2018. "The Player and Pokémon Go: Examining the Effects of Locative Play on Spatiality and Sociability." *Mobile Media & Communication* 7 (2): 232–247.

Saker, M., and J. Frith. 2018. "Locative Media and Sociability: Using Location-Based Social Networks to Coordinate Everyday Life." *Architecture_MPS* 14 (1): 1.

Saker, M., and J. Frith. 2019. "From Hybrid Space to Dislocated Space: Mobile Virtual Reality and a Third Stage of Mobile Media Theory." *New Media & Society* 21 (1): 214–228.

Schmitz, B., P. Schuffelen, K. Kreijns, R. Klemke, and M. Specht. 2015. "Putting Yourself in Someone Else's Shoes: The Impact of a Location-Based, Collaborative Role-Playing Game on Behaviour." *Computers & Education* 85: 160–169.

Schwartz, R., and G. R. Halegoua. 2015. "The Spatial Self: Location-Based Identity Performance on Social Media." *New Media and Society* 17 (10): 1643–1660.

Serino, M., K. Cordrey, L. McLaughlin, and R. L. Milanaik. 2016. "Pokemon Go and Augmented Virtual Reality Games: a Cautionary Commentary for Parents and Paediatricians." 1040-8703 Wolters Kluwer Health, Inc.

Shennan, R. 2018. "Digital Twins are Growing Up." *Opinion.* Infrastructure Intelligence. Accessed January 24, 2019. http://www.infrastructure-intelligence.com/article/dec-2018/digital-twins-are-growing.

Simonofski, A., S. Serral, J. De Smedt, and M. Snoeck. 2017. "Citizen Participation in Smart Cities: Evaluation Framework Proposal." 19th IEEE Conference on Business Informatics.

Sukhov, A. 2016. "Ethical Issues of Computer Games." 3rd International Multidisciplinary Scientific Conference on Social Sciences & Arts SGEM.

Tao, W. 2013. "Interdisciplinary Urban GIS for Smart Cities: Advancements and Opportunities." *Geo-spatial Information Science* 16 (1): 25–34.

Togawa, T., T. Fujita, L. Dong, S. Ohnishi, and M. Fujii. 2016. "Integrating GIS Databases and ICT Applications for the Design of Energy Circulation Systems." Center for Social and Environmental Systems Research, National Institute for Environmental Studies (NIES), 16-2 Onogawa, Tsukuba, Ibaraki 305-8506, Japan.

Tranfield, D., D. Denyer, and P. Smart. 2003. "Towards a Methodology for Developing Evidence-Informed Management Knowledge by Means of Systematic Review." *British Journal of Management* 14: 207–222.

UN (United Nations). 2015. "Sustainable Development Goals SDGs." *Sustainable Development.* Accessed February 15, 2019. https://www.un.org/sustainabledevelopment/sustainable-development-goals/.

Vasconcelos, M., J. M. Almeida, and M. A. Gonçalves. 2015. "Predicting the Popularity of Micro-Reviews: A Foursquare Case Study." *Information Sciences* 325: 355–374.

Vemuri, S., C. Schmandt, W. Bender, S. Tellex, and B. Lassey. 2004. "An Audio-Based Personal Memory Aid." In *'UbiComp 2004: Ubiquitous Computing' 6th International Conference Nottingham, UK, Proceedings*, edited by N. Davies, Mynatt El, and I. Siio, 400–417. Nottingham.

Virrantaus, K., J. Markkula, A. Garmash, V. Terziyan, J. Veijalainen, A. Katanosov, and H. Tirri. 2002. "Developing GIs-Supported Location-Based Services." International Conference on Web Information Systems Engineering. IEEE, Kyoto. Japan. ISBN 0-7695-1393-X.

White, J.D. 1992. "SIMCITY: The City Simulator." *Simulation & Gaming* 23: 120–123.

Whittermore, R., and K. Knafl. 2005. "The Integrative Review: Updated Methodology." *Journal of Advanced Nursing* 52 (5): 546–553.

Woessner, M. 2015. "Teaching with SimCity: Using Sophisticated Gaming Simulations to Teach Concepts in Introductory American Government." April 2015 American Political Science Association.

Wohn, D. Y., and R. Wash. 2013. "A Virtual "Room" with a Cue: Detecting Personality Through Spatial Customization in a City Simulation Game." *Computers in Human Behavior* 29: 155–159.

Xiao, Y., and M. Watson. 2019. "Guidance on Conducting a Systematic Literature Review." *Journal of Planning Education and Research* 39 (1): 93–112. doi:10.1177/0739456X17723971.

Yigitcanlar, T. 2015. "Smart Cities: An Effective Urban Development and Management Model?" *Australian Planner* 52 (1): 27–34.

Yigitcanlar, T. 2018. "Smart City Policies Revisited: Considerations for a Truly Smart and Sustainable Urbanism Practice." *World Technopolis Review* 7 (2): 97–112.

Yigitcanlar, T., M. Foth, and M. Kamruzzaman. 2019. "Towards Post-Anthropocentric Cities: Reconceptualising Smart Cities to Evade Urban Ecocide." *Journal of Urban Technology* 26 (2): 147–152.

Yigitcanlar, T., M. Kamruzzaman, L. Buys, G. Ioppolo, J. Sabatini-Marques, E. Costa, and J. Yun. 2018. "Understanding 'Smart Cities': Intertwining Development Drivers with Desired Outcomes in a Multidimensional Framework." *Cities (london, England)* 81 (1): 145–160.

Yigitcanlar, T., M. Kamruzzaman, M. Foth, J. Sabatini-Marques, E. Costa, and G. Ioppolo. 2019. "Can Cities Become Smart Without Being Sustainable? A Systematic Review of the Literature." *Sustainable Cities and Society* 45 (1): 348–365.

Yue, P., P. Baumann, K. M. Bugbee, and L. Jiang. 2015. "Towards Intelligent GIServices." *Earth Science Informatics* 8: 463–481.

Zhao, L., L. Chen, R. Ranjan, K. K. R. Choo, and J. He. 2016. "'Geographical Information System Parallelization for Spatial big Data Processing: A Review." *Cluster Computing* 19: 139–152. Springer. US.

Zhou, X., and L. Zhang. 2016. "Crowdsourcing Functions of the Living City from Twitter and Foursquare Data." *Cartography and Geographic Information Science* 43 (5): 393–404.

Zica, M. R., A. C. Ionica, and M. Leba. 2017. "Gamification in the Context of Smart Cities." International Conference on Applied Sciences ICAS Series: Materials Science and Engineering 294 (2018) 012045. IOP Publishing.

Index